B   Yarborough, Cale
YAR
BOROUGH Cale

DATE			

Cale

𝔊imes BOOKS

Cale

THE HAZARDOUS LIFE
AND TIMES OF AMERICA'S
GREATEST STOCK CAR DRIVER

by Cale Yarborough

with William Neely

Published in the United States by Times Books, a division of
Random House, Inc.,
New York, and simultaneously in Canada by Random House
of Canada Limited, Toronto.
Library of Congress Cataloging-in-Publication Data
Yarborough, Cale.
Cale: the hazardous life and times of America's
greatest stock car driver.
1. Yarborough, Cale.
2. Automobile racing drivers—United States—Biography.
3. Stock car racing—United States—History.
I. Neely, William.
II. Title.
GV1032.Y36A33 1986 796.7′2′0924 [B] 85-40732
ISBN 0-8129-1261-6
Manufactured in the United States of America
9 8 7 6 5 4 3 2
First Edition
Book design: Elissa Ichiyasu

Foreword

■

It has been twenty-six years since I first saw a young Cale Yarborough drive a race car, and somehow, even though it was one of his earliest NASCAR races, I knew that I was watching greatness. My reaction hovered somewhere between admiration and disbelief. I mean, here was a brash young kid I had met minutes before in the pits at the old Darlington Raceway, who looked like he was straight out of *Happy Days,* and he was working that granddaddy of stock car tracks like he was born there. That was 1959, long before they modernized Darlington, when it still was the toughest track anybody had ever seen.

Actually Cale *was* born there; well, just a few miles from Darlington, in the Pee Dee Region of South Carolina. From the time he drove a Soap Box Derby racer, his only plan was to "run Darlington someday." By the early sixties, many were wondering if they actually had built the track for him, because he seemed more at home on it than most of the great stars of the sport who had preceded him. He raced wherever he could go fastest, in places where angels feared to tread, places where great names like Fireball Roberts and Speedy Thompson and Marshall Teague and Tim Flock and Joe Weatherly were reluctant to go.

As I got to know Cale better over the years, I began to realize that he had a confidence that was outsize even for race-car drivers, and this is a sport in which confidence is easily the prime requisite. Cale's colossal confidence, combined with a determination that bordered on the fanatical, quickly made him a favorite of racing fans all over the South.

There is no doubt in my mind that Cale Yarborough will go down in history as the hardest charger who ever lived, the most aggressive race-car driver of them all. Perhaps it was Richard Petty who said it best: "There's one thing about Cale: You know what he's gonna do. He's gonna run just as hard as he can. With a fellow like [David] Pearson—or me, sometimes—you don't never know when he's runnin' hard or not. He might just be keepin' up and not even runnin' near as hard as he can. But if Cale's just keepin' up, you know he's runnin' as hard as he can that day; otherwise he'd be in *front* of you."

It is important to know what a man's peers say about him, and that is exactly why I talked with so many of them about Cale.

"Cale's a terribly physical driver," says Darrell Waltrip. "I mean, he's strong in the chest and shoulders . . . and he can just lay on top of that steering wheel and drive all day. He don't never seem to get tired."

Buddy Baker said: "You'll find that most of the problems are with the cars, not the drivers. It's not like a ball player that goes into a slump. If Cale's car is handlin' good, he's really hard to beat. He don't have no flaws to work on, and you just can't wait for him to make a mistake. No, I never bank on that. Cale's like a machine when he's racin'. He just don't make mistakes. Unless something in the car itself changes during the race, you can't outfox him. You've got to win with your race car."

There simply aren't many drivers in the sport of automobile racing who command such respect from their competition. When you get right down to it, Cale Yarborough is the footprint of the NASCAR star of the past twenty-five years.

That day I met him at Darlington, he acted like a veteran of the world's toughest sport—tough, confident, just a little cocky. And by then he had won only one Grand National race. Yet he was typical of the successful stock-car driver. Somewhere there's a mold. For one thing, he had come off a Southern farm. The sport of stock-car racing has always been dominated by rural Southern men. It seems to have been designed for them. And just in time for Cale. If it had been in the 1870s—or even the 1930s—there would have been no place for him to go. He would have ended up with some sort of aimless life; he would have gone nuts in rural South Carolina and probably would have headed for Texas.

If you go back and look at the number of people who migrated out of the Carolinas after the War Between the States and before the Industrial Revolution, you'll find that a tremendous number of them ended up in Texas, and a lot of them wound up as cowboys. I don't know what Cale would have been, but I do know that he would have been one of the first to leave, because he needed something more than the rural Southern life had to offer. All of these superstar stock-car drivers did.

The death of Cale's father had a tremendous impact on his life; it made even stronger the need to rise up above the crowd that is typical of race-car drivers, especially in the South. There wasn't much a kid could do there to distinguish himself. Oh, there was football and basketball, but those were things you did to pass the seasons. You could box and play baseball. And you could race cars, because every small town had a dirt track. Every one.

But the dirt tracks didn't fulfill the need Cale had to excel. The fact that Darlington was just a stone's throw away kept him from ever being satisfied with local fame. He had a siren call—the superspeed-way. And the way he drove it when he got there was almost like he had been destined to drive that kind of track right from the start. It makes me wonder if the system they have for starting kids on small local tracks and gradually working them up to the big time is right after all. Maybe the ones who belong at the superspeedway belong right from the start.

But where did Cale's fanatical desire begin? His mother says it's because "he's a Yarborough. They're all like that. There's never a thing they didn't think they could do." Interesting, but I personally suspect that it was Cale's mother who had the major influence on him. I think it's true with the mothers of most stock-car drivers. They were typical of the Southern white mother of the forties and fifties. They had been brought up in the Depression, and they were fully aware of the fact that they were trying to raise their kids over the sharecropper/textile mill existence. The only thing these women had to work with was their minds, because nobody had any money. Nobody. I doubt that any mothers in history had as much influence on their sons as Southern white mothers.

Put yourself in Cale's shoes. You're in Sardis, South Carolina, in the fifties, living a cloistered existence, and you're not even sure what the rest of the world is really like out there. The whole South, in a certain sense, was still recovering from the Civil War. There was farming and textiles and nothing more. Still there was a strong desire in these mothers for their kids to do better. But how could they? It took a lot of confidence—more than the kids could muster up by themselves—so the mothers had to instill it in them.

This book is about all of that—the tough early years, the tough middle years, and the tough later years. Stock-car racing is a tough sport; just look at it. Stock-car racing people are physically big people —the drivers, the crew members, the fans. The Japanese would love Grand National stock-car racing; to them it would be Sumo wrestling on wheels. If they could see Cale and Buddy Baker and the rest of the guys wrestling around those 3,700-pound cars, they would go bananas.

Through all the fame, though, Cale Yarborough has remained one of the most private stars car racing has ever had. He is an enigma to many. Even his most ardent admirers—and his following may be the largest in all of motor sports—don't even know much about the man *off* the track. Sure, they know all about his hard-driving style and his fanatical desire to win, and they know where he lives—but that's all. They don't know that he has done more wild things and more dangerous things off the track than he has on. But they will now. That's why I was excited when Cale and I first started talking about this book.

It's high time the world knows the complete story of the boy who came out of a tobacco field to become one of America's greatest sports stars. But you're going to find out that the road to the top wasn't easy. It seldom is. For one thing, this road was punctuated with great mixed emotions. As his fame began to spread, Cale found that it was tough to be a hero to a certain segment of the South—the working man—and not be the hero of the genteel set, the group who still looked to Atlantic Coast Conference basketball for its idols. It was tough coming up through that, knowing that there still were people who were bicycling through the hydrogen age, people who simply didn't know what the new South was all about. Cale Yarborough opened a lot of eyes. And not just in the South; he's a national hero. National? Hell, he's an *inter*national hero.

Bill Neely

I HAD MY FILL OF FIGHTING THE LAND

BY THE TIME I GOT TO NINTH–GRADE CIVICS.

Prologue

■

I'll guarantee you that this isn't going to be a slick, Hollywood–type adventure story, although a lot of the things that have happened to me—on *and* off the track—sound like some movie guy wrote them. But I promise you, they're true. All of them. I can't explain why, but weird things have always seemed to happen to me; I've been struck by lighting, I've been shot, I've fallen out of an airplane, I've been bitten by a rattlesnake. In between, I've won a lot of races. We'll get to all of that.

What I intend to do is take off my cowboy boots and get myself a Coke or two and just sit back and tell you how I happened to get where I am, which is in the twilight years of a career that most people would consider successful and glamorous, if not downright danger-ous. Actually I told it all to Bill Neely, who has put it down on paper, with the words in the right places. You see, I've known him for a long time; he was there when a lot of the things were happening, so together we've tried to remember as much of it as we could.

The fact that this story begins in the loamy soil and the tobacco fields of the Deep South makes it all that more improbable. The fact that I came right off one of those farms, without any knowledge about a race car or even anybody to help me get it, makes it hard for me to believe it even now. Nobody I grew up with believed it while it was happening, because, well, because a whole lot of people I knew when I was growing up were still fighting the War Between the States. They were content to stay there, doing the same things their ancestors had; somehow I knew there had to be a better way to make a living than digging around in the dirt and picking tobacco worms off leaves by hand. There had to be.

I had my fill of fighting the land for survival by the time I got to ninth-grade civics. I knew there was more to living than the Cotillion Ball once a year.

What I really want to tell you is how I knew the difference and what I did to climb out of the bean patch, and what it was like on the way up. I guess that makes it an autobiography, but it won't be an I-did-this or I-did-that story, I promise. No, I want to tell you what it was *really* like in the South in the forties, fifties, and sixties. I also want to tell you what it felt like to succeed in the only life I ever wanted, which, if you haven't figured it out by now, is racing cars.

The fact that this all begins in an area of the country that was still trying to pull itself out of the effects of a war and a depression makes it even more dramatic. It's the part Hollywood would have put in, anyway, even if it didn't happen.

I've never completely understood why people around home always referred to the War Between the States and the Depression as "great," but they did; you know, the Great Depression. I didn't sound great to me. Besides that, I couldn't tell much difference between what they talked about and the way things were when I was growing up. Life was always tough.

I want to tell you about where I work, which is the Grand National Circuit of the National Association for Stock Car Auto Racing—

NASCAR, for short. And I'll tell you right now, a NASCAR stocker is about as fierce a piece of equipment as, say, the space shuttle.

A lot has changed since I started driving NASCAR in the late fifties. It's calmed down a whole lot, for one thing, and I'm sorry to say that a lot of my good friends from those early days have been killed. I miss both the good ol' days and the good ol' boys. You know, the boys that are coming up today have missed a lot by not having the chance to know this period and these people, so this book is as much for them as it is for anybody else. I'll tell you, boys, you wouldn't believe how tough it was back then. There wasn't the big money in racing that there is today, and the cars, well, the cars were a far cry from what you're driving now. I mean, if a car didn't handle right, you didn't bring it into the pits and turn it over to a crew of engineers like we do now; no, sir, you stayed out there and you *made* it handle. It's almost a lost art.

There are a lot of drivers around today—some of them successful drivers—who couldn't have made it in the fifties or sixties. You had to come up through tough little old dirt tracks, or you didn't make it at all. Cars and equipment and tracks are sophisticated now, but there wasn't a single thing that was sophisticated about racing back then.

Another thing this book is about—at least part of it—is the guys who *could* and did handle those primitive race cars; people like Curtis Turner and Fireball Roberts and Little Joe Weatherly and Tiny Lund. Man, I can remember seeing Curtis come down a dirt track. It was something. A lot of people have said that I'm the only one who ever changed as hard as ol' Pops. All I can say is, "I sure hope so."

Those guys are all gone now, and we'll talk a lot about the days when they were here, but we'll also talk a lot about some of the guys who are still around—some retired and some still driving—from Ralph Earnhardt to Dale Earnhardt, and from Lee Petty to Richard Petty to Kyle Petty. And a lot of names you may never have heard of.

I'm definitely not going to take you race by race through a career that has spanned more than thirty years. That would be nothing more than a record book, and if you want to know how I feel about it, I think it would be boring. Instead I want to tell you how much fun a lot of it has been and how tough it was at other times. We're going to spend more time on the fun times and the tough times and the significant times—those races that were turning points in my career. Or stepping-stones.

There were many years, particularly in the late sixties and through all of the seventies, when I was very successful. There's no other way to say it. I won race after race, so pardon me if I don't blow my own horn about those years. You can check the records for that. It's all there if you're interested.

It's the other years that tell you more about what I'm really like. They're the ones a psychiatrist would try to get out of me if one ever got me on his couch—which they won't, I assure you.

So fasten your seat belt and sit back. It might be a bumpy ride at times, but I sure hope it's going to be as much fun hearing about it as it was living it. And remembering it. At least, *most* of it.

Cale Yarborough

Cale

THE WOOD SMOKE MIXED WITH THE SMELLS

OF BACON AND COFFEE IN THE WINTERTIME.

1

■

It was a long walk to school, about three miles each way, but I didn't mind it because the air was always cool at six-thirty in the morning when I left home, and that was about the only time of day that it was. By nine-thirty or ten the sun shined directly into the classroom, and I had to shade my eyes even to see the blackboard. But the windows were all up and, thank goodness, there were a lot of them. South Carolina is hot.

It's morning I remember most about my childhood; maybe it's why I still get up early. You see, I shared a room with my brothers—Jerry, who is two years younger than I am, and J.C., who is nine years younger. Daddy always came into our room and woke me first, by gently shaking my shoulder back and forth a few times. "Wake up, Cale. Mama's 'bout got breakfast ready," he would say.

And I would sort of half open one eye and mumble, "Awright, Daddy, I'll get the boys up." Then I would roll over for another few minutes' sleep. "Now!" he would say as he went out the door, and I knew he meant "now." So I got up. I can still feel that cold linoleum as my feet hit the floor. And I can still smell the bacon frying. It was the same every morning as I went over to shake Jerry and J.C. awake. There's maybe nothing that smells as good as bacon frying.

"Get up!" I yelled as I about shook them out of bed. I wasn't as easy on them as Daddy was on me, and they would throw their pillows at me and yell, "We're awake. We're awake. Get outta here." So I would pull on my jeans and go out to the kitchen.

"Good morning, Caleb," Mama would say, turning from the wood-burning stove. "You get your brothers up?"

"Mornin', Mama. Yes, ma'am, they're up." And I would head for the back door and the thirty-foot walk down the dusty path to the outhouse. The dust felt good between my toes.

"You better hurry, boy," Daddy always called after me as he looked over his steaming coffee cup. "Gotta get washed up."

I always met Jerry and J.C. heading down the path as I was coming back, and just as regular as clockwork, we tried to push one another off the path. J.C. was real little, so he would howl and laugh, and that always brought Daddy to the back door. He would yell at us through the screen door, "Cut it out, boys. You gotta get movin'."

It was the same thing every morning, winter, spring, and fall. The only difference was that for a couple of months in the winter it got cold, and then we wore coats and always ran like crazy down the path, and Daddy always had a big wood fire going in the kitchen. The wood smoke mixed with the smells of bacon and coffee in the wintertime. I think I liked winter best.

But that wasn't what I started to tell you about. It's just that I never think about my childhood without thinking of the bacon and the wood smoke and the cold lineoleum. And Mama, standing there at the cook stove in her housedress and apron. And Daddy, standing there behind that old screen that had tiny patches of other screen sewed on it in three or four places with black thread. "Cut it out, boys. You gotta get movin'."

The reason I think a lot about the mornings at school is that it was a morning when I was in the fourth grade at the Sardis Grade School when I learned what courage was. It has stayed with me all my life. There aren't many people who can pinpoint a thing like that, but I can.

From the time I was in the first grade I always liked walking to school. I'd kick in the dust and throw pinecones and just generally have a good time. I wasn't too excited about the school part, and once I got there, the fun was over, but I always made a sort of adventure out of getting there. I guess I knew I was going to be bored stiff once the school bell rang.

But, like I said, it was in the fourth grade, and the school year had just started. I got there about the same time the school bus did. You see, the bus brought some of the kids who lived several miles away. Three miles didn't count. It was a different era.

There was a kid whose name was Jimmy Humphries, and he was about twice as big as any kid in the class. He had grown about a foot over the summer. He was as strong as an ox. I was terrified of him. If you want to know the truth, I was terrified of everybody. I was small for my age, and if anybody said "boo" to me, I would scat. That morning I did about the worst thing anybody could have done; I was running up the school steps and I ran smack into Jimmy Humphries. I mean, I ran *into* him. It knocked him down. "Oh, Lord," I thought. "I'm in for it now."

I couldn't have been more right. Jimmy punched me right in the eye. He knocked me clear off the steps and into the dirt. The other kids laughed, and Jimmy looked down at me. From where he was standing he looked ten feet tall. "I'm gonna whip you every day," he said. And I knew he meant it.

From that day on Jimmy picked on me all the time—before school, at recess, and after school. And he started every day by putting a whipping on me. Lord, I hated to go to school. The trips were no longer adventures to me; they were like the steps a man takes up to the gallows, but I didn't tell anyone.

It got to the point that Daddy couldn't get me out of the house. I would find every excuse known to mankind, so that I would get there after Jimmy's bus arrived, and he was already in the schoolhouse. He still picked on me the rest of the day, but at least I got the day started a little better.

If my timing was bad and I beat the bus to school, I hid behind a big old live oak tree beside the school until I saw him get off the bus. He always looked up and down the dusty road for me, but he never discovered my hiding place.

Jimmy always looked surprised when I came in the room about ten seconds after he did. I didn't say Jimmy was the *smartest* kid in school, I just said he was the biggest.

This thing went on for about six weeks, and then one day I saw the most beautiful sight I had ever seen. Jimmy's bus arrived on time, and the kids started to get off. Jimmy was last, and there was one beautiful, fantastic, wonderful difference this time. Jimmy's right arm was in a cast. Clear up to his bulging bicep. I thought, "Thank you, Lord, thank you." And then something came over me. I don't know what it was, but I came flying out from behind that tree, and I ran straight for Jimmy. He had just reached the wooden steps to the school when I got to him. I grabbed him by the left shoulder and spun him around, and I came up with a right uppercut to his chin. He moaned and tried to get up the steps, but I was on him like white on rice. I hit him with everything I had, and he went down in the dirt, reeling in pain as he landed on his right arm.

I went back over to the tree, picked up my books, and went inside the school. But before I went through the door, I looked back. Man, I'll tell you, the view from up there was fantastic. I went on in.

"Jimmy'll be right in," I told the teacher. "I think he fell down the steps."

My life, from that moment on, was a bed of roses. Once more I enjoyed the walk to school. I left a little early every day because I didn't want to miss Jimmy's bus. I was right there waiting, out in the open, when it pulled up. And every morning, just as regular as clockwork, I laid a whipping on Jimmy. I was the hero of the school.

You can probably see what's coming next: It turns out that Jimmy had broken his arm when he fell off a tractor. Bones heal fast when you're a kid. And casts come off. So one morning he got off the bus, and I started over to administer his daily whipping to him, but as he came toward me, my heart sank.

There was no cast.

"Oh, Lord, two good arms again." But, somehow, the confidence I had built up hung in there. I surprised myself and everybody around —Jimmy included—when I lit into him again. I hit him square under the chin with the uppercut. Jimmy was a sucker for the uppercut. He fell backward. I hit him again and he went down. I was right on top of him, hitting him with everything I had. Jimmy didn't even fight back after a while, and I got up.

I took a few steps toward the school, stopped, and turned around. I felt sorry for Jimmy. I went back over and held out my hand, to help him. He took it and we went into the schoolhouse together, friends. We were friends from then on.

That one thing changed my life as much as anything ever did. I found out that day that if I made my mind up, it didn't matter how big the problem was. So, I'm telling you right up front where the confidence comes from. Jimmy Humphries gave it to me.

I think it changed his outlook, too, because he never again used his strength and size to get what he wanted. He became a different person. We both did.

Jimmy was killed in a car wreck a few years later. I lost a good friend, one that helped me get where I am today.

■

Tobacco is beautiful. It grows with big, wide, velvet-brown leaves. But it is hard to grow. First you burn off a patch for the seed bed, cultivating it until the soil and ash mixture is a powder. Then you plant the seeds. When they show leaves about the size of elm leaves, you transplant the sets in plowed ground. You make a hole in the ground with your finger, fill it with water, and then pack the plant in. Even now, when I drive past a tobacco field, I can remember the feeling of the soft soil as I patted it tight around the tobacco plant. The mud oozed up through my fingers, and it felt like I was making mud pies.

As the tobacco grows it has to be suckered—taking the small leaves off the stock so that the large ones will get even larger. When I did it, the tobacco juice got all over my hands and overalls; it took me about half an hour to clean up every evening.

And then the worms come—big green worms three or four inches long. I had to go down every row and pick off each worm and mash it in the dirt. We never had any poisons to do the job, so it was up to me, but it had to be done because one worm could eat an entire leaf in a day.

If you get past all these hurdles, the tobacco is ready to be gathered, which is another terrible job. After it is cut it's split on top and strung on poles. Then it is carried to the tobacco barn where it is hung up to be cured.

About November or December, when it is really damp and the tobacco has gotten softer so it won't break when you handle it, you hand it off—pulling the leaves from the stalks and putting them in bundles about the size of hands. These, in turn, are put into bales, which we took to Gregory's Tobacco Warehouse in Timmonsville, where an auctioneer like L. A. "Speed" Riggs sold it for us. Speed Riggs was the guy who used to do the Lucky Strike cigarette commercials on radio.

I worked in the tobacco field from the time I was five. I can't remember much before that, but I knew right then what was in the small world around me—dirt. A lot of it. And a lot of old wooden buildings. All of it meant work. You might think that little kids don't know what's going on beyond their own little world, but I can tell you right now that I knew this wasn't going to get it.

You have to realize where all of this was happening. I was right smack in the middle of the Pee Dee Region of South Carolina, a strictly rural area that has rich soil and tabletop-flat fields. There are great cypress and water oak swamps and big longleaf pine forests. It is a land that is rich in timber and cotton and tobacco and soybeans. But there wasn't much in the way of machinery around our place, so we had to wrestle it away from nature by muscle and sweat.

Our farm was about two miles off the main highway, which, if you want to know, is Route 403. There was a dirt road that ran right in front of the house. In fact, that road ran into another dirt road at the north edge of the farm, so we had dirt roads on two sides and the hard roadway over on the front side of the farm. The community of Sardis —population 150—was only a couple of miles from our house. The hard road went to Timmonsville to the north and Olanta to the south, about six miles to either one. I figured that the road went somewhere beyond that, but those were the towns we got to once in a while, and nothing beyond that really mattered.

Those trips to town, which meant Timmonsville or Olanta—Sardis was "home"—were the highlights of my early youth. They usually were on Saturday, and most of the time we went to Timmonsville, which had about two thousand people. It was two or three times bigger than Olanta.

There was a movie theater in Timmonsville. Mama and Daddy would let us out in front of the theater, and they knew we were good for the day. Gene Autry or Roy Rogers would watch out for us while they went about their shopping and visiting. They knew that they could take as long as they wanted, because we would stay right there, through show after show, helping Gene or Roy round up the bad guys. They could have gone on *vacation,* and we would have been right there.

We played out the movie the rest of the week. I was always Gene Autry. I got to wear the white hat.

Daddy always came in and got us, and I can remember how it felt coming out of the theater into the bright South Carolina sun after being in the Old West for about five hours. There was a feeling like somebody was inside your head, pulling on the muscles that work your eyeballs. We would squint like moles.

There's a railroad track that runs right beside Main Street in Timmonsville. On the other side of the track there's another street. That's where the drugstore is, and we always got an ice-cream cone or a Coke. Saturdays were special.

■

The one-story wooden house we lived in was old, but it was clean and neat. There was a big porch in front, and the house sat up on brick pillars, about three feet off the ground, just like all the houses in that part of the country.

Our home life was real good.

Out behind the house was the biggest field on the farm; it's where we grew tobacco, and I figured it had to be the biggest field in the world. It was about seven or eight acres, but that's big, I guarantee you, when you're going up and down those rows. The field, just like all the fields around, was bordered by hedgerows. Some of it wasn't even fenced off because the pine trees and scrub oaks and brush was so thick that nothing could get through, even if it wanted to. That's the reason for the hedgerows.

It wasn't all work, even though it seemed like it at times. One of the things I loved most was riding in the old Ford pickup truck. From as far back as I can remember I was in love with anything that had wheels and a motor. Daddy had an old "colored" man working for him; his name was Son Ham. Actually he was a sharecropper, and his house was on the edge of the farm nearest the hard road. His sons, Donnie and Willie James, and I were the best of friends. You see, we didn't really know enough about the outside world to think that there was anything wrong with a person who wasn't the same color as we were. We all worked together, side by side in the field, and there wasn't a one of us who ever thought of hating someone because he wasn't like us. We called them "colored" because that's what they called themselves.

One of my fondest memories is when Son drove the pickup to town to get groceries or seed or whatever. He always let me sit on his lap and steer the truck. And one of his boys would sit in the seat beside us and keep saying, "That's good, Cale. That's real good."

By the time I was seven or eight, we would wait until there wasn't anybody around, and I would drive the truck myself, up and down the dirt road and through the fields. I had to sit right on the front edge of the seat so that I could see through the steering wheel and reach the pedals. I was almost standing up. It wasn't long before I could run that old truck about wide-open. Naturally I ran it into ditches and hit a few trees, and one day I even ran it into the barn. It was a beautiful, long, dusty, broad slide, but it didn't matter much, because another dent or two in that truck wouldn't even be noticed. Daddy knew I was doing it, but he never said anything to me about it.

It was about this time that I decided I wanted to be a rodeo cowboy, so I went down to the pasture behind the tobacco barn and cornered the bull. I climbed up on his back. Nothing happened. I reached back and got hold of his tail and twisted with all my might. Something happened. He threw me right off his back and I landed on my head. It made me mad, so I got right back on him and twisted his tail again. And off I went again.

The hardest part was cornering the bull so I could get back on; that is, if you don't count hitting the ground as "hard."

It didn't take me long to decide that truck racing was way ahead of bull riding in the fun department.

Daddy owned the general store and the cotton gin in Sardis. You have to understand, we weren't poor; it's just that we weren't rich, either. Everything we got, we worked hard for, just like everybody else around us. My Grandfather Yarborough had been sort of rich. He had been a real big farmer, and he owned hundreds of acres of land that had actually made him a lot of money. He didn't spend much of it, so all fourteen of his kids learned to live pretty simple. But he did believe in education, so Daddy had gone to Carlisle Military School.

The general store was a great place where you could buy anything from feed to lantern globes to gingham by the yard to groceries to you-name-it. Inside, right smack in the middle of the store, there was a potbellied Burnside stove, surrounded by some old wooden chairs and nail kegs. The farmers sat around it and told hunting and fishing stories and spit tobacco juice into a cardboard box beside the stove. During the cold periods the belly of the stove glowed from the wood fire inside, and every once in a while you'd hear a sizzling sound and you knew that one of the guys had missed the cardboard box and hit the stove. It was part of the ritual.

The store was old and wooden, and it needed a coat of paint. It had a screen door with MERITA BREAD stenciled on it in red and yellow

11

paint, right in the middle of the screen wire. The bread company gave Daddy the door. There was a Royal Crown Cola sign and a Mail Pouch tobacco thermometer on the front of the store and a Clabber Girl baking powder and Camel cigarette signs on the side. There wasn't even a sign saying what the store was, but everybody knew it was Yarborough's Store.

I spent a lot of happy times in that old store. When I was there, I was in charge of working the old brass National cash register, which was so big I'd have to get up on a nail keg so I could crank the handle around to ring up the sale and open the cash drawer.

Just down the road, about a quarter of a mile, was Daddy's cotton gin. I'll tell you, I had fun there, too, but I also worked there. During the time the cotton was being picked, I spent more time there than anywhere else. It was a big old two-story building, covered with corrugated tin. It had a high, pitched roof, and inside it looked about as big as the National Guard Armory in Timmonsville. It wasn't, of course, but it looked that way because it was two stories high in there, and dark. It made it look mysterious to us kids.

The cotton came in mule-drawn wagons. They drove under the shed, and a great big suction pipe sucked the cotton right out of the wagons. When they turned on the suction, the mules always bucked, so the farmers had to hold on tight to the reins. The cotton went inside, where the seeds were removed and taken to a storage building out back. The cotton went to the press room where it was pressed into big bales.

I liked working in the press room best. The bales were wrapped in burlap and banded with steel bands. Each one weighed about four or five hundred pounds and looked as big as cars to me. Son worked back there, and he was determined to get me to the point where I could roll one of the bales over. Every day I came in and pushed and strained, and every day I moved it a little more. The day I finally rolled it over, Son put a big arm around my shoulder and he said, "Boy, you gonna be strong when you grow up. And determined too." That meant a lot to me.

I can't honestly say that I was always a help around the gin. At times I was an absolute menace; it depended on how many of my friends from school came over to "help" me—the more that came, the less work I did. If enough came over, Daddy ran us all off, so we spent the rest of the day playing around outside the gin. We made tunnels in the cottonseed piles and propped up pieces of wood to make rooms and played there. When the novelty of that wore off, we got the idea to jump off the two-story roof onto the stacks of cotton bales. From that came the barrel idea. We carried a big barrel up the ladder to the roof—which, in itself, was a feat—and then one of us would get in it and roll down the roof and sail through the air, onto the cotton bales below. I was the first to try it. After the barrel hit the bales it would roll across the grass in front of the gin. It was fun until I rolled across the grass *and* the highway, right in front of a bread truck. I didn't get hurt from the ride, but I sure couldn't sit down for a while after Daddy got through tanning my hide with a cane switch.

It's probably a real good thing that I didn't live near Niagara Falls.

I'll tell you, there wasn't much we didn't think of. Claude Springs, who lived close to me, was over to my place a lot. When he wasn't at our farm, I was at his. We made parachutes out of sheets and jumped off the barn. I wouldn't recommend that, either. And Claude and Jerry and I played in the mud swamp, out near the edge of the woods. That got us a whipping every day, in spite of how much we tried to wash up before we got home. I could never understand how Daddy knew we had been in the mud, except that maybe he could tell by my blond hair and brown scalp. Jerry got the idea of washing his head real good and drying his hair with the vacuum cleaner. It came clean, but his hair stood straight up. He looked like Stan Laurel. We got another whipping.

What Daddy was afraid of were all the snakes back there in the woods and around the mud swamp, but it was obvious that whipping us wasn't going to help, so one day, while we were wallowing in the mud, he sneaked back there and took all of our clothes. Of course, we took them off; I mean, you didn't think we were going to have clothes to wash, too, did you?

When Jerry and I got home, covering ourselves as well as we could with modified versions of grass skirts we had made out of leaves, he didn't even have to whip us. We were cured.

■

An important year for me was 1950. It was a year of great highs and lows in my life. The high point was building my first Soap Box racer. That was important. For one thing, it finally got me into direct competition with other kids; for another, it kept me off the roofs of the gin and the barn. But, more than that, it was a project that Daddy and I worked on together. That means more to me than almost anything I can remember about my childhood, because it's one of the very few projects we ever worked on together.

I suppose half the fun of any job like building a Soap Box racer is the planning, and I made a big thing out of that. I started long before school was out in the spring, and I spent many hours working on the plans. In school. (We won't go into that.) By the time school was out for the summer, I must have redesigned that race car a thousand times. As far as I was concerned, I had the best design this side of Indianapolis.

The next step was finding the material, so I started scrounging up lumber from everywhere. That's one of the good things about living on a farm: There's always a supply of wood, providing that you don't need pieces too long. By the time I got ready to build the racer, I had a stack of wood in the barn that was big enough to build a house. It might have looked a little like a patchwork quilt, but there was enough there.

I sat down in the middle of the dirt floor in the barn and spread out my plans for the "Cale Yarborough Special," which was going to be the Soap Box racer that people would talk about for generations to come. I could just hear the announcer: "And here it is, ladies and gentlemen, the breathtakingly beautiful racer you've all been waiting for, driven by the Sardis Flash, Cale Yarborough." And the crowd would cheer and throw their hats—people threw their hats a lot in those days when they got excited. "And there they go! Yarborough's car shoots out to a big lead. I've never seen a racer go that fast. I can't believe it. Why, he must be going a hundred miles an hour. He's across the finish line even before the other racer gets out of the starting gate." I fantasized a lot.

In my moment of glory I hadn't realized that Daddy had come into the barn and was standing behind me, watching as I waved to the crowd and thanked the president as he gave me the trophy.

"Okay, champ, you ready to get started or are you past that point already," he asked.

Back to reality. "Er . . . uh, I mean, you see . . ." I stammered. But I didn't have to explain. Daddy knelt down beside me and looked at my plans once more, and then he looked at the lumber. "I was lookin' for that lumber there," he said, pointing to the only boards longer than two feet, "over at the gin yesterday." It seemed like a good time to change the subject.

"Whatta'ya think of this?" I asked as I pointed to the plans for the frame.

"Well, for one thing, I think you're gonna need a bench saw to do it right," he said. "Why don't we take it over to the shop at the school and see if they'll let us cut it out there? We can take it in the truck."

I had a partner in my race-car project. A crew chief. We both knew that fathers were not supposed to be anything but advisers in the Soap Box project, but we also knew that there probably wasn't a racer that had ever been built where an adult wasn't directly involved to one degree or another. It definitely fell into the white-lie category.

We laid out the widest and longest pieces of wood on the barn floor and marked off the proper angles for the shape of the basic frame. And then we took it over to the school shop and cut it out. The next step was up to me, which was nailing together the pieces and making the ribs that formed the body. Again I went scrounging, this time for nails. There were a few here and there, but I had to pull a lot of them out of the barn and some of the other buildings. After all, a used nail is as good as a new nail. Besides, what's a few nails here and there in a building as big as a barn? I didn't take them all out of one place. I spread it around. The hardest job I had was straightening out those old, bent, rusty nails.

Since the racers were gravity-type cars, which means that they coasted down a hill, all of the wheels, axles, and bearings had to be the same. This was supposed to give some uniformity to the whole thing. What it really meant was that it kept the fathers from cheating any more than they already did. You had to buy your wheels and axles from your local Chevrolet dealer, since Chevy sponsored the whole Soap Box Derby. But they only cost a few dollars, so it kept it within the reach of almost anybody. Listen, I had saved that much on nails alone. Not to mention the lumber.

Daddy got more and more involved as the project went along, and when the racer was completed, we both stood back and admired it. If I do say so myself, it looked pretty good. I painted it white, for a very good reason: That's the only color enamel we had enough of to paint the whole car. White's a good-guy color, so why not?

The race was held in Darlington, which was some coincidence. While I was getting ready for my race they were putting the finishing touches on the very first superspeedway ever built for stock cars. That Labor Day, they were going to hold the first Southern 500—in Darlington.

There were some basic differences—I knew that—but I still imagined my race to be as important as the big stock-car race. When race day came, we loaded up my racer in the back of the Ford pickup and headed for Darlington. Mama and Daddy rode in the front seat, and Jerry and J.C. and I rode in the back where we could keep an eye on the world's greatest race car. I was eleven, Jerry was nine, and J.C. was two.

The Soap Box Derby was held on one of the only streets in Darlington that had a hill on it. It wasn't much of a hill, but it was a hill— South Carolina–style. There was a really big crowd in Darlington by the time we got there, and there were red-white-and-blue banners across Main Street and around the Courthouse Square. And there were pickup trucks with race cars and little kids in the back, coming from every direction. "Man, there's gonna be a lot of racers to beat,"

I thought. "This'll be harder than I figured, but the Cale Yarborough Special will get the job done." I was long on confidence.

We sat in a line of traffic, waiting to get in the lot where the cars were to be unloaded. After half an hour we were parked, and the car was unloaded and pushed over to the area where they inspected it. I guessed they were looking for big rubber-band motors or something. What they were doing was checking wheels and weighing the cars. There was a maximum weight limit; otherwise, the first two-ton Soap Box Derby racer would be the world's champ. I don't even remember anymore what the weight limit was, but it was a combined weight of car and driver. We had taken mine down to the scale at the gin about fifty times to weigh it, and I had it down to the exact weight. It was so close that I even wore the same clothes on race day that I had worn the day I got the weight down perfect. I didn't want to take any chances.

It weighed in perfect. But I had protected myself, in case their scales didn't agree with ours. I had attached some lead weights that could be taken out, one by one, until the weight was right. And I had some more in the truck that could be added if necessary. I wasn't going to give up an ounce.

I drew one of the earliest heats, and I was glad because I was really nervous. I was pacing around like a tiger in a cage. As I waited for the first heats, two cars at a time, my heart beat faster and faster and my hopes rose higher and higher. Finally the time came.

I didn't even listen to the name of the kid I was to race against. I only had one thing in mind, and that was getting the car set just right in the starting gate and getting my head down below the windshield —low enough to cut down on the wind resistance and high enough so that I could, at least, see where to steer.

The officials helped me get the car in place. I was on my own after that. Mama and Daddy and the boys were in the crowd. The cars were resting with their noses on the starting gates so that when the gates swung open, it was all up to gravity; that and design, graphite, aerodynamics, and skill in keeping the car in as straight a line as possible. Daddy told me before the race, "Keep it going perfectly straight, boy. Anytime it goes off to either side, you're losing speed."

I wiggled my behind down in the seat a little more, and I adjusted the helmet they had given me. I had my hands on the steering wheel just where I wanted them, one at ten o'clock and one at two o'clock. The man walked up between the two cars and asked the other boy if he was ready. I heard him say, "Yes, sir."

"You ready, son?" He was talking to me. "Yes, sir," I said. "I sure am." I took a big breath.

The man stepped back, and then I saw the gates start to open. It was almost like everything was happening in slow motion. It seemed to take forever for the gates to clear the front of my car, and then it seemed to take even longer for the car to start rolling. "Go! Go!" I said to myself. "Why doesn't it go?" Then it started rolling, slowly at first and then faster. I could feel the air coming in around the tiny windshield and hitting me in the face. You know, up until now I never really thought of that. Maybe I didn't even remember it, but I remember it now. I remember thinking, "Man, that's a great feeling." I didn't know it, but I was hooked.

I glanced over to the left lane, and I could tell that I was ahead by a little bit. But, as we got to the line on the track that they had told us was the halfway mark, the other kid had pulled up even. I was holding onto the wheel with all my might, and the car was going as straight as an arrow. The other car was rolling away from me.

The last thing I can remember was seeing that yellow car cross the finish line about two feet ahead of the nose of my car. It was a little hard to see what happened after that, because it's always hard to make things out too clearly through tears.

I don't know how long it was before Mama and Daddy and the boys got there, but nobody said a word at first. Daddy just held me tight to his body. And then he said, "You sure did keep it straight, boy. I never did see anybody drive a car any better."

I never forgot how bad it felt to lose.

■

Daddy's generation was tough, the entire family. But they were kind people too. You just didn't cross them. I found that out at an early age, but I was about as determined as Daddy, so that led to a lot of lickings. But the Yarboroughs were a close family, and anytime any one of them needed help, the others were there.

There had been the usual amount of tragedy for a family that size, but most of it had happened before I was old enough to remember. One of Daddy's brothers was killed when a farm tractor turned over on him, and another was killed when he was blasting out some tree stumps. One of the dynamite caps he had placed between his teeth went off while he was stringing wire. I don't remember any of that. In fact, I don't even remember my Grandfather Yarborough, because he died when I was real young.

But I do remember my Grandmother Yarborough. She was a lovely Southern lady. After Granddaddy died I guess she sort of drifted around from one of her children's houses to the other, staying a few weeks with this one and a few weeks with that one. I always looked forward to the times when she came to stay with us, because she always took a lot of time with my brothers and me. She told us stories of "how things used to be." They always started with, "Back when I was your age . . ."

Sunday was always a big family day for the Yarboroughs. We all went to church, and then we all had Sunday dinner together. All of the clan. It was always held wherever Grandma was staying. She definitely held the family together.

The Sundays were nice, even though it was a little tough sitting up straight and keeping quiet in church. But after church all of my cousins and I sat under the trees at whichever aunt's or uncle's place we were at. We talked and laughed and played games, waiting for Sunday dinner to be ready. After what seemed an eternity, Grandma always came out on the porch and called us in to "wash up and get ready to eat." I can see her as plain as day, standing there in her Sunday dress with the big apron tied around her waist and up around her neck. It's funny, but I can hardly remember my grandmother when she didn't have an apron on.

The meal was always the same, but I'll never complain about that. Grandma always fried the chicken, and it was done just right—crispy and golden brown on the outside and soft and steamy on the inside. I don't know what herbs and spices she used, but I do know, even now, that I wouldn't trade one piece of her chicken for a barrel of anybody else's. That's a taste you don't forget.

I always tried to get the drumstick, and for some reason, there always seemed to be enough for all the kids. Those chickens must have had eight legs each. The rest of the family brought the mashed potatoes and candied yams and gravy and black-eyed peas and turnips and greens. And there was always lots of sweet iced tea. The pie was the only thing that ever varied, and that depended on what was in season; it was either peach or apple or pumpkin or rhubarb or mincemeat. Any one of them was fine.

We moved when I was nine years old, into an old house over near the general store; but it was a temporary move. Daddy was going to have a new house built. While they were building the new house I used to go over there and sit on the ground, right in the middle of what was going to be the living room. I looked out through where the front window was going to be, and I figured that I was right where I wanted to be. That house was right on the main highway and right smack in the middle of Sardis. Even though it was a tiny community, it was a "community," and that meant a lot to a kid who had grown up on a farm. I was going to live in a community. It made a big difference, even though it was only a mile or so across the field from where I had lived all my life.

I was so anxious to get in that new brick house that I spent about as much time over there as the carpenters did. Man, what a house. It was even going to have indoor plumbing.

When the day came to move, I was as happy as a lark. But I knew I was going to miss the old house that had always been my home. As young as I was, I was sure that I was going to miss the smell and feel of that old house. It was a bittersweet experience.

THE HURT I HAD WAS A PRIVATE ONE,

AND I WASN'T GOING TO SHARE IT

WITH ANYBODY IN THE WORLD.

2

All my relatives tell me that I am a lot like my Daddy. I guess he was a daredevil too. He must have been, because the things he did as a youth were a lot like the things I found myself doing. For one thing, he was a good athlete, particularly in football. He kicked the ball barefooted, and he could kick it a country mile; I've seen him do it. And he was one of the first to fly an airplane in our area. He got the bug, so he went down to M. B. Huggins Airport in Timmonsville, which had a grass strip and a couple of hangars and a Piper Cub, and he took a lesson or two. That was all he needed, because he picked up everything so fast.

There were several people interested in flying and even a few who made a living out of it by crop dusting. I'm really surprised that he never got into that end of it, because it was the daredevil type of thing he loved to do.

Flying any kind of a plane in the Pee Dee Region was a dangerous thing. In fact, it has to be one of the toughest things man can do. It sounds easy because there's so much flat land around home, but it isn't, because there are horrendous thermal drafts everywhere, and during much of the year, thunderstorms can come up in a minute or two. It's dangerous. I'll tell you, a lot of pilots bought the farm because of the bad flying conditions in that South Carolina sand country.

Daddy got the bug so much that he bought his own plane, a Piper, and he spent hours teaching himself the finer points of flying. He took me up with him often, and I watched everything he did, because, after my first flight, I knew that I, too, was destined to soar like an eagle. I loved the feeling it gave me, particularly the sudden drops when we hit an air pocket or some turbulence, which was often. The feeling it gave me in the pit of my stomach made my skin tingle.

Daddy and all of the rest of the pilots around there did all of the mechanical work on their planes. I mean, where were you going to find an airplane mechanic in Timmonsville? You just did the work on the plane yourself, like you did on the tractor or the pickup truck. Simple. Even the crop dusters did their own mechanical work. But most of them kept their planes right on their own farms, so why not? They landed on the public highway and taxied to the farm and got out and pushed it over behind the barn. Nobody thought a thing about it.

If you happened to be driving down the road and you saw a plane coming in for a landing down there in front of you, you simply said, "Well, there comes ol' Tim in from dustin', better pull over and let him land." So you pulled your car way off to the side of the road and let him land. And ol' Tim waved to you as he taxied by.

You could always tell where a crop duster lived, because all of the trees were gone from either side of the road around his place. Daddy knew all of the crop dusters, and he learned a lot of his techniques from watching them fly. He really admired them, and I think that if it hadn't been for the general store and the cotton gin and the tobacco farming keeping him so busy, he would have been a crop duster. He could fly just as well as any of them. I watched him come in over the treetops many times. He came in low over the tobacco field and banked it at a sharp right at the end of the field and lifted it right over the row of longleaf pines at the far end. Then he took it up high, almost into a stall, and pulled it out and glided back across the farm and out of sight. We knew he was headed for Huggins Airport and that he would be home in fifteen or twenty minutes. Daddy loved that plane more than anything.

I remember Mama saying to him, "Julian, you're thirty-one years old and you act like a kid. Why, at times I think you care more about that airplane than you do me." He laughed and said, "Aw, c'mon, Annie Mae, you know I like you a lot better. Besides, that ol' plane can't cook." And she shook her head and went back in the house. But I don't think she was convinced that she was number one and that the plane was number two.

Daddy taught me two loves: flying was one; automobile racing, the other.

There were dirt tracks everywhere when I was a kid, and once we started going to the races, we never stopped. We went as far away as Columbia, where they raced on Thursday nights—that was seventy-five miles away—and we went to Florence on Friday nights and Sumter on Saturday nights. They were close.

Qualifying heats started at about seven o'clock, and the first heat race was usually at eight or eight-thirty. We were always there by six o'clock or so, and we went over into the pits and looked at the cars and even talked to some of the drivers. What a thrill it was to actually talk to some of the guys. Once, in Columbia, I got to talk to Junior Johnson and Cotton Owens on the same night. It wasn't often that we got to see names like that, but occasionally they came to Columbia, or even Sumter, and that was a special treat. Oh, Junior and Cotton weren't the names they later became when they started running Grand National, but to me they were about the closest thing to living legends that I ever expected to see.

About the time the cars were ready to qualify, we went back across the track and got us a good spot along the fence so that we could see the cars as closely as possible. There was a spot down past the far end of the grandstands where you could stand and still be out of the way of the people sitting up there. And we got a good view of the cars as they came down the front straightaway and slid through the first and second turns.

On all of the tracks there was a ten-foot-high wire fence in front of us and a wooden guardrail in front of that, so there wasn't much danger. But you did get sprayed with dirt pretty good when the cars got up high in the loose stuff near the fence.

Daddy and I used to stand there and hook our fingers through the old fences and get as dusty as could be. It was almost like being in the race car, I thought. By the second or third heat I got hungry, so we would get hot dogs and Cokes and come right back to the fence. Of course, the hot dogs got covered with dust before we could eat them, but that didn't make a bit of difference. It made them taste better.

Sumter and Florence were quarter-mile tracks, so you didn't even have to move your head much to watch the cars go around. Columbia was a half-mile track, so the cars went faster. I'm not sure which one I liked best; I think it was the one where I happened to be at the time. But I would watch Daddy; I would watch his eyes as he followed a certain car around the track, and I could tell, even by the time they qualified, which one he was going to cheer for, and that's the one I chose. So, when the race started, we both yelled like mad for our hero. If he won, we yelled even louder.

Once in a while we sat up in the old wooden grandstands if it was particularly dusty, but it was never the same as being down near the fence. Actually you could see more of the race from up there, especially if you sat up high, so we always tried to get in the back row. It was one extreme or the other. But it didn't matter where we sat; we had a good time. We were buddies, and that's all that mattered. The fact that we were watching a race was just icing on the cake.

The racing season was a long one, because the weather stays warm through November, and then it starts warming up again around the middle of February, so, I'll tell you, we went to a lot of races once we got started. I'll bet we averaged two a week.

I missed the races when I went to church camp, but I loved the camp, so it was worth it. The Sardis Baptist Church had a summer camp that was open to kids between the ages of eleven and seventeen, and 1950 was the first year I got to go. It was in Aiken, one hundred miles from home, but it was like a different world because we got to sleep in cabins and they had a camp fire every night, and, well, it was just different from anything I had ever done. It was an adventure. But I missed being home for the first few days.

The camp fires were the most fun. We sat around them every night, and the leaders told ghost stories and just generally scared the wits out of all of us. There were six boys and a leader in each cabin. The leaders or counselors, or whatever they were called, were high-school kids, but they seemed very old to us. I can remember how spooky it was going back to our tents every night after the ghost stories. I imagined that I saw something behind every tree. After the lantern was turned out there was always something outside the tent going, *"Whooooooo, whoooooo."* Everything always got real quiet, and then someone said something funny and the giggling started. It was the same every night.

It took me a day or so longer than the rest of the boys to get over being homesick, because not only was *I* away from home, but Mama and Daddy and the boys were too. The boys were too young to go to camp, so Mama and Daddy had taken them to Myrtle Beach for a few days. I knew that Daddy was going to fly back to the farm every day to check on the tobacco crop, because he had some men working for him, but still, it was sort of a strange feeling, knowing that there wasn't anybody at home. What if I got sick?

There was a lot of joking at camp on Friday, because it was Friday the thirteenth. I learned to believe in the superstition that day. My family had been a little superstitious, so I guess I was inclined that way, anyway. But I got through most of the day without anything serious happening to me, and I convinced myself that Friday the thirteenth was no different from Friday the twelfth or Friday the fourteenth. The day wasn't over.

We were at the camp fire, and the ghost stories were a little wilder than usual, when the camp director came over to me and took me by the arm.

"Cale, come over here, son," he said. "I've got to talk to you." His voice was very serious, like when you've done something wrong, but I knew I hadn't done anything, so I thought he was just trying to scare me. Another ghost story. But when he led me over to the edge of the clearing, away from the others, and put his arm around me, I got the same feeling in my stomach that I always got when we hit an air pocket in the plane.

"Cale, I'm taking you home, son," he said. "There's been an accident. Now, son, you've always got to remember that God acts in mysterious ways, and none of us—not a single one—can explain why some things happen, but they do, and, well . . ."

"What is it? What's happened?" I asked. Tears were already welling up in my eyes, and I brushed them aside with the back of my hand. "What is it?"

"Cale, your daddy's been killed. His plane crashed." I think he said more, but I'm not real sure. In fact, I'm not real sure about anything after he led me away from the camp fire. After he told me what had happened everything just sort of went blank. There wasn't any feeling in my body at all.

I didn't say a word on the way back home. I just sat in the passenger seat and stared out at the darkness. I was eleven years old, and I thought my world had ended. I wanted to cry, but, well, I don't know how to explain it; I hurt too bad to cry. I had never felt like that before. The tears wouldn't come. When I got home, Mama and the boys were there, and when I saw her and the house, I thought my heart was going to tear out of my chest. The pain was real bad.

Mama hugged me close to her. My aunts and uncles were there, and everybody was crying. And everybody told me how I had to be "the man of the house" now. I had to be strong. I heard it a dozen times, and I didn't want to hear it again. I didn't want to hear anything. I didn't even want to hear what had happened, but Mama told me.

"Your daddy came to check on the workers," she said, "and he got started back late, after dark. Nobody knows what happened. He just went down in the woods, between here and the beach. He loved you a lot, Cale."

"I know, Mama," I said. "Can I go to my room now?"

She nodded, and I went in my room and closed the door. I laid down across my bed and cried harder than I have ever cried in my life. The hurt I had was a private one, and I wasn't going to share it with anybody in the world. I didn't understand one bit of it.

■

There was so much to do on the farm after Daddy's death that I guess I didn't have time to grieve too much. At least, that's what I told Mama and my aunts and uncles. I can remember saying, "I really miss Daddy, but I've got to take over" or "I've got the boys to worry about now and all the other chores." It was all a show. I did have time to grieve; it's just that I did it all on the inside while I smiled on the outside. You remember that old song that goes, "I'm laughing on the outside and crying on the inside"? Well, that pretty well sums up the way I felt.

I couldn't understand why the world around me was still going on. But, while I worked in the tobacco field or helped with the chores or played with my friends, I laughed and held my head up high. When I was alone, I thought my heart was going to break. I mean, I thought Daddy was God Almighty, and all of a sudden, he was gone. It took me a lot of years before I began to feel complete again.

But Mama was strong, and she took over everything. That gave us all a great incentive. She ran the general store and the cotton gin and the farm. She hired men to help us plant tobacco and to do a lot of the heavy work. I'll have to admit, things ran smoothly. A lot of women in her position would have knuckled under and sold everything and moved us away but not Mama; she was determined to keep our lives as close to the way they had been as she possibly could.

Nobody could ever take Daddy's place, but my mother filled the gap better than anybody can ever know. She never left us alone, and she paid attention to us and fussed over us like an old mother hen. Jerry and I both became restless sleepers; we woke up a lot during the night. I never asked him if it was because he was having bad dreams, but I'm sure it was. I know it's why *I* woke up.

We just didn't talk about Daddy's death. If someone brought it up, Mama would immediately change the subject. And when we started waking up so much, she moved her bed in with us and slept there with us from then on. Jerry started sleeping through the night; I know, because I was awake and I could tell. Nobody knew that I wasn't sleeping. There was one good thing about the dark: You could let the hurt show and nobody could tell.

■

Oddly, it was racing that helped me get over the hurt. With the spring of 1951 came the desire to run in the Soap Box Derby again. This time it was going to be held in Florence, and this time I didn't intend to lose, so I hauled the trusty racer out of the barn and began planning on what it would take to make it a winner.

The aerodynamics had to be the problem, since the weight of all the cars was the same and the wheels and bearings were identical, so I spent the next few weeks working on new designs. In school, of course. I decided that the front end needed to be a little more streamlined and that the windshield could be an inch or so lower. After all, I could scrunch down some more.

This time I did all the work on the car myself. I reshaped the front end and cut down the windshield to the point that there wasn't much left of it. I toyed with the idea of eliminating it completely and using a periscope, but Jerry talked me out of it. Still, I cut it down a little more.

When the modifications were complete, I painted it red, white, and blue.

There weren't any hills around, but Jerry and J.C. pushed me up and down the dirt road so that I could tell whether or not I was going to be able to see. I could see enough. But the important thing about the test runs was that the steering felt tight to me. Maybe that was the reason I had lost.

I took the front end completely apart and sanded and filed all the parts until they worked more smoothly. I was ready.

On race day Uncle Dwight came over and helped us load the racer in the old pickup. He and Mama and the boys went along again; the three of us in the back, just like before.

They held the race just outside of Florence, on a back road that had the only hill in the whole area. It still wasn't the steepest spot on earth, but it had a little more of a grade than the course in Darlington. The cars would run faster. All of them.

Some of the cars were works of art, and you had to know that the fathers, and Lord knows who else, had a lot more to do with their design and construction than the kids did. Some of them even had sponsors. There were names of companies painted on the sides of them. Listen, some of them looked like the race cars I had seen at Sumter and Columbia. I wouldn't have been too surprised to hear some of them fire up an engine and go *up* the hill. But it didn't dim my enthusiasm one bit. I had all the confidence in the world in my design and in my ability to keep it going straight.

Once more I got an early starting spot, and once more I had butterflies in my stomach. I paced up and down the area where all the cars were lined up, and I looked at each one, particularly my opponent in the first race. His was one of the nifty-looking ones. It was sponsored by some Chevrolet dealership, and I wondered if they had built the car for him. I even imagined the mechanics working day after day in the shop to build all sorts of trick devices. But I couldn't see any of them, so I didn't let it worry me.

Two by two, the cars began to disappear in front of me, and after twenty or thirty minutes it was my turn. Uncle Dwight and Mama and the boys wished me luck and went over where they could get a good view of the race. The officials helped me get my car in position, and I climbed in and put on the helmet. It felt good.

I scrunched down in the seat so far that it looked like there wasn't a driver. It was perfect, except that I was looking straight into the inside of the racer. I scooted back up enough so that I could at least see out over the cowl.

The starting gates were painted red, white, and blue and had Chevrolet bow-tie emblems on them. I looked straight at the Chevy emblem on the gate in front of me. I didn't even glance at my opponent because I didn't want him to think I didn't have confidence. The butterflies were stirring around so much that I thought I was going to throw up. Terrific.

Everything happened quickly this time. The gates swung open, and the car started to move immediately. The steeper hill was going to be exactly what I needed. I could see the other car right beside me, and as we rolled faster and faster, he was still right there. He was still there at the halfway marker and beyond. We were both running as straight as arrows. I knew I was moving much faster than that first race.

The hill got a little steeper three-quarters of the way down, and it still looked like we were in a dead heat. I could really feel the wind coming over and around what little windshield I had. Man, I loved that feeling. Now, if I could only pull away from this kid, everything would be fine. But I could see the finish line coming up, and we were still wheel-to-wheel. When was my racer going to pull ahead?

We crossed the finish line in the same dead heat. At least, that's how it looked to me. I really couldn't tell who had won. I braked my car to a stop at the proper place and waited. All of a sudden I saw two officials running toward us. They ran right past my car and over to the other kid. They were slapping him on the back. I had lost again, and again in the first heat. I'll tell you, losing was getting old in a hurry.

This time there weren't any tears in my eyes. I was just plain mad. And I promised myself that I would never run in the Soap Box Derby again. But I knew even then that I would race again. And I knew that I would be a winner. Only I would never compete again in anything where driving skill had so little to do with the outcome. I needed a motor in front of me. I just had to wait a few years, until I was old enough. From that day on I knew what was down the road for me. And losing wasn't in the cards.

I think the rest of my childhood must have prepared me for what I figured would be the wild and dangerous life of a race-car driver. I really don't know if I had some subconscious idea that the more wild-and-woolly things I did, the easier it was going to be for me to race a car, but as I look back at it, it certainly appears that way. I became a real daredevil in everything I did.

THERE'S NO WAY A PLYMOUTH
CAN BEAT A CADILLAC. NO WAY!

3

■

Darlington was about fifteen miles from home, and from the time I was eleven years old, it became a mecca for me. You see, that's when they built the Darlington Raceway—in 1950—and it's when they ran the first Southern 500, which was to be stock-car racing's answer to the Indianapolis 500. Well, that first year it not only became the answer, but to everybody in the South, it became the most important sporting event in the world—the World Series, the Kentucky Derby, *and* the Indianapolis 500 all wrapped up into one.

From its first race, Darlington Raceway set the standard for cars for the next year. I mean, whatever car won that race was king of the highway until the next race. That race alone kept Hudson in business for years, because if it hadn't been for the success of the Hudson Hornet, the company would have gone belly-up long before it did.

And the race was the perfect launching pad for the Rocket 88 Olds.

I know that if Daddy had lived, he would have become a race-car driver and would have driven at Darlington. There's also no question in my mind that he would have been a good one, because he had that Yarborough determination.

Daddy and I listened to that first race in 1950 on the radio, and I'll have to admit that it was hard for me to picture a track as big as a mile and a quarter. To me a half-mile track was big. But we sat with our ears glued to the radio and pulled for guys like Red Byron in the Cadillac and for Joe Weatherly and Curtis Turner and some of the drivers we had seen at short tracks around home. I felt like I knew many of them. After all, I had been sprayed by their dust many times.

That race was important to all of us who were ever to have anything to do with racing, so I think it's important to tell you about it; we got the story from the radio and from some friends of Daddy's who had been there.

The real story began a few days before the race. Bill France, Curtis Turner, Alvin Hawkins, and Johnny Mantz bought a new Plymouth sedan in Winston-Salem, North Carolina, on the way to Darlington. They paid $1,700 for it, and they bought it just to get there and to have something to run around in once they got down there.

They figured that they would either race it on a short track somewhere later or sell it. They really didn't know what they were going to do with it. But that car came in handy. It was always parked outside the Darlington Motel, and anytime anybody needed to go for food or drinks or whatever, they took the little black Plymouth. They took it back and forth to the Elks' Club in Florence. Everywhere. It was their hack.

Well, Mantz was a hotshot Indy driver who had come down to find a ride for the Southern 500, but by the day before the race, he hadn't found one. He came back to the motel, looking for the Plymouth.

"Where's the Plymouth?" he asked.

"I think somebody took it into town," Bill France said.

"Well, tell them to leave it here when they get back," he said. "I'm gonna race it tomorrow."

Everybody thought he was crazy, especially on race day. There were Oldsmobiles and Fords and Cadillacs and Lincolns. Everything. And there was Mantz in that six-cylinder Plymouth. He had come up with some Indy Firestones, and he was the only one in the race with anything that even remotely resembled racing tires. But everybody doubted that it would make up for the lack of horsepower.

But Mantz put on a show. He just drove around the track, out of the groove, at a steady pace all day—about 70 or 75 miles an hour —and he did everything right. He pitted under caution—which is something he had learned at Indy—and generally he made everybody else on the track madder than a wet hen. Particularly after he got the lead.

Red Byron in Red Vogt's Cadillac and Fireball Roberts in an Olds 88 would blaze right by him and roar down the back stretch, and then, *ker-boom!* a tire would blow and into the pits they would go. And there would be Mantz, tooling along at about 72 miles an hour, right through the turns and down the straightaway, past the pits where everybody was frantically changing tires. Curtis Turner said after the race that he knew exactly how many pit stops he had made—twenty seven—because he counted the blown-out tires in his pit.

When the checkered flag came down, Mantz had built up a two-lap lead on the field. Everybody was in a state of shock, especially Red Vogt, who was over in the garage where they were checking the Plymouth. He kept saying, "I know there's something phony. There's no way a Plymouth can beat a Cadillac. No way!"

They checked everything. In fact, they worked all night, while Vogt paced the floor, muttering, "No way." Everything was torn apart— the carburetor, the exhaust, the heads. The pistons and valves were taken out; even the gas tank was taken off. And the wheels and brakes. Everything.

As a car owner, Vogt had a right under NASCAR rules to protest, so he made them go through all of it again. Finally they said, "Red, there it all is, you check it."

"Yeah, I know," he said. "There it all is, but there's no way. . . ."

During the night they had been to the Plymouth dealer four times; they got him out of bed twice. They compared valve springs and heads and carbs. They even compared mill marks on the heads to see if they were turned in the right direction. They had everything off the car that would come off. After another hour of looking at everything, they dumped all the parts in the back of the Plymouth and declared Mantz the official winner of the first Southern 500. In the hack. But they never did convince Red Vogt that a Plymouth could outrun a Cadillac.

You can see why the excitement was so high when time came for the 1951 Southern 500. Daddy and I had planned to be there for that race, but as race time drew near, I gave up hope of ever getting there. With him gone my hopes died.

By then I was going to school in Timmonsville, because the Sardis School only went up to sixth grade, and I rode the bus the six miles each way—when I didn't ride my bike. I really preferred the bike because I liked the wind in my face as I raced other kids to school. If there weren't any other kids, I raced imaginary people, such as Red Byron or Curtis Turner.

But one morning when I was riding the bus (it must have rained), I overheard a bunch of the bigger boys talking about the Darlington race. They were going. I was out of my seat and into the middle of their conversation in a flash.

"Hey, fellas, you got room for me? I mean, can I go to Darlington with you?" I pleaded. "I won't get in your way and I'll pay my own way and . . ."

They looked at me and then at each other, and one of them said, "Sure, I guess so, but you're gonna be on your own once you get over there. We don't want no little kid hangin' around us, you understand?"

"It's a deal," I said. Man, did I understand. The Southern 500! But then they started talking about some girls that they were going to meet over there, and I didn't understand that. I couldn't figure out why in the world anybody would want to fool around with girls when there were race cars around. But I figured that it was their life. If they wanted to mess it up with girls, that was their business.

Around lunchtime it hit me. What about Mama? What if she wouldn't let me go? I spent the afternoon planning what I was going to tell her. Let's see. . . . "Mother, I won an essay contest in school today, and the first prize is a trip to the Southern 500." No, she would never buy that, because she knew that I'd never get interested enough in school to win anything. It would have to be a better story than that. "Mother"—I always called her Mother when I had done something wrong or when I wanted something—"I have been asked by the school to represent them at the Southern 500." Why? I didn't *know* why.

The direct approach was the only one that had a chance, so when I got home that evening, I went right up to her and said, "Mother, can I go to Darlington for the race on Labor Day? It's a holiday, you know. I've got a ride, and I've saved up enough money to pay my own way, and I'll be careful, and I'll wear clean underwear, and—"

"Slow down," she said. "Who are you going with?"

"Some of the boys from school," I said, mentioning their names. "They're good drivers, and they really want me to go. They *asked* me."

"I'll have to think about it," she said.

Think about it? *Think* about it? Man, it would be like some guy waiting for the jury to come back. My life was hanging in the balance, because if I didn't get to go, I would die. There was no question. Just before bedtime she said, "Cale, I've made some phone calls, and from what I can find out, the boys you're going with are good boys, so I guess you can go."

I went straight up in the air. Darlington! The Southern 500!

"But you make sure about the clean underwear," she said.

Listen, I would have been willing to wear *two* pairs of clean underwear.

The trip from Sardis to Darlington seemed like it took a week. I'd made the same trip a dozen times, but this one seemed like they had moved Darlington to somewhere up near New Jersey. When we got there, traffic was lined up for miles and people were starting to park in fields two miles from the track. The roads were lined on both sides with parked cars, and there were people walking, coming from all directions. I had never seen anything like it. I figured that everybody in the entire world was there. We finally found a place where we could pull off into a field and park, so in we went, and everybody abandoned the car.

"Remember where we parked, Cale," one of them said. "And we'll meet you right here after the race. And we ain't waitin' on you, so you'd better be here."

"I'll be here," I said over my shoulder. I was already well on my way to the track, running at a pace that would have gotten me in the Olympics. By the time I got to the track, there were huge lines at all the ticket booths. There were big signs that read, RESERVED SEATS $6. BOX SEATS $8. GENERAL ADMISSION $4. CHILDREN $2. I had the two dollars, that was no problem; but the lines drove me crazy. I mean, I could hear the race-car motors running, and I had to get in there. I wondered if I could figure out some way to get in without paying so I would have plenty of money for Cokes and hot dogs.

A kid was passing out pamphlets. He gave me one and I read it. And I reread it. Wow! I still have it. It read:

Darlington International Raceway today is the scene of the nation's greatest stock-car race of the year . . . the second annual "Southern 500" strictly stock car speed classic . . . under NASCAR sanction.

Darlington, the nation's finest raceway, that's how the new mile-and-a-quarter asphalt track is regarded by the race fans throughout the country.

Not another track in the United States of this size provides such ample facilities . . . a grandstand from which you can see every corner of the track from every seat . . . something that is better than any other track in the country.

For speed . . . Darlington ranks second only to Indianapolis . . . with its two-and-a-half-mile span.

"For beauty . . . there's none finer than Darlington Raceway!

Three programs were scheduled for the first year . . . 1950 . . . with Johnny Mantz of Long Beach, California, winning the Labor Day race . . . then Johnny Parsons, Van Nuys, California, won the 200-mile AAA big car race . . . the motorcycle program that included three events was cancelled due to rain after only the novice 50-mile race saw a new record established for all tracks.

The 1951 program includes only two events—the 250-mile AAA big car race on July 4th . . . won by Little Walt Faulkner of Long Beach, California. . . .

So far in the three major races at Darlington Raceway, the California drivers have monopolized honors . . . but can they do it today? . . . That's the big question . . . and the "Rebels" with their confederate flags flying . . . are out to upset the California fruit cart.

Who's the favorite today? Pick your own. Everybody else has . . . and they can't all be right.

I couldn't wait any longer. I went around to the side of the track, over where there weren't any gates or people, and I walked up and down until I found a spot where the fence was a little loose. I looked around to see if anybody was watching, got down on my belly, and slid under like a snake. Oh, man, I was inside the Darlington Raceway. And I had two bucks in my pocket. I was, at that moment, the happiest kid in the world.

Darlington was the biggest place I had ever seen. I knew that it had to be the best showplace of racetracks in the whole world. The grandstands seemed to go on forever, and a big portion of them along the start/finish line were the box seats. I figured that you had to be the luckiest person in the world—or the richest—to sit there. There must have been a lot of both, because the stands were already nearly full. And then I looked at the track. Man! As I stood above the first turn and looked over toward turn four, it looked like the other end of it was in another county. I could just imagine how it would feel to race around that.

It was hot at the track, about 95 degrees, and I saw the heat waves coming off the asphalt surface. There were people pouring in from all the gates, in T-shirts and dress shirts and some of them with no shirts at all. And the women, well, a lot of them were dressed like I had never seen. And some of them almost didn't have on any shirts, either. About every other person had a Styrofoam cooler, and I knew that there probably wasn't a piece of fried chicken or a can of beer left in South Carolina.

Over in the infield I saw the tents and pick-up trucks and scaffolds. There was smoke from barbecue fires and people were laughing and throwing footballs and Lord knows what else. It looked like a jungle in there. I figured that a lot of them had been there all night because about half of them were asleep in the grass and on blankets and on top of the pick-ups. There were bodies everywhere.

But the most important thing was happening in the pits. I could actually see the cars and the people in there, and I knew some of them had to be drivers. You see, it was hard to tell drivers from a distance, because they dressed just like everybody else in those days, even when they were driving. It was long before driving suits. Everything about Darlington was informal, so I knew that I could get over there in the pits. I was right.

I walked right across the track, in the stream of people going over there, and I went right into the pits. I recognized a lot of drivers from their pictures in newspapers; a few I had seen racing on the short tracks. I immediately recognized Fireball Roberts and Curtis Turner and Herb Thomas and Lee Petty and Fonty Flock. Man, I was right in the midst of my heroes.

All of the race cars were there. I touched Lee Petty's Plymouth and Marshall Teague's Hudson Hornet, and Frank Mundy's Studebaker and Buddy Shuman's Ford. I touched them. This was as close to heaven as I would ever get; or even wanted to, for that matter.

I went from car to car, saying, "Hello, Fireball," "Hi, Buddy," "How'ya doin', Fonty," and, do you know, every one of them spoke to me: "Hi, kid," or just "Hi," but they spoke to me.

If I hadn't been hooked before, you know, from the Soap Box Derby racing, and running the pickup and the motorcycle as fast as I could, I certainly was now. There guys were my buddies. I had rubbed elbows with them in their own environment, the pits at Darlington.

I leaned against the race cars with them and listened to them joking and carrying on, and I peered over front fenders into engine compartments with them. I really felt a part of it, because, well, because I *was* a part of it—in my mind, at least. Oh, nobody included me in their conversations and they didn't ask me how I thought the timing should be set or anything like that, but they didn't run me off either. That's being a part of it for a little kid.

I was brought back to reality when one of the guards said, "Hey, kid, you're gonna have to get back over there in your seat now. We're gonna be startin' the race right away." But it was all right, because I had been to the hub of racing—the pits at Darlington. As I walked back across the hot asphalt track, I turned and took one last look at the pit area, and I knew that in a few years I would be there with my very own race car. There was no question in my mind.

By the time I was back to the grandstand side of the track, they were starting to fire up some of the race cars and move them from the pits out toward the racetrack. I had to find a good place to watch the race, quick. I couldn't sit in the reserved section, and all of the unreserved seats were filled, so I headed for the fence, where I had watched most of the short track races with Daddy. I stopped near the first turn.

As I stood there I thought about Daddy and figured that if he had been alive then, I probably would be standing right where I was, by myself, because he would have been out there racing. He would have been.

It was reality time again.

"Hey, kid, you can't stand there," said some guy with an official-looking shirt on. "You're blockin' people's view. You'll have to get in your seat or move over there out of the way." He motioned with a big open hand toward the second turn. Well, I didn't have a seat, and there was nothing but bushes over there. I didn't have much choice. I headed for the bushes just past the first turn.

The view from over there was better, anyway, I told myself; and it was. I could see the whole track. I was content in my own reserved section in the boondocks.

I wasn't the only one over there, either. There were a couple of hundred people there who had probably stayed in the pits too long, just like me, or couldn't afford anything else. Just like me. I got myself a good spot, ready to watch the race. Somebody yelled, "Hey, kid, you're blockin' my view." It was definitely a "hey-kid" day. I moved a little farther down, but I could still see everything.

The cars started to move out on the track, and as they came toward me, I got goose bumps. Even though they were going slow, the noise was unbelieveable as they went by. All of them had their mufflers off, and they sounded like the most powerful cars in the world. But I knew that it was mostly because of the exhaust. Most of the time the muffler was off our pickup, and it sounded fierce, and the old Indian motorcycle that had been around the farm for years never had a muffler. I knew about exhaust sounds. Taking off a muffler always made you *feel* like you were going faster.

The man on the PA system said there would be another pace lap, and then they would go racing. They came by again. And the goose bumps popped up again. I could see the starter down at the edge of the track, the green flag behind his back. When the cars came out of the fourth turn, he was going to wave it and the race would be on. There were seventy-five cars on the track, and it was the most beautiful sight I had ever seen. They were in rows of two, all painted bright colors and all just raring to go.

The starter pulled the flag from behind his back and waved it like mad. All of a sudden it sounded like the biggest Fourth of July fireworks show in the world. You could *feel* the sound on your skin as the cars roared by. I'm sure my mouth was wide-open, because, I guarantee you, I was in seventh heaven. It was just like I imagined it to be. There were the guys I had been rubbing elbows with only a few minutes before. My buddies. Hot dog, I was watching big-time stock-car racing.

I didn't have one favorite driver. If you want to know, I didn't know too much about any of them. You see, NASCAR was still pretty new, and there wasn't a whole lot in the newspapers about the races. Besides that, I didn't see a newspaper too often, anyway. Once in a while one of the boys would bring a clipping to school or a photo from the paper, and I always tried to trade them out of it—you know, a couple of marbles or a baseball card—but I'll have to admit that my collection of driver's pictures wasn't too big. I was going to cheer for the drivers who had been the nicest to me in the pits. My friends.

Frank Mundy had started from the pole in his new Studebaker. Also up near the front were Marshall Teague in his Hudson Hornet and Fonty Flock in his Olds 88 and Fireball Roberts in a new Ford. I tried to pick out other drivers, but they were going by me so fast that their numbers were a blur. Man, oh man, what a race! Even though I wasn't completely sure who was who, I still waved to them like mad. Somehow I felt that they would know that the waves were for them. After the cars got past me and into the second turn, I could make out the numbers, so it took me only a few laps to be able to follow the cars I wanted to follow, all the way around the track.

Marshall Teague went past Frank Mundy right in front of me, and it looked like they scraped. The Hudson was in the lead, right where it stayed for the first fifty laps. My standing place was a perfect one to see the action, because most of it was happening right in front of me. There was a flat spot in the track in the first turn, so there were a lot of spins and crashes right there. And it seemed that most of the blowouts were there, too, and there were a lot of them because the temperature had gotten up to near 100 degrees. With the heat and the high speeds, the tires were popping like popcorn. Not to mention some of the engines.

Herb Thomas, in another Hudson, took the lead and held on to it for most of the rest of the race, but there still was a lot of real racing. They were averaging over 100 miles an hour, and when you're running that hard, there has to be excitement. I was enough of a race fan to know that. Unfortunately, a lot of my buddies left the race in exciting ways.

Herb Thomas won, Jesse James Taylor was second in another Hornet, and Buddy Shuman was third in a Ford. Because of all the caution flags, the race lasted six and a half hours, but it didn't seem too long to me. The truth of the matter is, I wish it had lasted another six and a half hours.

I stayed right there near the fence until all the cars were off the track and all the PA announcements had been made. I knew that Herb Thomas had won $8,800 that Fireball had won $800 for sixth place, that Tim Flock had won $300 for thirteenth place, that Lee Petty had won $250 for sixteenth place, and everything in between.

And I knew that 35,000 people had been there. I knew it all. You learn things like that when you outlast everybody.

What a day. What a race.

It was only after the PA went off that I remembered that I still had two dollars in my pocket. I had been so wrapped up in the race that I hadn't even eaten. I had been in the same spot all day, yelling my head off.

I bought a Coke and two hot dogs. I stuffed the hot dogs in my jeans pockets and headed for the car. As I moved along with the crowd I kept wishing that I had time to go back over to the pits with the thousands of people who had gone over there from the grandstands, but I was afraid that the boys would leave without me. I hadn't seen them all day. So I filed out with the crowd, eating my hot dogs and drinking my Coke. And smiling. It had been, I figured, the greatest day of my life.

I used to fantasize a lot, wondering what it would be like if I had a million dollars, and right then, I knew exactly what I would do with some of it: I would buy a six-pack of Hudson Hornets, just like the one that had won the race. I would have one for almost every day of the week and maybe a Cadillac like Red Byron's for Sunday. I wasn't alone. I heard lots of people talking about the Hudson, and I was sure that a lot of them would probably buy one, just because it won the race. Winning that race had to mean a lot to auto manufacturers.

The boys weren't there yet when I got to the car, so I waited. And I waited. Almost an hour. I knew that they were fooling around with those girls. I mean, I could understand it if they had gone to see the *cars*, but girls? Yuck! I was young.

I could have gone back to the pits after all.

**IT TURNS OUT THAT MY ENTIRE
LIFE WAS MADE UP OF DOWNRIGHT
BIZARRE HAPPENINGS.**

4

■

About a year and a half after Daddy's death Mama started seeing Vernon Floyd, who was from Olanta. He was a kind and polite man, and he came to the house a lot. He treated the three of us boys real good, and we all accepted him just like Mama asked us to, as a friend. But I was old enough to see that it wasn't going to be too long before Vernon—that's what we all called him, even little J.C.—was going to be moving in and taking over Daddy's place.

The pain had started to go away a little—until Vernon, and then it came back strong. It took on a deeper, duller form, and there was a period when I just didn't think I would be able to conceal my hurt and my anger because someone had the nerve to try to take the place of my daddy.

Mama confirmed my greatest fears one day when she called us boys together for a family meeting. I knew what it was going to be about, and Jerry knew, too, but we had never talked about it among ourselves. As a matter of fact, we never talked about Daddy's death or Vernon and Mama or all the work there was to do or anything. We just went along like the "good little troopers" everybody kept telling us we were.

"Boys," Mama said in that tone of voice that is reserved for church and other serious times. It's not the same one she used when she was upset with us, it was the one when we were about to be told something that was "for our own good."

"Boys," she repeated, "you know that Vernon and I have been seeing a lot of each other, and you know that we need some help around the farm, don't you?"

"Yes'm," we said on cue.

"Well, you know, too, that people's lives do go on after a great tragedy. God wants it that way, doesn't he?"

"Yes'm."

"Boys, there's nobody in the world that can ever take your daddy's place in your hearts," she said, "and I would never try to have anyone do it. But Vernon and I are going to get married, and I want you to try to accept him as a friend and a companion, not as somebody who's taking Daddy's place. Just as a friend. You understand?"

The "yes'm" was smaller, almost a whisper. I, for one, didn't know if I could do it. In fact, I know I couldn't have done it if Mama hadn't done what she did next. She went out on the porch and brought Vernon inside.

He looked at each one of us slowly, one at a time. And he said, "Boys, I think a lot of your mother, and I think a lot of you. In fact, I feel like, oh, I don't know, like, say, a big brother to you. That's what it is, I want to be a *brother* to you. I want to help you out on the farm and with your schoolwork and, well, with anything you need help with. And, boys, I promise you, I'm never, not for one minute, *ever* going to try to take your daddy's place. That's a very special place, and nobody can fill that." And then he left.

There wasn't a thing he could have said, not a thing in the world that would have made me feel better than "I want to be a brother to you." We didn't need a daddy, but we sure could use another brother around the place, especially a big brother.

Vernon lived up to his word. From the time he and Mama got married, he was a good friend and a companion to all three of us. A big brother. There's just no other way I would have accepted him, because Yarboroughs are independent people who don't cater to outsiders telling them what to do. It was nice having someone around to work with us, side by side.

Now I could go back to growing up. And, for the most part, I resumed life pretty well. But there were times when, out of the blue, I would hear a familiar sound or see a familiar sight, and the emptiness would return for a moment. I would be doing just fine, and then I'd hear something, like a car door close, and I'd think, "There's Daddy now." Then I would remember that he was gone.

■

I don't have the slightest idea why I did some of the things I did when I was growing up. In fact, now that I think of it, I don't even know how I happened to *grow up,* considering some of the things I did. For example, some of my friends and I used to catch water moccasins—that's right, *catch* them. We got ourselves a forked stick and headed for the river—there were always snakes down there, and they were usually pretty lazy from lying around on logs or on the riverbanks in the sun. If you sneaked up on them, it was easy to put the forked part of the stick right behind their heads and pin them down. But you had to keep the pressure on them, because they would flop their bodies back and forth, and if you weren't careful, they would get loose. And, I'll tell you, they weren't too happy at that point.

So we kept them pinned down and then reached down and got them by the back of the neck and held them up. Not every kid was as enthusiastic about the snake catching as I was, and there was always one who was a little more squeamish that the rest, but they never said anything. They went along with the rest of us who were having fun. At least we said we were. We carried the snakes around for a while, and then we would see how far out in the river we could throw them. It was just a kid's game. We didn't know any better.

I did have one encounter with a snake that wasn't planned. It was when I first became a teenager, right after I had discovered that girls might be all right after all. You knew the day would come. Well, I had met a cute little girl down by the river one day, and I was surprised to learn that she had lived right up the road from me for years. I couldn't understand why I hadn't noticed her before, as cute as she was.

Now that I look back at it, I guess I was carrying on a little more than usual, and one of my buddies had said, "You showin' off for the little blonde, Cale?" I really was.

That evening I was watching television, when I heard someone call, "Cale, you home?" It was her, Mary Ann. I jumped out of the chair and ran out on the front porch. Sure enough, there she was, out in the front yard. I jumped over all of the front steps and landed in the grass. There was the rattlesnake. It was too late to turn back, so I figured I could jump once more, right over the snake, and be out of danger. It wouldn't react that quick. Wrong. I was directly over it when it struck me in my bare foot.

Mary Ann screamed, the snake slipped away, and I grabbed my foot. "I've gotta go now, Mary Ann," I said, and hobbled back into the house and headed for the bathroom. I had already slit my foot open with a razor blade and was sucking on it when Mama came in. I remembered from somewhere that you were supposed to make an X cut on a snakebite and then suck out the venom. I didn't remember reading about feeling like you were going to faint.

Mama knew exactly what had happened. "Oh, Lord," she said, "we've gotta get you to the doctor." She wrapped a towel around my foot and helped me to the car. I was careful where I stepped.

There were a lot of poisonous snakes around our part of the country, so nobody ever thought the world was coming to an end if someone got bitten by one of them. Although I'll have to admit that I paid them a lot more respect after that encounter.

The doctor fixed me up in short time, drawing the rest of the venom out and bandaging my foot. I was well in a few days. If you want to know, I made the most of it, though. I was a hero with my buddies. And the story kept getting bigger and bigger: the snake got bigger; the battle between man and beast got tougher. Why not? I mean, after all, I didn't get a chance to be a hero too often, and I was going to make as much out of it as I possibly could. I was Tarzan. Superman.

It turns out that my entire life has been made up of downright bizarre happenings. The thunderstorm incident is a perfect example. It was the very same summer; lightning was cracking all around, which wasn't unusual, so I wasn't paying any attention to it. I never was afraid of lightning; in fact, it always fascinated me. I guess that's why I had gone over to the window to watch the many streaks in the sky. It was just about dusk, so the zigzags seemed very bright. They looked pretty to me.

I was standing with my nose pressed against the windowpane when a huge ball of fire hit the ground about thirty feet from the house. I saw it coming toward the window where I was standing. I don't remember much after that, except the sound of breaking glass and a feeling of flying. I must have been thrown clear across the room, because when I came to, I was laying beside the television set. My back hurt a little, and I was kind of numb all over. There was broken glass everywhere, from the window and the television picture tube.

I worked my fingers and toes and checked everything out. Every part of my body was there and it all worked. Man, I had been struck by lightning! And I didn't even have a broken bone. I was starting to feel like Captain Marvel. Boy, you talk about a "Shazam"!

The rest of *The Hazardous Happenings of Cale Yarborough*—that's what I decided I'd call the book on my life if I ever wrote it—I brought on myself without any help from nature. I guess that next phase started with the old Indian motorcycle. You could have predicted that, right? I had been riding that old bike around the barnyard since my legs were long enough to reach the foot pedals, but it hadn't been started for a long time when I got the idea to learn some trick riding.

Jerry and J.C. helped me push it outside where we could see to clean it up. The cleaning-up part was easy; the starting part was hard. It had a big, strong kickstand, but I wasn't very heavy, so I got up on it and kicked and kicked. And kicked. Then Jerry kicked some.

J.C. was definitely too little, or we would have had him in on the act too.

Vernon came to our rescue. He suggested that we take the spark plugs out, and he would take us down to the filling station to get them cleaned. They had one of those old spark-plug cleaners down there, where you put the plug in the top of this barrel-like thing and press down on the part that looked like a little umbrella. Air and sand blasted the tip of the spark plug clean, and if you were lucky, it was as good as new again.

We were lucky, I guess, because with clean plugs the motorcycle fired right up. My motorcycle days were under way. I wasn't allowed to ride the bike on the highway, which is probably a good thing, because that bike was powerful. So, if I laid it down, it wouldn't hurt as much in the dirt as it would on the asphalt. And I laid it down some; it had to happen, what with jumping gulleys and dry creek beds and anything that could be jumped. You didn't expect me to keep riding it around the barnyard like I had been doing for years, did you? I wanted to learn trick things. And it wasn't long before the good jumps far outnumbered the bad jumps. For one thing, I found out that while you're in the air, you had to make sure the front wheel was headed straight, because if it wasn't, the landing was sure to separate you from the bike. And that hurt, even in the sandy soil of South Carolina.

When I wasn't racing around on the bike, I was racing around in the truck, bouncing off trees and jumping some of the same gullies that I'd jumped with the bike. My playtime was starting to become motorized. Of course, I didn't realize it at the time, but the mold was being cast.

But, wait a minute, I've overlooked the ol' swimmin' hole. Every kid that ever grew up in the South—and I'll bet in most areas, outside of cities—had a swimmin' hole. Somewhere in the manual it says, "Kids have to have a swimmin' hole." Well, ours was a mile or so from my house, on Lynches River, which is a fairly good-sized stream that runs mostly through the swamp.

Now, you have to realize that when we talk about swamps in South Carolina, we're not talking about some little old marshy area where you can't drive your car or where you're going to get your sneakers dirty if you walk through it. I'm talking about a *swamp.* A swamp with a dense population of cypress trees and water oaks and palmettos. It's dark in that kind of swamp, and it looks like the kind of swamp they had in that Humphrey Bogart movie. In the movie, there was a sheriff's posse, complete with bloodhounds, and they were chasing Bogie, and he was falling down a lot. There were alligators slithering off into the water and water moccasins all over the place. Our swamp had all of those things; well, with the exception of the posse and the bloodhounds and Bogie. But we had the alligators and the water moccasins and everything else. The Spanish moss on the trees made everything seem darker, I guess, but none of it bothered us because we grew up with the swamps. There was no particular mystery to us; it was the swamp where our swimmin' hole was. Simple. There were others like it all around the Pee Dee region.

Ours was a little better than most, because Lynches River was fairly deep—about five feet—and wide. It made a good swimmin' hole. There was a little sandy road down to where we swam, about a hundred yards or so off Route 403, and a sandy little beachlike area. We spent a lot of time down there in the summertime.

We made a swing by tying a rope to the upper branch of one of the oak trees near the water, and we had a tire tied to the end of it so you could hold on and swing back and forth until you got going real high, then you could drop off into the water.

The swing got too tame for me, so I suggested that we build a diving platform on the tallest cypress tree. It was a good eighty feet tall, and it was right at the edge of the water, so it was a natural for the platform. We nailed boards up the side of the tree, one about every three feet, to make a ladder.

At about thirty feet Jerry said, "Let's build the platform here."

"Not high enough," I said. "Let's keep going."

At fifty feet Claude Springs said, "This oughta do it, Cale."

"Not high enough," I said. "Let's keep going."

When we got almost to the top of the tree, I said, "This'll do fine." Nobody else even commented. They were just holding on to the steps right below me with all their might. I will have to admit, eighty feet does look pretty high when you're up in a tree. But there was a good strong limb up there, so we carried up enough boards to make a little platform. From the ground the platform looked like a postage stamp. Listen, from the platform, *every*thing looked like a postage stamp.

"Who's gonna be the first to try it?" I asked. Everybody looked at me like I was crazy for even asking.

"It's your damn platform," Claude said. Somehow I knew that that was going to be his answer. I also knew that the longer I stood around, looking way up in that tree, the harder the first jump was going to be, so I said, "Okay, boys, here goes," and I started up the tree. And when I got to the top, I took a big gulp of air, held my arms out in front of me, just like Johnny Weissmuller did in the Tarzan movies, and I dove off. With the water only about five feet deep I knew I was going to have to hit just right. All the way down I was planning it: I couldn't do a belly-whopper because that would hurt like mad; I also couldn't go straight in like Tarzan always did because I would end up buried in the sand bottom up to my waist. I was short enough already. What I had to do was hit the water at about a forty-five-degree angle. I wasn't sure how I was going to do it, but I didn't have much time to think about it because the water was there in a hurry.

I think that all of the planning I did on the way down kept my mind off being afraid. Had I stood up there on the platform and planned it, I might never have taken the plunge. But, as it turned out, I hit the water just about right, and when I came up twenty or thirty feet downstream, my buddies were yelling and clapping their hands, which, of course, was exactly what I had wanted.

I went right back up and did it again, only this time I felt the wind in my face and the sinking feeling in my stomach on the way down. From then on, every time we went swimming, I went off that platform about ten times an hour. None of the other boys ever went from the top, and it got so that people would stop their cars to watch me. I liked that.

Before we leave Lynches River, let me tell you about the time I wrestled an alligator there. I know, this is beginning to sound like fiction, but these stories are all true, I promise. Like I said, it wasn't unusual to see gators around our area, but they were usually downstream from the swimming hole. Usually.

On one of my high dives I hit something under the water. The water was clear and I opened my eyes. It looked like a log. I had only brushed it, but when I came to the surface, the log did too. It was an eight-foot alligator. Well, I figured that I probably had scared him more than he had scared me. I also knew that about the only time a gator would hurt a person was if he was either scared or hungry. This one looked both.

There was no way I could outswim him to the bank, so I did the only other thing there was to do: I grabbed him around the head. I had always been told that you couldn't pry open a gator's mouth once he clamped down on something but that you could easily hold it closed. All of the muscles were supposed to work on keeping a hold on something. Lord, I hoped I had gotten the story straight because I had that gator's mouth under my arm, and I was holding on with all my might.

It started rolling around in the water. It rolled and rolled. First I saw the sky, and then my vision was blurred by splashing water and the sandy river bottom. Then I saw the sky again. And then the river bottom. And all the time he was whipping his big tail back and forth, I was trying to hold on, keep his mouth closed, and stay out of the way of his tail. All at the same time.

For some reason he worked us over near the shore. That was good. I yelled to the boys—between dunkings—to get some clubs and beat on him. I figured that if they scared him enough, he might swim away instead of having me for lunch. When we got near the beach and I felt my feet on bottom, I stood up and gave a mighty heave, pushing the gator away from me. The boys were in the water, beating on him. And, do you know, that old gator flopped over and headed back toward the other riverbank.

Aside from having swallowed about half of Lynches River and looking like I had been in a hatchet fight, I was all right. There were only scratches but a lot of them. I hoped I had given up alligator wrestling for all time.

I don't think it was as dangerous a thing as it sounds. I mean, that old gator had just been floating down the river and I jumped in on him, that's all. And all he wanted to do was get away. That's what I tried to tell myself and the other boys. We all agreed; otherwise, I don't think any of us would have gone swimming there again. And another thing: I made them promise never to let my mother hear about it or, I'll guarantee you, *I* never would have gone swimming there again.

I guess it's all right for her to know about it now.

THE ROAR OF THE CROWD WAS LIKE

SUMMER THUNDER FROM ACROSS

THE GREAT PEE DEE SWAMP.

5

■

I can honestly say that my high-school days were fantastic. They would have been even better if I could have eliminated the classroom part of it, but I guess you can't have everything. As it was, I got through the studies, just so I could enjoy the sports and the girls, and pretty much in that order. I did just enough studying to get by.

Football was the part I liked best.

I went out for the team as a freshman, and I would have done it sooner, but there were rules against it, so I waited impatiently until I could become a "football hero" and get all of the girls.

I was fourteen years old, and the first thing I did when I got off the school bus on that first morning of school in 1953 was head for the gym. Wallace Walkup was the football coach, and he was in the gym, sorting through uniforms.

"Hi, Coach," I said. "I'm goin' out for the team. I'm a freshman now, you know. Can I get my uniform?"

"I know, I know, Cale," he said. "But I think they want you in homeroom right now. We'll let you know when we're going to pass out the uniforms."

That wasn't what I wanted to hear. I mean, *homeroom?* The next thing they were going to expect me to do was study. I could see the pattern. Do you believe I had to wait until lunchtime just to find out when practice was going to be held? They obviously had their priorities all mixed up.

At 130 pounds and 5′ 5″, you might expect me to be the smallest boy on the team, right? Well, I wasn't. When you have only fifteen boys on a team, there aren't many big ones. The coach couldn't afford to turn anyone away. After all, it was a very small school, and I was glad because I was sure I would get to play a lot that first season. If desire had anything to do with it, I would be on the first team.

We met at three o'clock in the gym, and Coach Walkup told us to pick out pads, pants, a jersey, shoes, and socks.

"Just sort through the piles until you find what fits you," he said, and he pointed to stacks of what looked like the remnants from a rummage sale. The jerseys and pants were all patched and stained. I couldn't believe it.

"We're gonna look like the Timmonsville *Bums,*" I said to one of the boys.

"They're just practice uniforms, Cale," he said. "We'll get the game uniforms before the first game."

I felt a little better, and I took my armload of gear down to the locker room and picked out a locker, just like the coach told us to do.

I'll never forget the smell of the locker room; it was a musty, heavy odor—the collection of smells from years of sweaty jerseys and sweat socks mixed with the dampness of the showers. It was the smell of football. Of competition. I liked it immediately.

I got into my pads and uniform and went out to the football field behind the school. I stood there and looked at the bleachers on each side of the field and at the scoreboard down at the far end. I was one of the first kids out there. I could hear the announcer saying, "Yarborough's loose at midfield. He's down to the forty! the thirty! the twenty! He's in the clear. It's another touchdown for the Timmonsville Flash!" I had a really good imagination when I was a kid. I think it comes from growing up on a farm.

The coach came out, and we all huddled around him. All fifteen of us.

"Boys," he said, "this is a small school and we don't have many players. In fact, we don't even have enough for a complete scrimmage, so I want to tell you one thing right now: I want all of you to be in the best physical condition you can get in. I mean, I want every one of you to be able to play sixty minutes if you have to. We can't afford to have anybody hurt, so we're going to work hard every day at getting you in shape. The rest is up to you. I don't want any smoking or drinking pop or abusing yourselves in any way, if you know what I mean."

"Yes, sir," we said in unison. We knew what he meant.

I didn't know about the rest of them, but *I* meant it. From that moment on I was a committed athlete, and nobody ever had to tell me to stay in shape. I was so small that I knew I would have to make up for it by being tough. And fast. It didn't take me long to prove the fast part.

Coach lined us up in a row to run wind sprints, which are a whole lot like the 100-yard dash, except that you do them in full uniform and you do them over and over. I lined up on the goal line with the other kids, down on one hand; the fingers supporting my weight were turned under; my left hand, with fist clenched, was resting on my left thigh. My head was high. That's exactly how real football players looked in pictures, and I wanted to look as much like a football player as I possibly could. I felt like one.

"Ready?" Coach asked. Everybody nodded. I took a deep breath. "Go!" he yelled.

I got off to a fast start, and by the time we got to the twenty-yard line, I was leading. This was going to be easier than I thought, because I was used to running everywhere on the farm. I never *walked* anyplace. I won easily. The coach lined us up on the other goal line and yelled "Go!" again. Another good start, but the twenty-yard line seemed farther away. It took me to the forty before I took the lead, and I won again, going away.

"Okay, boys," Coach said. "It looks like Cale's the fastest one out here, so let's see how fast he is. Cale, I want you to line up five yards back this time. Think you can still beat them?"

"I'll try," I said. I knew I could, but I didn't want to brag. By the time I got to the fifty-yard line this time, I was starting to get a pain in my left side, but also I was almost in front. At the twenty, I *was* in front. I won by two or three yards. Lord, I hoped that was the last one, because the pain in my side had gotten worse.

"One more," Coach said. And then he looked at me. "You're fast, son."

"Thanks, Coach," I said.

"*Ten* yards back," he said.

Ten yards. Ho, boy. I got a perfect start. The pain started just as quickly. By the thirty, I didn't see how I could possibly make midfield, let alone the other goal line. But I got to the fifty, although I was way behind. That's the only thing that kept me going; there was no way I was going to finish that far back. The pain was bad, but I ran with everything I had. I guess I was running on pure adrenaline. Whatever it was, at the twenty-yard line I caught the boy who was leading. It was him and me. My legs were aching as much as my side, but I knew I had to beat him. If it had been a horse race, they would have said I won by a nose, because that's about how much I beat him. But I beat him. We all fell to the ground.

"Okay, boys," Coach said. I held my breath. "That's it for today." Hallelujah! "Tomorrow I'll give you the plays and we'll start practicing for real. Take a shower. And, Cale?"

"Yes, sir," I said.

"Good job."

Everybody, including the coach, walked in the back door of the gym. When all of them were inside, I threw up.

We practiced hard every day, and all of us got in good shape. We really took to heart what the coach said about nobody getting hurt. When it came time for the first game, we were ready. Fortunately, that first game was against Lamar, which was the only school on our schedule that was smaller than Timmonsville. We played on our field. Both of those things made me feel better because I was starting the game. At fullback. I really wanted to get my football career off to a good start.

It was a Friday night game; I don't remember the date, but it was around the first of September in 1953. We were told to be at the gym by six o'clock to get our game uniforms and to go over the plays "one more time." I was one of the first ones there. I was sure I knew every play as well as I knew my own name, but I wanted to go over them again. If I had spent that much time on my studies, I would have been a Rhodes scholar.

Coach came in the dressing room with a stack of jerseys. He tossed me number 35. And then we went over the plays again.

We won that game, and I even scored a touchdown. It was an end-around from the fifteen-yard line. It's as clear to me as if it were yesterday, because I remember exactly how I felt when I heard that hometown crowd cheering as I scored. It was like the high dives and the thrill of riding the motorcycle fast and every other thrill I'd ever had, all wrapped up into one. It was what I would have felt like if I had won the Soap Box Derby. Everybody on our team was slapping me on the back, and I could hear people yelling and clapping for me, and I'll tell you, I liked the feeling a lot. For a kid who grew up back in the sticks, it was a great feeling to have a day in the sun.

We won more than half our games that season, which wasn't a bad record, considering the fact that most of the schools we played were bigger than Timmonsville High. I played fullback on offense and linebacker on defense, and I played sixty minutes of every game.

The following season I was up to 140 pounds and in good shape when practice started. We had eighteen players that year, almost enough for a full scrimmage. The first-day wind sprints weren't a problem for me that year; I had run them all summer, because I was going to make sure I never again had to go through those "first-day pains" again. I actually counted the days until school started, because my whole life was wrapped up in football.

I would have been better off if part of my life had been wrapped up in my studies. Needless to say, they started to suffer, so Coach had to call Mama to discuss American History. You see, that's the class where I studied my football plays. But I wasn't going to be on the team if I didn't shape up, so he felt he had to call her. He took me to the principal's office when he called her.

"Put him on the phone," she said. He handed me the phone and I thought, "Oh, boy."

"William Caleb Yarborough," she said. I knew that when she started a sentence with that, I was in for it. "I'm right put out with what Coach Walkup's told me. How do you ever expect to make anything out of yourself if you don't have an education?"

"But, Mama," I said, "I—"

"Don't you but-Mama me. I'm not going to stand for it. You're going to study, and you're going to bring those grades up. Or *else,*" she said.

Or else? "But, Mama, I said, "I mean, but, Mother, I don't need that ol' history. All I want to do in life is play football and race cars."

That did it. She lectured me for about five minutes, about family pride and my heritage and everything from the War Between the States to the current tobacco crop. When she was finished, I felt so bad that I had to turn my back on the coach, because I didn't want him to see me crying. I might have been tough with the coach and the boys on the team, but she knew that she could shame me into tears. She had tried whipping me to tears, but that didn't work. But I guess I'm softhearted, and she knew it.

I promised her I would work on American History and would make a better grade, and I meant it. Well, a passing grade, anyway. It's the last time anybody ever had to call her; all they had to do was threaten me with it.

As I look back at it, it was probably a bad thing that studies came so easy to me. I mean, all I had to do was spend a few minutes at my homework and I could pass. If I had had to work harder at it, maybe I would have gotten more out of it. But all I wanted to do was pass, so I could play football. And so they wouldn't call Mama. So I guess sports are important, after all. I wouldn't have studied at all if it hadn't been for that threat.

It was more than winning—not that that wasn't important, it was

—it was the competition with other boys that appealed to me. Besides that, it was fun, especially the road trips.

We played schools like Bishopville and Hartsville and Sumter and Darlington, all of which were about fifteen or twenty miles away, so we went by school bus. Most of the games were played on Friday night, so we didn't have practice after school on that day. We just hung around after school and met at the hot-lunch room at about four-thirty so we could eat supper early enough for it to digest before the game.

They always served us a lot of vegetables and some kind of meat. And baked potatoes. We always had baked potatoes, and I always took an extra one and put it in my jacket pocket so I could eat it later. I had a big appetite.

After we ate we went to the gym and laid around on the bleachers or the mats on the gym floor. We told jokes and talked about girls and cars. It was fine with Coach. He told us we could talk about anything we wanted to, except football. He wanted us to get our minds off football as much as possible, because he didn't want us to be uptight when we got to the game. The only thing he said was, "Don't cuss." So we didn't; at least, not that he could hear.

Actually none of us cussed much, anyway. Not like kids do today. Maybe that was part of growing up in the rural South back then; I don't ever remember hearing more than a *damn* or a *hell* once in a while, or if we were really mad or extra excited, maybe a *sumbitch*, as in, "Look at that sumbitch run!"

We did sing some songs on the bus that wouldn't have gone over too well in church, but for the most part they could be considered only a little off-color and not "dirty" by any standards. We had a good time on the bus, going and coming. Of course, we sang a lot more coming back if we won, but most of the boys weren't even too dejected if we did lose. I tried not to show that I was.

I'm glad that I didn't have to suffer the pains of losing too often. We had an exceptional record, and that suited me just fine.

■

Probably the most important date in my entire childhood was March 27, 1953. I was always counting the days until something or other, but this was the big one. It was to be my fourteenth birthday. You see, you can get a driver's license in South Carolina when you are fourteen. I had been driving for years, but on that date I could do it legally. Since I was five years old I had been dreaming of that day and steering the truck while I was sitting on Daddy's or Son Ham's lap.

Driving a car would fill in the period between football seasons—the Dark Ages. I played basketball and baseball, too, whatever was in season, but they weren't like football. I needed something else to make my life complete, and driving a car would do well.

While I was waiting to drive I took up boxing, and I liked that almost as much as football. Every town in my part of the country had a big interest in the Golden Gloves program, and if the town wasn't big enough to have a team, the boys who were interested went to the nearest town that did. I went to Florence and signed up for the welterweight class.

I took to boxing as quickly as I did to football. The speed I had developed helped a lot, but again, I think it was more desire than anything. I always had that, and it helped. Sure, I got hit a lot and knocked down some at first, but that made me that much more determined. I wasn't one to "cover up" when I started getting hurt; instead, I got like a tiger and came right in, throwing everything in the book. Once in a while I got knocked down again, but it didn't take me long to learn that it's all right—great, in fact—to come back strong after being nailed a good one, as long as you know what you're doing.

I worked at "knowing what I was doing" as often as I could get Mama or Vernon to take me to the gym in Florence. I worked on the bags and shadowboxed and watched the other kids. I developed a style that helped me start winning fights. It was good for passing the time.

The day finally arrived—March 27, 1953. It was the day I could get my driver's license. It also happened to be my birthday, but that was secondary, for the first time in my life.

I'll never forget as long as I live how I felt that morning when I woke up. It wasn't even daylight yet when I opened my eyes; I don't know, it must have been four or four-thirty in the morning. I laid there in bed for a few minutes and thought, "Hey, buddy, you're fourteen. Wow!"

I had to tell someone, so I got up and went over to Jerry's bed. I shook him. "Jerry. Jerry, wake up. I'm fourteen." He rolled over, opened one eye, and said, "Good for you, Cale. Now lemme sleep." And he rolled back over. I could tell that he wasn't as enthusiastic as I was, so I woke up J.C. "J.C.! J.C.!" I said as I shook him. "I'm fourteen. It's my birthday." He sat up in bed and said, "You got a birthday cake?"

I couldn't believe it. "Not yet," I said. "Nobody else is even awake."

"Good night," he said.

Some birthday this was going to be.

Finally the sun came up, and I could hear Mama and Vernon in the kitchen. I knew things had to pick up; I jumped out of bed and ran in there. "Happy Birthday," they said. Mama hugged me and said, "It doesn't seem possible. Fourteen. What do want to do today?"

"I want to get my driver's license," I said.

"Aw, you don't want to drive a car," Vernon said.

"I do! I do!" I said. "I really do."

They both laughed, and Mama said, "Well, I reckon we're going to have to get you into Florence to get you a learner's permit. How 'bout after school today?"

"How 'bout lunchtime?" I asked.

"I think you can wait until after school," Mama said. "We'll pick you up in front."

It was a long day, but I got my learner's permit, and I started to study the booklet with the questions in it with as much enthusiasm as I had for my football plays. It goes without saying that I gave it far more attention than American History. In fact, that booklet was inside every textbook I held up in classes for the next week. I had those questions mastered in a few days, and I got my buddies to quiz me. I almost never missed one. I knew exactly how far I could park from a fireplug, and I knew who had the right-of-way at every imaginable intersection. I knew it all.

"How's your parking?" my friend Russell DeFee asked me.

"Whatta'ya mean, *parking?*" I asked. "I'm going to drive a car. I'm not going to work in a parking lot."

"I hate to be the one to break the news to you," he said, "but they're going to make you parallel-park the car. I mean, you don't just go over there and drive around the block and they hand you your license. You've gotta park."

I had never parked a car. Parking. Why couldn't you just drive around until you found a place you could just *pull* into? If you didn't want to park a car, I couldn't see any reason you had to. I asked a dozen people, and they all told me I had to park.

I went home that evening and laid out my parking course, right beside the general store. I sat a couple of nail kegs out from the store, about the width and length of a normal-size car, plus a little room to maneuver, and I started practicing. There wasn't anything to this. Or so I thought.

In no time I was back in the store after a couple more nail kegs.

"What happened to the first two?" Vernon asked.

"I don't know," I said. "Somehow they got crunched."

"I'll give you some help," he said.

He got in the passenger side of our '51 Buick, and he told me exactly when to turn the wheel and when to go forward and backward. Then he stood outside the car and guided me some more. I got much better; in fact, I got to the point where I only *knocked over* the nail kegs. Well, that was a whole lot better than *running* over them.

"Cale, you're gettin' better," he said, "but remember one thing: They're not going to give you a license for the fastest parking job, just the best. Slow down." That was going to make it a whole lot easier.

I kept practicing at a slower speed, until I could do it time after time, without even touching a nail keg. I practiced until dark, and then started in again the next day after school. I figured I was so good that I could get a job parking cars if all else failed. I was ready.

I passed my test the next Thursday in Florence.

The next step was obvious; I had to have my own car, so I got a job after school at Gregory's Tobacco Warehouse in Timmonsville. I did odd jobs, but mostly I moved tobacco around a lot. It was heavy work, just like I had done around the farm and the gin, but I think it's what gave me strong arms and a big chest. I only made a quarter an hour, but I saved every cent of it. It didn't take long, because I hadn't set my sights too high. All I wanted was a set of wheels, and I wanted them as soon as possible. I would have gone crazy if I had to wait until I saved up sixteen or seventeen hundred dollars for a new Ford or Chevy. I would have been an old man.

I found a 1930 Model A Ford coupe for $75. It was a little rough —well, if you really want to know, it was a *lot* rough. The fenders were banged in and the top was dented and the front bumper was gone and the rear window was broken out, but it ran pretty good. Besides, I was going to strip it down, anyway, and things like fenders and top and rear windows were going to go, anyway.

It doesn't take much time to take things *off* a car, so it was ready in no time. Penetrating oil on the rusty bolts did wonders. If that didn't work, a hammer and chisel sure did. I hacksawed the top off, and when I had everything off, I painted it red. It looked just like a street rod.

I kept saving money until I could buy lowering blocks and some hop-up parts for the motor; then I put a straight-through Smitty muffler on it. Man, was I eager for school to start. The girls were going to love it.

With the summer job and the stripped-down Model A, the time passed quickly. I spent as much time working on the car as I did moving tobacco; $75 cars require a lot of attention, particularly if you drive them flat-out, which I did. Most of the time. Picture this: I would pull out of the drive at home, just as slow and careful as anybody ever did, and I drove about 35 miles an hour for a mile or so down 403, down to where Son Ham lived. There was a little rise in the road there; after that you couldn't see me from home, so it was hot-rod time from then on. The Timmonsville Flash rode again. I went sliding into the parking lot at the tobacco warehouse every day.

When football season started, I had to give up the job, but I had saved up enough money for gas, at least, until after the end of the season. Boy, did that car make a difference. Here I was a football player with a car. I had it made. On weekends—Friday nights after the game and Saturday nights—I cruised over to the Bright Leaf Grill or the 76 Grill in my rod and held court with the other guys in their cars. Those were the two drive-ins in Timmonsville, and every kid in town was there, especially the girls. Anything I spent came out of my gas fund, so I usually had a milk shake and made it last all evening. When it was gone, I kept the paper cup and straw in my hand, and if one of the curb-service gals asked if I wanted anything else, I'd say, "No thanks, sweetie, I'm still working on this one. Besides, one's my limit. I'm driving, you know." I got a lot of mileage out of a twenty-five-cent milk shake and a corny line.

It's obvious that life was different in the fifties, particularly in the rural South. It certainly was simpler, I know that. We never even heard of drugs, and as far as drinking whiskey or anything like that, the teenagers I knew just didn't do it. Oh, once in a while someone would get hold of some beer—a can or two—but that didn't happen often. I never did smoke cigarettes. I chewed tobacco from time to time, but that was mostly to show off for the other boys. I can't say that I was addicted.

That brings us back to cars. And now it can be told: We did race on the highway from time to time. The truth is, we ran the daylights out of anything we had. Our cars might not have been the fastest ones in the world, but we ran them as fast as they would go, every time we got a chance. And I guarantee you, if we could find any way to make them go faster, we did it. Every cent that we had went toward our cars. And milk shakes.

The races usually started at the Bright Leaf or the 76. I don't mean we actually raced there, but it's where the "Listen, my Ford can outrun your Olds any day of the week" arguments turned into action. Out to the edge of town we'd go, to where 403 branched off from Highway 76. It was a six-mile straight shot from there to Sardis. There was never much traffic on that road, and you could always see at least a mile ahead. At night you could tell for two miles if something was coming. That was our race track—the world's longest drag strip, we called it.

You could run wheel-to-wheel with a guy all the way to Sardis. There were times when you could make several trips and never see a car. If anybody ever had a better proving ground, I never saw it.

The cars we had were mostly older cars, so the speeds were seldom much over 100 miles an hour, but as we saved our money the speeds went up, because we had more hot-rod parts. It's like all forms of racing—it doesn't matter if it's street or strip—the faster you go, the more it costs. Cubic dollars will win every time.

Street racing got dull after a while, because everybody had raced everybody else so many times that we all knew to the mile an hour what the other guy's car would do. There wasn't any challenge to it. It was only when somebody got a different car or a new modification to the old car that there was any excitement. After he ran everybody in town it was back to milk shakes at the drive-in again—back to *talking* about racing. I'm sure it was the same in every town around us.

Since most of our cars were borderline junk, we were always looking for diversions, anything we could do with them. It didn't matter much what it was, as long as it was different. I remember coming back from Olanta one night in Murdoch Lynn's black '51 Chevy convertible when he decided to take to the fields. He saw a bunch of big haystacks in Eli Benton's field, so he figured that running through them might be fun. Actually they were stacks of oat straw that had been blown into forty-foot piles after the oats had been thrashed. Perfect targets. Murdoch wheeled the Chevy off the road and right into the field. He drove right smack into the middle of one, and straw flew in all directions. The car went in to about the windshield, and we all thought it was fun, so we decided to see how far we could drive the car into the stacks. Murdoch got way back in the field and drove like mad while Pete Workman and I sat up on the back of the front seat so we could see better. It got so that we could drive clear through the stacks. Of course, there was straw all over the field, but it kept us occupied for an hour or so.

We didn't think anything about it, because it wasn't half as wild as some of the things we did with cars on the highway. We didn't think anything about it, that is, until the next time we were over that way. The straw had been burned, and where each pile had been, there was a big pole, the size of a telephone pole. That's what they blew the oats around. How we missed those poles that many times, nobody ever knew. It was the last time any of us ever strayed off the highway. Racing had to be a lot safer than that.

If you don't count blowing up a few mailboxes with cherry bombs or putting an occasional dog in a mailbox to scare the daylights out of the mailman—not to mention the dog—we didn't get into too much trouble. Living in a small town like that, it was hard to do anything, because everybody knew what everybody else was doing. You couldn't get away with anything. I mean, I paid for a lot of mailboxes.

We spent a lot of time coon-hunting and fishing for brim in the farm ponds. And we raced on the highway. That was about it. I had a reputation, even then, for fast driving, and, you know, it hasn't been too long since one of the old-timers in Sardis said to me, "Every time we heard a fast car go by at night we'd say, 'There goes Cale.' But, you know, after you grew up and moved away, we still heard fast cars go by, so I guess it wasn't always you."

But it *was*—most of the time.

By my senior year at Timmonsville High I had saved up enough money to buy myself a used Ford convertible, a 1955 with a strong V-8 engine. The first thing I did was to make it stronger by putting in a higher-lift cam and a bigger carburetor and freeing up the exhaust system. It was quick, but the top end wasn't right for the Timmonsville–to–Sardis drag strip. I got a set of taller gears, and, man, that car would flat get it. I was the champion for a long time, until somebody got hold of a really hot Olds 88. Then it was back to the drawing board.

Cars had to take a backseat for a while, though, because it was football season and we were expected to have a world-beater of a team, maybe the best team Timmonsville had ever had. By the time the season opened, the Florence paper was listing us as the team to beat in Class A football in the entire state. They were touting me as a shoo-in for All-State honors. The team and I had some high goals to shoot for. But all of us were ready to try.

There had been so much publicity that Bishopville had my name painted on their tackling dummy the week before we opened the season against them. That tickled me when I heard it. And, if anything, it made me run even harder when we played them.

A lot of times publicity like that will ruin a team, get them cocky, but it didn't affect us like that. A team from Timmonsville had never gotten publicity like that, so I guess it made us all proud. We all seemed to try harder. We charged out on the field at every game like we were a bunch of wild men, and I think we psyched out about half the teams we played. We won some of those games before the first whistle blew.

By the end of the season we had been selected to play Summerville for the championship of the Lower State. Even though Summerville was a much bigger school than Timmonsville, there was no question in any of our minds that we could beat them. We sure didn't lack for confidence, none of us.

In the couple of weeks before the game we practiced harder than we ever had. Coach Walkup had us about as finely honed as any high-school football team I ever saw. It was a good period of my life. The whole town was behind us. I mean, I couldn't drive down the street without everybody I met yelling something at me: "Go get 'em, Cale" or "We're countin' on you, boy." For a small town that kind of team is a real shot in the arm.

There were photographers at our practice sessions almost every day, and newspaper reporters around, talking to all of us. I was spending as much time talking as I was practicing. Coach finally put a stop to it because it was really cutting into our practice sessions. He told the reporters and photographers that they would have to wait until practice was over before they talked to any of us. The whole thing made his job harder, because not only did he have to keep us fine-tuned, he also had to keep our heads from swelling, and that was a hard job when everywhere you turned, somebody was telling you how good you were.

Coach constantly reminded us that we were the underdogs, because our school was so much smaller than Summerville's.

"It's going to take perfect football on our part to win that game," he said. "But I'll tell you right now, we can do it. *If* we play perfect football. You'll have to play better than you've ever played before. And that might not even be enough."

He had a way of bringing you back to earth.

We all knew he was right. Beating a school like that was something out of a book. If we played sixty minutes of the best football any of us had ever played, we could do it. Anything less than that would be disaster. But I knew, deep down inside, that we were going to do it. We had to. We had worked four long, hard years to get to the championship, and we weren't going to blow it.

On the day of the game—a Saturday—we met at the high-school gym as usual, only this time we had big steaks to eat. I don't think I really appreciated the meal as much as I normally would have because I was so charged up for the game. I could have eaten *raw* meat. I didn't even take an extra baked potato that day.

We didn't even sing any songs on the way to Summerville. The coach started a couple, just to liven things up, but he wound up singing by himself. In spite of everything he had done to keep us loose, we were as tight as fiddle strings. I had more butterflies in my stomach than I had had during both Soap Box Derbys, the first high dive, my first football game, and the Golden Gloves, all wrapped up into one.

We filed off the bus and went straight to the dressing room that had been assigned to us, and we quietly suited up. When we were ready to go out on the field, Coach said, "Okay, boys, I want you to charge out there like the dressing room was on fire. No, I want you to charge out there like *you* were on fire. I want you to look like champions because, well, because you *are* champions. They'll never stop talking about this team in Timmonsville. Remember that! Let's go!"

He kicked the door open with his foot, and it was like kicking open the chute at a rodeo. Man, we went charging out of that dressing room and onto the field like we were possessed. We were, in fact.

The crowd roared as we ran onto the field. I guess all the publicity in the local papers had helped. Everybody from Timmonsville and all the other towns around must have been there. The more they cheered, the more charged up we got. There were banners and signs everywhere. And a lot of them had my name on them.

I didn't think it was possible to have any more butterflies than I already had, but when I saw those signs, a whole 'nother batch arrived. "Oh, Lord," I thought, "what if I blow it?"

There wasn't much time to think about it, because in about another minute, a roar went up that made the one for us sound like polite applause. We just thought that we had the most fans there because never before had we had that many. Summerville apparently had twice as many. The stands went wild when they ran onto the field. One look at them and I could see why.

I couldn't believe the size of that team. There were twice as many of them, and they were twice as big as our team. In addition to that, their uniforms were better-looking. They had guys in their *band* that were bigger than most of our players. We didn't even have a band.

We all just stood there with our mouths open. I guess coach realized what was going through our minds. He said, "Okay, boys, now we know what we're up against. We can do it. Right? Let's run some patterns. And, hey, those guys don't look so tough, do they?"

Was he kidding? They looked like the Green Bay Packers.

We ran some patterns and we kicked some and we got as psyched up as we could get. Coach gave us the signal, and we ran into the dressing room. I didn't know if it was for last-minute instructions or last rites.

Next time we came back to the field, the battle would be on.

Coach didn't have too much to say in the dressing room, but what he said was serious. We knew how much the game meant to him too.

"Boys, I don't have to tell you a thing," he said. You're the best ball team I ever coached. You all know your plays, and you can carry them out to perfection. You've proved that many times. You can beat this team. I mean it, you've beaten better teams. Now one thing: If we win the toss, I want you to receive. I don't care who catches the ball on the kickoff, just get a good hold on it. And I don't care what it takes, but get the ball to Cale."

Oh, Lord.

"Let's get out there and win that game," he yelled. This time we almost took the door off the hinges. We were ready.

We won the toss.

We huddled in front of our bench—the one with the five substitutes on it—and Coach said, "Remember, boys, get the ball to Cale. They're not going to kick it to him, you know that, so you have to do it. And, Cale, run like the wind, boy. We need to break their spirit right off the bat. If we do, we've got 'em.'"

I don't even remember what was going through my mind as the other team lined up on their forty-yard line, but I remember hearing the official's whistle. After that I saw the ball sail high in the air. It came down right in Ramsey Mellette's hands. He tucked the ball under his arm and ran in my direction. When he was about ten feet from me, I saw the lateral coming toward me. It was perfect. I grabbed it and stuffed the ball into my left armpit. And I squeezed it so tight with my left forearm that I thought it was going to burst the ball. I was on our own fifteen, and I headed upfield.

I could hear the roar of the crowd, but it sounded like it was coming from a couple of miles away. It was a dull roar, like summer thunder from across the Great Pee Dee River Swamp. I was near the left sideline; I cut diagonally across the field. The entire Summerville team was headed in my direction; in fact, two of them were almost on me. I knew that they were the fast ones, the ones I had to shake first. Just before I got to them, I could see that they were ready to lunge for me. Perfect. They would be off-balance.

I spun around and headed for the near sidelines. They were faked out completely, and to my complete surprise, so was the rest of the team. I turned on the speed and raced up the sideline. Eighty-five yards later I crossed the goal line. The thunder had gotten closer. But nobody was coming to pound me on the back. I looked down the field. There was a yellow flag. One of our guys ran up to me. "They got us for clipping, Cale."

My heart sank. Naturally they accepted the penalty, and the touchdown was called back.

The guys didn't even get the ball to me on the next kickoff. I don't know what happened. In fact, we never really got rolling again. All night. We were in the game but not like we would have been if we had had the momentum of that first touchdown. We lost the game by two touchdowns.

I made All-State that year. And I won the welterweight championship in Golden Gloves for the entire state. I was excited about both, but all of it was just a tad hollow. I wanted to win that football game more than anything in my whole life. Except maybe the Soap Box Derby.

But they're still talking about the team we had.

**IN THE SOUTH IN THE FIFTIES THERE
WERE CERTAIN THINGS THAT WERE TABOO:
HILLBILLY MUSIC, COCKFIGHTING,
DRINKING, AND DRIVING A STOCK CAR.**

6

■

With football season over my thoughts naturally turned to racing. It started on the spectator side of the sport, but we all knew that this was only a temporary situation. Bobby Weatherly and his brother Irby had put together a race team, Palmetto Racing. I tagged along wherever they raced—Florence, Sumter, everywhere. Listen, I even had a red satin jacket that said "Palmetto Race Team" on the back and "Cale" on the front. I was an official crew member; I didn't get paid anything, but I had a jacket. In fact, that's the way it was with most crew members of most teams. The drivers didn't even get much, for that matter.

Stock-car racing was not a sport where many people got rich; still, it was how I planned to make *my* livelihood. But my sights were set high—NASCAR.

Bobby had some road-grading equipment, so he built some short tracks himself, one at Ashwood and one at Hemingway and one each in Sumter and Darlington. There wasn't any sort of sanctioning body connected with any of these tracks. They were called "outlaw tracks," and they were about what the name sounded like. Anybody who wanted to, could run there, and there wasn't much order at all. There were fewer rules. The fans loved it because they never knew what was going to happen. Since most of the drivers were fairly inexperienced, the fans always saw an exciting show.

Being around racing without being in a race car was more than I could stand. I got my old job back at the tobacco warehouse and started scouring the countryside for a car that I could build into a race car. I looked in junkyards and in old barns and everywhere cheap old cars lived. I found one right under my nose. It was over behind the Ford Garage in Timmonsville—a 1935 Ford coupe, up on blocks. The body was good enough and the engine ran; well, if you want to know, it wheezed and coughed, but that wasn't any problem, it would have to be rebuilt, anyway. I paid $50 for the car and towed it away.

Building a race car for those tracks wasn't as big a job as it sounds. Probably the hardest part was installing the roll bar, mainly because I didn't have a welding torch. In fact, I didn't even have the pipe. I talked Ashton Phillips and his cousin Lynwood into going into the race-car business with me. They worked with me at the warehouse, so we decided to tow the car over there and work on it inside, out of the hot sun.

Bobby brought his welding equipment over, and we bought some used inch-and-a-quarter pipe. The first part was easy; we ripped everything out of the interior, the seats and headliner and door panels and glass from the side and back windows—everything.

We heated the pipe and bent it to the right shape, and then we welded the roll bar directly to the frame. I'll guarantee you, it was as strong as a battleship.

"Better make it strong," Bobby said. "You'll probably spend as much time on the roll bar as you will on the wheels."

Very funny.

We got some of the old four-inch-wide seat belts from the army surplus store, the kind they used in tanks. Most of the racers used them because they were strong. And cheap. We anchored them to the frame too. Who knows? Maybe Bobby was right.

That's all we had to do to the inside of the car. We needed some expert advice on the rest. Bobby told us what we needed to do to the engine, so we pulled it out and started rebuilding it. It was back to the junkyards again, looking for pistons and all sorts of parts for the old V-8 engine. And I made nightly trips to the drive-ins, to see if any of the guys had turned up any cut-rate speed parts. I had guys all over the country looking for parts for me.

The simple way would have been to make a doorstop out of the old engine and replace it with a newer overhead valve V-8, or even a bigger Ford truck engine, like an F-8, but that took a lot more money than our meager racing budget would allow, so we were stuck with patching up. If we had the money, we could have found a motor that would have powered the first rocket to the moon. I mean, this was hot-car country, but the economics of the whole thing didn't add up. You just don't spend a couple of grand on a motor to put in a race car that might win twenty-five bucks, max, and that's if you won a heat race *and* the feature. This kind of racing was a far cry from the Southern 500. It was a far cry from the Columbia Speedway. From anything.

Keep in mind that this whole operation was taking a long time— several weeks. It wasn't just jerk out the interior, weld in roll bars, stuff in the rebuilt engine, and go racing. I had to do it in stages, for many reasons: I was still in high school; I had a job at the tobacco warehouse after school; I was about broke; and I had to keep up my social life. The race car got its fair share of time but not all of it. Man cannot live by four-barrel carburetors alone. Besides all that, we had to save up our money and take everything a step at a time.

A lot of the steps had to wait until we could get someone over there to show us what to do; like the suspension. Things like that don't require a lot of money—we could buy used truck springs or shocks or whatever we needed to stiffen up the suspension—but it took time. For a while we were towing the car all over town, putting on this part here and that part there, wherever we could get someone to help us.

Much to the relief of everybody in Timmonsville, we got the car finished. We painted it white and then we painted a number on the side of it—35. That number had always been lucky for me. If it worked as well in racing as it had in football, I would make NASCAR in no time.

We were ready to go racing.

We decided to start on the quarter-mile dirt track in Sumter, where you could "run what you brung." In other words, there weren't any restrictions at all. I might be running against something real strong or I might be racing cars right out of the parking lot. Probably both.

We rigged up a tow bar to the bumper of my Ford convertible and towed old Number 35 to Sumter. When we got there, the pits were already crowded. Of course, it doesn't take too many cars to crowd the infield of a quarter-mile track. We pulled the car across the track on the back straightaway and found a place where we could unhook the car and get it ready to race. It was my very first pit.

Over the PA system the announcer said that qualifying would start in twenty minutes and that we could practice until then. The time had come. I said, "Well, boys, let's see what we've built."

Ashton and Lynwood slapped me on the back, and I climbed through the driver's window and buckled up the army surplus belt. I pulled on the crash helmet I had borrowed from Bobby and scrunched down in the seat a little. I felt right at home in those surroundings.

The engine sounded good when I cranked it up. I rubbed my hands together, got a good grip on the steering wheel, and looked over toward the fourth turn, where the cars entered the track from the pits. *What was I supposed to do now?* You know, I had never given any thought to what I was going to do when it came time to race. I guessed that I would do just like the other guys did, the ones I had been watching out there on the dirt tracks since I was ten years old. I had to have picked up something.

The whole thing was a lot like the high-diving platform on Lynches River. I was going to jump in without thinking about too much. I pulled the floor-mounted shift lever down into first gear and let out on the clutch. And I headed for the track.

The clay surface felt strange to me. Somehow I expected it to be more slippery, but it was sort of tacky, not at all like the old country roads I had learned to drive on. On this stuff the tires got a bite when I expected them to slide. Cars were going around me on both sides as I drove down the front straightaway, so I nailed it pretty good, and the car shot into the turn. It got nearly sideways, and for some reason unknown to me, it slid right through one and two, which, on a quarter-mile track, are one and the same—it's one going in and two coming out.

"I hope I can remember what I did," I said. Out loud. Right away it was time to try it again. I cocked it sideways again, by pulling the steering wheel hard to the left and standing on it, just like I had seen all the drivers do over the years, and the car came around. "This ain't so tough," I said. I don't know who I was talking to, but I seemed to be doing a lot of it.

By the time I got back around to one, I figured I was a seasoned race-car driver. I cocked it again and it came around; only this time it came *clear* around. I was sitting in the middle of the corner, facing about a dozen race cars that were coming straight at me. They went by on either side, and I said, "Damn, this is embarrassing."

I decided that it was time to slow down a little and get the feel of the car and the track before I stood on it hard again. It was a lot like learning to park the car; it helped to learn at a slower speed. After a dozen laps or so, I had a general idea of what I was doing.

The man with the flag came over to the inside edge of the track and waved us all in. It was time to start qualifying. I watched as the first few cars qualified, studying exactly where they were running on the track, which ones went faster, and trying to figure out why. I noticed for the first time that the ones who went the fastest were the ones who also went the smoothest. They knew where to run and where to cross the car up, and they did it the same way every time. I didn't know if I could remember everything that I had seen, but I was going to try.

When it came my turn, I went right out there and turned a time that was about in the middle of the pack. I wasn't excited about it, but I guess it wasn't bad for a first try.

"You were faster'n half the field," Lynwood said.

"Yeah, but I was *slower* than half the field too," I said.

It was the old half-full/half-empty thing.

There were eight cars in my first-heat race; I started fifth. It was an inverted start, where they lined the cars up in reverse order with the fastest ones in the back and the slowest ones in the front. It made a better show for the fans, if not the drivers, because it meant that the ones who were most likely to spin were going to be out front, spinning right in the path of the rest of the field.

My strategy was simple. Simple strategy: Pay attention for the first couple of laps, until I could see which cars I needed to stay away from and which ones I was going to have to race, then stand on it and finish up front. You see, it never occurred to me that I might *lose*. It didn't make a bit of difference if this was my first race or not. I had confidence in myself, and I had confidence in the race car we had built. What more did I need?

There really wasn't much preparation for the race; it all happened very fast. They lined us up, the guy waved us around, and when we got back around to the front straight, he dropped the green flag. A fraction of a second before he dropped the flag, two cars shot past me like I was standing still. "Write that down in your book, Cale," I said. "Don't wait for the green flag to drop. Catch it on the way up."

I pushed the accelerator hard and started to put the car into a broad slide, but it wouldn't go sideways because there was a car banging me on each side. We went into the turn three abreast, and the car on the outside hit the fence. I could see the boards fly. The one on the inside slid down toward the infield and hit one of the tires that was half buried at the edge of the track, to keep the cars out of the infield. He bounced back on the track, right in front of me. I banged him in the rear, and somebody hit me. There was metal scraping and dust flying everywhere. Man, this sure beat anything I had ever done. I was as happy as a kid in a candy store.

The yellow flag came out because of the car that went into the fence in one and for another car that was turned over on its side in three. "That's two down," I said.

They just pushed the two cars into the infield and waved the green flag again. I watched the starter this time, determined to get the jump on him. When he raised the flag, I stood on it. Another car shot past me. How early was I going to have to start?

Every time I tried to get a good line on a turn, somebody hit me from either the side or the back. It was like dodge-'em cars at a carnival. I was sideways one way and then sideways the other—all the time. I completely gave up trying to look smooth in the turns. That kind of driving was for qualifying only. I started slamming and banging myself, and I was holding my own in no time at all. Man, I'll tell you, I was having the time of my life.

It ended about as quickly as it had started. I saw the checkered flag waving, and I couldn't believe it was over. I finished third.

Now, before you think, "That ain't half bad for the first race," I think it's only fair to tell you that I also finished last. There were only three cars running at the finish of the race. But I was one of them. Of course my pretty, white race car didn't look quite as good as it had when we towed it in there. If you want to know, it looked about like it did when I first saw it out behind the Ford Garage in Timmonsville.

Racing got me good that first night, and I never got it out of my system.

I ran old Number 35 for all it was worth for the next several races, and I was really getting the feel of the sport. I learned to accelerate past the slower cars—when I could—before I got to the corner, so I could get a better line on it. I didn't have nearly as much power as many of the cars, so I had to do some fancy maneuvering through traffic to get myself in the right spot to get through the corners best. In some odd way I had a feeling that the *lack* of power was a help to me in getting started. And, now that I look at it, I think it taught me a lot in a hurry about learning to handle a loose race car on dirt.

I was only able to console myself like that for a little while longer. The time came when I could no longer convince myself of how much I was learning. I wanted to go faster; I was only fooling myself. I had learned about as much as I was going to learn at that speed. I was ready for the next step, so I started looking around for another ride. I hated to give up my first race car, but progress is progress, and I wasn't making any.

I went through the pits at every race, asking if anybody needed a driver. And when someone wasn't doing as much with a car as I thought they should, I went right up to the guy who owned the car and offered my services. There weren't any takers. Of course, I wasn't exactly the Fireball Roberts or the Junior Johnson of the Pee Dee, but I felt I had talent. And, Lord knows, I was ready to unleash it on the right machine. How long was it going to take these guys to discover me?

Winning a race might have helped my cause, but I couldn't win a race if I didn't have a better car, and I couldn't get a better car if I didn't win a race. To say that I was bewildered would be the understatement of the century.

Several weeks later, during one of the heat races at Sumter, one of the cars got upside down—a *lot* of the cars got upside down all the time, but this one had a particular significance to me. The driver pulled himself out, stomped over to the pits, threw his helmet down, and said, "You can have this sumbitch, I quit."

I couldn't believe what I had heard. This was a good race car, just the kind I had wanted to drive; I mean, a *good* car. Big V-8 and everything. Why would anyone give up a ride in a machine like that?

"Who owns that car?" I asked one of the guys in the pits who looked like he knew what was happening. You can always tell the guys who belong there, they have the T-shirts with grease stains on them.

"J. N. Wilson," he said. "Right over there." And he pointed over to the other side of the pit area.

I was never one to be bashful, so I went right over and said, "Mr. Wilson, I'm Cale Yarborough. I drive Number 35, that white car over there, and I was wonderin' . . . I mean, I thought, well, you know . . ."

"You want to drive my car," he said.

"Right."

"Well, I ain't got nothin' to lose. Come on over next week and give 'er a try. I'll have it ready to go again."

It goes without saying that I figured this was a big step toward NASCAR. And, you know, I think it was.

J. N. Wilson was from Camden, South Carolina, and he built good race cars. The engine was far more powerful than mine, and the suspension was a whole lot more than the junkyard parts we had bolted on. I could tell the minute I got the car on the track the next week at Sumter that I had something under me. I felt that I finally knew what real racing was, and I was sure that nothing would stop me now. Get out of the way, here comes the Timmonsville Flash!

I qualified third fastest in J.N.'s car. "Not bad, kid," he said.

"You just wait," I thought. "That was only my first time out."

I lined up in the back row in my first-heat race, and when they dropped the green—no, *before* they dropped the green—I was on the gas and moving up front. All of a sudden I found myself in a familiar situation. I had accelerated right into the middle of the pack of slower cars, and I was up high, on the outside. I was in exactly the same spot that the guy had been in when he'd tried to go around me in my first race.

Hello, wall.

The boards flew and the car stopped. I couldn't believe it. "Damn," I said. I couldn't sit there, looking like a dunce, so I got the engine restarted, put it in reverse, and backed up. It would still run. I gunned it and roared around to catch the pack, which was moving slowly, under yellow—because some gung-ho kid had knocked down the fence.

They cleared away the splinters and we were racing. This time I moved up fast, but I used my head. I didn't try to go through a hole unless there was going to be a place to come out.

It was only a fifteen-lap race, so I didn't have time to get up front where I knew I could run fast, but I learned an important lesson that night: Don't let your right foot outrun your brain.

When I pulled myself out of the car in the pits, J.N. said, "Well, if you don't count the first lap, I guess you did all right."

"Let's not count the first lap, Mr. Wilson," I said. "I'll get it right from now on." We both knew I would.

It took me two more races, but I finally got it together. And, you know, even on that little old quarter-mile dirt track, back in the sticks of South Carolina, it's not an easy thing to do to "get it all together." You have to qualify well, get just the right jump on the flagman, work the traffic, and, more important than anything else, try to stay out of the way of the crazies. If you can do all of that, you *might* win.

Well, I did it all. And I won. I took the second-heat race one night, and I was leading the feature when some wild kid—you see, I wasn't a wild kid anymore; no, sir, I was a veteran driver—well, this wild kid knocked me into the infield.

The important thing is that I finally won a race. I only got $15 and I had to split that with Mr. Wilson, but I was a *professional* race-car driver. I could see it right under my Senior picture in the yearbook: "Cale Yarborough, captain of the football team, all-state; baseball; basketball; boxing; glee club (we'll just let that one pass, thank you); student council; professional race-car driver."

I might be a professional, but I hadn't outgrown fantasizing. And I doubted that I ever would.

There was one other thing that they could have put in the yearbook: bus driver. I know you're not going to believe it, but they actually hired me to drive the school bus during my last year. Why not? I had driven about everything there was, so a school bus shouldn't be any problem.

I went down to the bus garage the first day to check out my bus, and the guy said, "Aren't you the one who drives race cars?"

"That's me," I said.

"And you're gonna drive a school bus?" he said with a puzzled expression on his face. "Man." He shook his head.

"Look, I'm not gonna *race* it, I'm gonna drive it," I said.

"Sure," he said. "Sure."

Well, he was wrong. I didn't race the bus. The kids were never late getting to school again, but I drove it safely. Keep in mind, I didn't say "slow," I said "safe."

In fact, the most unusual thing that happened during my days of driving a school bus is that nothing unusual happened. That, in itself, was different for me. I mean, my life had always been so strange that I could be minding my own business and something unusual would happen—like getting struck by lightning and bit by the rattler.

One night Wallace Jordan and I had a date with a couple of local girls; we went to the drive-in in Florence to get some hamburgers. Nothing could have been more innocent. As we sat in my convertible under the cover at the drive-in, some guy in a trench coat—a *trench coat*—came out of the alley and exposed himself. Can you believe that? Right by the FLASH LIGHTS FOR SERVICE sign.

It really bugged me, so I got out of the car and said, "Listen, buddy, you shouldn't do that. You should be *ashamed* of yourself. I mean, there are girls around here."

"Of course there are girls around here," he said. "You don't think I'm flashin' you, do you?"

He was drunk.

When I tried to move him away, he pulled a gun. I said, "Now why don't you just put that away and leave. You don't want to cause any trouble." And I reached for it. Mistake. The gun went off, and the bullet richocheted off the pavement. It must have scared him more than it did me; he ran away.

The guys came running over to see what had happened, and I said, "Man, that guy was crazy. I could have gotten shot. I mean, look, the bullet went right there beside my foot."

One of the guys said, "You did get shot, Cale. Look!" And he pointed to my right foot. Blood was oozing out of my cowboy boot.

"I *did* get shot!" I yelled.

It turned out that the bullet went right between my big toe and my second toe and just clipped the skin. It didn't even touch a bone. But it sure ruined my cowboy boot. Maybe not—it was a really good conversation piece. I showed it to everybody.

You may have the impression that nothing good ever happened to me. Well, you're wrong. It did.

One night I got a call from a girl I knew, and she asked if I would do a favor for her. "I'll try," I said. "What?"

"Well, this girlfriend of mine would like for you to take her to the prom," she said.

"Why doesn't *she* ask me?" I said.

"Cale, she's afraid to ask you. She's afraid because she admires you so much and she thinks you'll say no," she said.

"Why would I say no?" I asked.

"Well, you see, uh, she's crippled. She had polio when she was real young," she said.

I told her I would have to think about it. "Call me back tomorrow," I said. And I did think about it. I thought, "What would everybody think if Cale Yarborough showed up like that, you know, with a *crippled* girl?" I guess I had gotten a little too big for my britches because when she called back, I said, "No, I don't think I can do it."

She said, "Well, that's the reason she wanted me to call you, because she *knew* you wouldn't do it, and she didn't want to hear it from you."

I don't think anything anybody had ever said hit me as hard. There was a long pause. And then I think I grew up on the spot. "Well, you tell her she's wrong," I said. "You tell her I accept."

I didn't know what to expect on the night of the prom. I got her a corsage, and I went to her house to take her to the dance. I rang the door bell and held my breath. Her mother answered the door. "Hello, Cale," she said. "I'm so glad you came. You come in and sit down, I'll go get Nancy."

She was back in a few minutes, helping her daughter, who walked unsteadily on aluminum crutches.

She was as pretty as a speckled pup.

Her mother helped me put the corsage on her, and I helped her down the steps and into the car. All the way over to the gym I wondered what my buddies would think.

I opened the door to the gym real slow, and I held it for her until she got through. There was a long sort of aisle formed by the tables, and we had to walk all the way to the other end of the building. I thought it was going to take forever; I could tell that everybody was watching us. But a strange thing happened: Instead of being ashamed, I found myself with a different feeling—I was proud. When I went through that door, I was five-seven, but by the time I got to the table, I was ten feet tall.

That evening changed my whole outlook on life, and I'm sure I became a better man because of it. I don't think I ever thought about it much before, but after that, I realized that not everybody was as fortunate as I was. Even though I never had to suffer being hungry or cold and was never really deprived, I always wished that I had more money, that I had come from a wealthy family. I never wished that again.

We had a wonderful time that night. We sat and talked and even tried to dance. I held her tight and almost dragged her. We both laughed about it. And, you know, before the evening was over, I think about every couple at the dance had come over and sat with us for a while.

■

One of the advantages of living in an area like I do is that warm weather lasts so long. There are a couple of months where it gets down to freezing a few times during the night, and there's always what we call Blackberry Winter, when it frosts a couple of times after the spring blooms come out, but for the most part you can work outside or hunt or do almost anything year-round. And that includes racing.

I raced through most of the winter, and by spring I had won several races. I still wasn't making much money at it, but I was having a wonderful time. And as time for my high-school graduation drew near I was ready to swing into racing full-time. I figured that I might have to have another job for a while; you know, until I made it to the big time—NASCAR.

I was running every track around, so you could figure that there would be a race on the night of my graduation. It couldn't miss. I toyed with the idea of trying to get out of going, but I couldn't come up with a story that wouldn't have gotten me skinned by Mama. I might just as well plan to go to the ceremony because I could hear Mama if I even suggested that I miss it: "William Caleb Yarborough, if you think that I am going to be denied the thrill of seeing my first son graduate from high school, well, you've got another think coming."

I never did know why I always had "another think coming," but I did. And I knew that she would give it to me if I even thought of missing any part of graduation.

I avoided the grief and went to graduation. It was held on the stage at the end of the gymnasium on a Friday late in May of 1957. I wore a white sport coat, and I did what every kid in the world does: When my name was called, I walked across the stage, took the leather-bound diploma folder in my left hand, shook hands with the principal with my right, and walked off the stage. From there it differs slightly: I turned right instead of left, where the rest of my classmates were sitting on folding chairs on the gym floor. I went backstage, pushed up a window, and climbed out, dropping the eight or ten feet to the ground. And then I ran over to my Ford convertible and raced to Bishopville. And I mean raced, because I drove that Ford street car faster than the Ford race car would have run.

I got to the track just as the cars were lining up for qualifying. J.N. was pacing up and down the pits. I didn't say a word. I just ran over to the car, strapped on my helmet, and slid through the window of the race car.

"I'll say one thing, Cale," he said. "You may not be the most prompt driver here, but you sure are the best-dressed one."

I still had on my white sport coat and the dark gray gabardine slacks Mama had bought me for graduation. And the new penny loafers.

I qualified fastest that night. And then I went back to the pits and took off my white sport coat. It was the least I could do.

I won the heat race. In the feature I got exactly the right jump on the flag. I passed five or six cars before I got to the starter, and by midway through the forty-lapper, I was out front, well on my way to a feature victory. What a story it would make if I could tell you I won, put my white sport coat back on, and went back to the graduation dance at the gym, trophy in hand. It is the stuff movies are made of. But it didn't happen. I got spun out with two laps to go. At least I was one of the few race-car drivers with a high-school diploma.

My racing picked up after graduation, and Mama and Vernon went to almost every race I was in. They always did. And they went to the football games and the boxing matches. If Mama wasn't able to go, I mean, if she was sick or something—and that's about the only thing that would keep her away—Vernon went. There were rare times when neither of them could go, like some of the games and races that were a long distance away, but Vernon always waited up for me, to find out how I did. He always had me tell him about the game or the race or the boxing match. And he listened. He was a good friend and an inspiration.

I think one of the reasons I always had so much confidence, other than the fact that I was a Yarborough, was that nobody ever told me I shouldn't try something "because it's too hard" or "impossible." No matter how ridiculous what I wanted to do seemed, I was always told, "Go ahead and try it if you want to." And, you know, I could usually do it.

It was that way from the start. Daddy always encouraged me to "try," and so did Mama. And so did Vernon. Of course, they never encouraged me to do anything dangerous—I came up with that on my own—but my family always gave me the feeling that I was something special. I guess I believed it.

With people behind you pushing, rather than holding you back, you can do some mighty big things.

■

The whole idea of my being a race-car driver must have been very hard for Mama to swallow—as much as she wanted me to be happy —because, well, if you must know, driving a race car wasn't exactly the most respected thing there was to do; at least, not in the South in the fifties. There were certain things that were considered taboo. Hillbilly music was one of them, cockfighting was another, drinking any kind of alcohol was another, and, well, you already know the other one—driving stock cars. If you did any of them, you weren't considered "high-class," and Mama always wanted me to have class.

If your kids were involved in any of those things, you weren't too proud. It was like living in a log house; that was taboo too. I guess it was just too close to what a lot of people had come from. It didn't exactly spell progress.

Now, of course, if you *don't* do at least three of those things I just mentioned, you're not considered high-class. Times change.

But, as hard as it might have been for Mama to accept—as much as she wanted something better for me than all the people around us who had grown up in the Depression had—she always accepted the fact that I wanted to be a race-car driver. I don't know why, except that maybe she was a better predictor than most people. Maybe she had so much faith in me that she felt I *would* make it to the top. Maybe she felt I *would* make a lot of money and a name for myself.

Mothers sense those things.

She even got to the point that she rode to the races with me, and that took a lot of courage because I drove wide-open, all the way there, raced, and drove wide-open all the way home. More than once I heard her say, "Oh, Lord, if you'll just let me get through this one, I'll never go again." But she did.

Bless her soul, she never gave up on me. Not for one second.

**FUN–LOVING RACE–CAR DRIVERS WERE
SPREADING SPLASHES OF TECHNICOLOR
THROUGH WHAT HAD BEEN A GRAY
AND DRAB SOUTH.**

7

■

For so many years the South was dull. It seemed that there wasn't any spirit after the War Between the States; and don't think that because the war had been over for ninety years that things had changed all that much—at least, they hadn't around where I lived. And it was worse in other places: Charleston, for example, was still fighting the war.

Life in our part of the country was gray and drab, and sort of like a black-and-white movie, with nothing but cotton mills and farms and hard work. But that was starting to change, and stock-car racing— the sport that was once frowned upon—was part of the reason for the change. Colorful, fun-loving characters like Curtis Turner and Little Joe Weatherly were spreading splashes of Technicolor throughout the entire South, and the fans were eating it up. It was like a traveling circus, going from small track to small track and leaving behind it a little hope. And a lot of pleasure.

Many of the guys raced around home. That gave me even more determination to travel with them—right to NASCAR. I had so much determination, in fact, that I announced my plans to race at Darlington. Immediately the hometown folks got behind me. If I ever had any doubt about the merits of growing up in a small town, the "favorite-son" treatment they gave me wiped that out. They even collected money to help me buy a new car.

There was one major problem, however: the NASCAR rules stated that a driver had to be twenty-one years old to race. I was seventeen. No problem. I knew a girl who worked in the Court House, so I had her make me a phony birth certificate. I mailed it in, along with my application and five dollars, and in about ten days my NASCAR license arrived. I had it laminated.

Bobby Weatherly really felt that I was ready for the Southern 500, so he put together the money that had been donated and went to White Pontiac in Darlington to make a deal. We didn't have nearly enough for a new car, but they gave us one, anyway—a brand-new 1957 Pontiac.

I had a NASCAR license and a race car. I was on my way, at seventeen.

In 1957, the NASCAR rules were still very strict as to what you could do to a car. You could beef up the suspension and put on a bigger radiator and modify the exhaust system and do a few minor things to the engine, but the cars were still stock cars. Of course, you had to have roll bars and headlights and side windows, and most of the interior had to be taken out. And there were real racing tires by then. Firestone had developed a stock-car tire a year or so before that, and that had gotten Goodyear into the act, so we went to Thompson Oil Company, who was the local Goodyear distributor, and promoted a few tires. It became a community effort.

We ran out of money, so we had to use some junkyard suspension parts like springs and spindles, but we felt they would do. When all of the modifications were completed, we took the car to a professional sign painter and had it lettered with White Pontiac on each side and a big 30. You see, Number 35 wasn't available in NASCAR, because that's the number Bill Champion was using, so I just picked a number that was available. The car was white—the good-guy color.

There were times I just sat around and looked at the car. I couldn't believe that I had my own Grand National car and that I was on my way to Darlington. My life's dream was about to be fulfilled. At seventeen. I had expected it sooner.

The car was completely ready two weeks before the Labor Day race, so I took it out on Route 403 and ran it a lot, just to get the feel of it. After each run we tinkered until we had the car running as fast as it ever would run. Then we checked all the parts, to make sure that there weren't any flaws. If we found anything that looked questionable, we replaced it. You see, we had access to parts through White Pontiac; we could replace a part on a sort of informal warranty situation. Through that same plan we had balanced the engine, which means that we went through hundreds of pistons and working parts to find those that weighed the closest to one another. We spent more time in the parts bins than the parts manager did.

When we were putting the engine back together, we turned it over by hand thousands of times, just to make sure that all of it matched and worked perfectly. The engine was as perfect as we could possibly make it, and we had enough clearance on all the parts to make it run like a well-broken-in motor.

We picked up about 30 miles an hour on Route 403.

When it came time to go to Darlington, I just drove the car up there. I knew that most of the top cars would be hauled on a truck, but we didn't have a truck that big, so driving it would have to do. Besides, that would give me a few more miles of practice in the car —fifteen, to be exact.

The day before I left for Darlington I got a letter from NASCAR. They had found out that I wasn't twenty-one, and they wanted their license back.

"What should I do?" I asked Bobby Weatherly.

"About what?" he replied.

"The letter," I said. "This damn letter from NASCAR." I was shaking it in his face.

"I don't see any letter," he said. "You know what lousy mail service we have. Lissen, are we gonna stand here all day and talk about the mail or are we goin' racin'?"

"We're goin' racin'," I said.

We decided that if they gave us any trouble, we would put the entry in Bobby's name. He had a legitimate NASCAR license. He followed me in his pickup with our small supply of spare parts and our large supply of tools.

I can't begin to count the number of times I had driven to Darlington, but this time it was entirely different. For one thing, I seemed to be noticing things a lot more. Maybe I was looking around more to see if anybody was looking at the Pontiac with 30 painted on the side. But I think it was more from a sense of pride I had for my part of the country. I was looking around, really appreciating where I had come from. And, you know, I was seeing a lot of beauty in it for the first time.

To get to Darlington from Timmonsville, you drive a couple of miles west on Route 403, then you head due north on Highway 344 for about ten miles. It's all flat country with long, straightaway runs. It's no wonder people drive fast down here. I mean, with all those long straights, a man just has to run it wide-open once in a while, just to see what she'll do. It's an obligation he has.

I looked around at all of the farming country and at all of the pine trees. Most of the houses are one story with high hip-roofs and big porches, and they're up off the ground three or four feet on brick foundation pillars. That day I looked at every house and at every hedgerow and at the cotton fields and the tobacco and the swamps and the Spanish moss and the kudzu. I wondered if people from up north would think it had been snowing, because there was cotton along the sides of the road that had fallen off wagons taking it to a gin.

I was doing about 90 miles an hour when I went past the High Hill Baptist Church. That wasn't unusual; we had a lot of highway races on that straight. It was a little different that day, though. I had so many butterflies in my stomach, I thought I was going to throw up. It was the destination, not the speed. I was used to speed.

All of the houses had clotheslines out back, and there were clothes on most of them—mostly work clothes—and I could see them in my rearview mirror as they fluttered in the wake from my Pontiac. There were a lot of shade trees around the houses and a pickup truck in every sandy drive.

About every mile or so, a dusty road led off the main highway, and I knew that it went to a farm very much like the one I grew up on. I remembered how all of this looked from Daddy's airplane; the dirt roads and hedgerows and cotton and tobacco fields and the stands of pine trees and the swamps made the whole country look like a giant patchwork quilt. It wasn't dull or ordinary at all, like I had thought.

I was proud of my heritage.

I thought about a lot of things as I drove up there—maybe I was trying to take Darlington off my mind. I looked at the sharecropper shacks, and I thought of all the trouble blacks and whites were having in Alabama and Mississippi and in many places. We hadn't had any trouble. In fact, from the time I could first remember we had always worked side by side with blacks—in the fields and in the gin, everywhere. We didn't have a whole lot more than they did, so there wasn't any great difference as far as I was concerned. I guess nobody told us that we couldn't get along.

My thoughts turned to the Darlington Raceway, as much as I tried to keep my mind off it. I got a few more butterflies when I thought of who I was going to be racing against: Speedy Thompson and Fireball Roberts and Curtis Turner and Lee Petty and Joe Weatherly and Fonty Flock and just about every great stock-car driver in the world.

"You've got your work cut out for you today, buddy boy," I thought. But deep down inside I felt like I was ready. I had to be; there were a lot of people back home counting on me.

The fifteen-mile trip couldn't have taken more than ten minutes; it would have been quicker if Bobby hadn't been following me in the pickup, because I wanted him to be able to keep up. No matter, it still seemed to take forever.

When we got to the track, I followed the signs that read PITS. I went through the tunnel under the track between turns three and four, and when I came up on the other side, I was a Grand National driver. I didn't go sailing into the pit area like I felt like doing, sliding sideways to a dramatic stop, because I didn't want to call attention to the fact that I didn't have a truck to haul my car on. You really can't blame me; I mean, I had this brand-spanking-new race car, and I didn't want to look like some kid from Timmonsville—some green-horn.

We parked the car and the pickup, and Bobby and I went over to the NASCAR office to sign in.

"Who's going to drive the car?" asked Norris Freil, who was in charge.

We both knew why he was asking. "I am," Bobby said.

"Uh, Bobby," I said, tugging at his sleeve. He slapped my arm away and shook his head at me.

"Okay," Norris said, "but make sure he doesn't," and he pointed to me. "He's too young."

"Sure," Bobby said. "Whatever you say."

I couldn't wait until we were away from there. I was jumping up and down. "Why did you tell him that?" I bellowed.

"Calm down, Cale," he said. "I've got a plan."

"What is it?" I asked.

"Well, I'll take the car out the first time," he said, "and then I'll bring it in the pits and you can practice in it and qualify it. They'll never know."

"What about the race?" I asked.

"Well, I'll start—"

"Bull crap," I said, "I'm drivin' the race." I was sputtering, I was so mad.

"Just hold on, Cale," Bobby said. "I wasn't finished. I'll start the race and you can take over after a lap or two. It'll work, believe me. They won't recognize you with the goggles and helmet."

I didn't like the plan very much, but I guessed that it was the only thing that would work.

I settled down to the point that I could look around. There were race cars everywhere, and here I was, right in the middle of them. I was about to be one of them, even if I was going to be the "Masked Marauder." It was all right—after the race everybody would know who I was, and then it would be too late for them to put me out.

I had been in the pits at Darlington before; somehow I expected it to be a lot different than it was this time. I mean, it was exactly the same: I was always looking over my shoulder and waiting for them to throw me out. This wasn't how I expected things to turn out.

While Bobby was out on the track with the car, I paced back and forth. Finally I went over to talk to some of the other drivers, and I even told a few of them about my problem, swearing them to secrecy. They all said about the same thing: "We don't give a damn how old you are, kid, just as long as you don't cause us any problems out there." Well, that would work out fine, because not only was I not going to cause any problems, I was also going to be one of the cars to beat. Monday, September 2, 1957, was going to be a red-letter day for me.

I thought Bobby would never come in. He was only out there for a few laps, but it seemed like it took forever. When he did bring the car in, I was right on top of him again, jumping up and down. "How'd it run? What's it feel like? Get out! Get out!" Everything I said was starting to run together.

We puttered around the car a little to make it look like we were making some adjustments. He started to answer my questions. "It feels good, Cale," he said. "There's a flat spot out there in turn one. . . ."

"I know," I said. "What about the rest of the track?"

"It's big," he said. "*Big.*"

I had the helmet and goggles on and was halfway in the car before he could say any more. And I was buckled up and had the engine fired up before Bobby could stand up from where he had been crouching at the left front fender. I wanted to get out of there before they caught me.

I pulled it down into first, waved to Bobby—who was still a little dazed from my sudden departure—and moved out of the pits and down toward turn one. The banking on the turn seemed much higher than it had from either the pits or the outside of the track, and when I came out of two, I couldn't believe how long that straightaway looked. It looked as long as our drag strip from Timmonsville to Sardis. I took a complete lap before I accelerated much, staying down low, out of the way of faster cars. Some of them went by me so fast that it rocked my Pontiac. But as I came out of two the next time, I punched it. I felt the power in the seat of my pants, and my head rocked back a little. I stayed on the gas until I got to three, and then I backed off, drove it up high near the wall, and got on it a little more, taking it wide into four, just like I had watched the other guys do. When it started out of four, I punched it hard again and brought it down near the center of the track, letting it go through one a little lower than most of the cars were going.

I had made my first lap at Darlington at speed and, man, it was a great feeling. I drove the same groove, lap after lap, until I saw the NASCAR official standing at the edge of the track with a black flag in his hand. I recognized him; it was Johnny Bruner, and he was pointing the flag at me. The black flag means "come in." The Masked Marauder had been caught.

Next time around I came into the pits. Johnny was standing there with his hands on his hips. As I brought the car to a stop he motioned me behind the pit wall with his thumb. "Get out of that car, kid," he said. "And stay out!"

I didn't say a word. I just tossed the helmet to Bobby and stomped off. As I went by Bobby he said, under his breath, "Don't worry."

That was easy for him to say.

Bobby brought the car back in a few laps later and said, "Did you get enough of the feel of the car to qualify it?"

"I don't think so," I said.

"Well, there are a whole lot of cars out there right now, so why don't you go out and run some more? They won't notice." He didn't have to beg me. I got in about ten or twelve more laps, and then I brought in back into the pits when there were a lot of other cars there. They didn't notice.

When it came time to qualify, Bobby made a big deal out of letting Johnny Bruner and Norris Freil see him bring the car out to the line.

He stayed right in the car, and just before it was our turn, he looked around to make sure that they weren't around and got out. I had been waiting inside on the floorboards on the passenger side.

When I took the Pontiac out, it felt great. I took a couple of fast laps, and I knew that I was really moving. I was sure I had qualified well up in the pack. As I inconspicuously got out of the car in the back of the pits, I heard the announcer say, "And that was Bobby Weatherly, ladies and gentlemen. Bobby's speed was 108.45 miles an hour. Not bad for a newcomer." Huh, they didn't know how much of a newcomer Bobby Weatherly was.

The speed I turned was only good enough for the forty-fourth spot out of fifty-three cars. What had seemed to me to be a record speed was more than ten miles an hour slower than Paul Goldsmith's, who was the fastest qualifier at 119.29.

I wondered if I was ready for this race.

There was only one way to find out. I was going out there and give it everything I had, and I would see what happened. I knew one thing: As big as the track was, I wasn't intimidated by it. Humbled a little, maybe, but not intimidated.

But I was about to be intimidated by NASCAR. Here came Johnny *and* Norris. Both of them had their hands on their hips.

"What are we gonna do?" I asked Bobby, panic in my voice.

"Beats me," he said. "Short of running over them with the race car."

"Very funny," I said.

They didn't say a word. They each took me by an arm and walked me across the track.

"Where you taking me?" I asked, dragging my feet.

"Outside the track," Norris said.

"Why?" I asked innocently.

"Why?" Johnny said. "Why? Because we saw you get out of that race car. And you're *out* now." They escorted me right outside the gate.

When they turned and headed back for the pits, I ran around to the side. I knew where there was a place to get in. I found exactly the same spot that I had crawled under when I was eleven years old. I was under the fence, across the wall, down over the track, and in the race car before Norris and Johnny even got back. "Gimme the helmet and goggles, quick," I said to Bobby.

"No, they'll catch you again, Cale," he said. "Let me start the race, when they'll be looking for everything, and then I'll come in right after it starts and you can get in. They'll be too busy watching what's going on out there to notice."

I knew it was the only way.

Besides, it would give me a chance to watch some of the other drivers in action. I had already talked with some of them, and they had given me some tips. These guys were my idols; I thought they could walk on water. If I saw them drive, I could put what they told me together with what I saw and, man, I would be a terror out there.

Most of the drivers were standing beside their cars when Johnny came through the pits, saying, "Okay, boys, let's get in the cars and get ready." As he passed our car he looked at Bobby and said, "And that doesn't mean your co-driver."

"I know, I know," Bobby said.

I was over behind the pit wall, blending in with a sea of onlookers, pit crews, press guys, whatever. It was easy to blend in, because none of the teams had uniforms or anything like that. Everybody was dressed the same, jeans and T-shirts.

Drivers started climbing in cars, and my heart rate must have doubled. I didn't think I was going to make it. Would it work? Would I ever really get in the car?" *Hurry up!*

Someone said, "Gentlemen, start your engines." I don't even know who it was, and a roar went up that could have been heard all the way to Charlotte. It was music to my ears, beautiful music that could have been improved only if I'd been playing one of the instruments. But it wouldn't be long. I hadn't come this far just to watch from the pits. I knew that I would be in there soon.

The cars started to move out of the pits in rows of two. It didn't take long before all the cars were gone. All but one. He was stalled at the pit entrance to the track. The NASCAR guys were all huddled around the stalled car. This might be the break if Bobby had seen it. He had! I was probably the only one in the whole place who was watching the back of the pack, and I saw car 30 drop down low. He was coming into the pits. I was at the top end of the pits as planned, and when I saw him come down on the apron coming out of four, I was ready. He came to a stop at the very top end of the pits and crawled out the window. I crawled in. Man, oh man, this was it. I came through the pits and was back in the pack before they got the stalled car rolling.

I could see a puff of smoke from the exhaust of the stalled car as we turned out of four for the back straightaway. This was it.

I kept my eye on the starter. I wanted to get a good start, but I didn't want to call any attention to myself by standing on it *too* early. It had to be just right.

There was the green flag.

All hell broke loose.

I accelerated past cars 88 and 71, but I could see another car that had started behind me, moving right up to my outside. I had my foot in it as far as it would go, and I was staying with the pack. Way up front I could see Cotton Owens in another Pontiac, moving ahead of the pack. He was going through turn two with Bobby Myers and Curtis Turner right behind him. They were pulling away from the field.

By lap thirteen, Turner had moved into first place. And he had lapped me. Two cars were already out of the race with mechanical problems, and I was beginning to wonder if maybe I should be out too. I wasn't getting anywhere. All of this was a lot tougher than I had thought it would be. Maybe I wasn't ready for the big time.

I could run with the cars in the back of the pack, where I had started, but I couldn't begin to pick up any ground on guys like Fireball Roberts and Curtis and Little Joe. Had they given me the wrong information? No, I knew better than that. I realized that it takes a lot of experience to drive race cars like they did, and I was afraid I wasn't getting it with the level of racing I was involved with. I was a little duck in a big pond at Darlington.

Fonty Flock's Pontiac spun, went into the corner, and hit the wall on the eighteenth lap. The yellow flag came out. I thought that maybe I could do better after the cars got bunched up again. But I didn't.

When the green flag dropped, my idols pulled away from the rest of us again, building up a bigger lead as the race went on.

On lap twenty-seven there was a bad crash between Bobby Myers and Paul Goldsmith. Myers's car was completely destroyed, and as I went by him, I knew that it was all over for him. He was slumped over the wheel, motionless. The yellow came out again, and I made several more laps, trying to keep from looking, or even *thinking* about Bobby Myers.

Before the green came out again I was in trouble once more.

There was that familiar figure at the edge of the track in the front straightaway—Johnny Bruner, his thumb pointing toward the back of the pits. I knew that this was it. There wasn't even any use to try to get back in the car again, but it didn't matter much at that point. I didn't belong out there with the big boys, anyway.

It was hard for me to swallow. Everything had come so easy to me in racing. I had jumped in a race car and, in a very short time, had become a winner. Great promise, everybody said. I had people back home who had so much faith in my ability that they helped me get a race car. But I wasn't ready for Darlington and I knew it. I had a lot to learn.

I might have been hot stuff on the short tracks, but that was a long way from Darlington. A long way.

It was decision time for the kid from Sardis.

Bobby took the car out, but four laps later he hit the wall in the first turn. The right front spindle—one of our "used" parts—had broken. All in all, it had been some day. I had started on top of the world and ended up with the weight of the world on my shoulders.

For the rest of the race I was a spectator. A dejected spectator. But, in spite of how bad I felt, I still was interested in how things were going. After all, I *had* been a part of it for twenty-seven laps. And I was still a racer at heart.

The lead switched back and forth between Curtis and Cotton and Lee Petty until the fortieth lap, and then it was Fireball and Lee, but both of them wrecked later on, so Speedy Thompson and Curtis fought it out.

Speedy was too much for the rest of the field in his '57 Chevy. He led the final 150 laps and averaged just over 100 miles an hour, which was a new record for Darlington and not that much slower than the speed I had qualified at. He averaged that for the whole race, yellow flags and pit stops and all.

It was a long trip home. The race had lasted five hours, and it had taken us a couple more hours to get the race car in shape so that we could tow it. Nobody had ever driven the Southern 500 at my age before. That should have been enough. But it wasn't.

It was quiet in the truck as we drove back down Highway 344. And the countryside that had been so colorful and beautiful only hours before had returned to black and white. Maybe even sepia.

Cale at one and a half years old.

Cale's first job—the tobacco warehouse—when he was in high school.

Reward Yourself

PALL MALL

Outstanding

One of Cale's first Pee Dee dirt races, this time at Bishopville, South Carolina. Cale was running in fourth place at the time.

A seventeen-year-old Cale Yarborough makes one last engine check at the 1957 Darlington Southern 500.

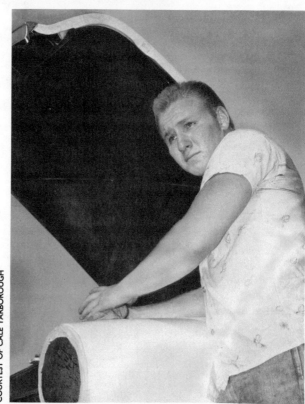

Betty Jo Thigpen at sixteen years of age. It's easy to see why Cale spent so much time at the drugstore.

Cale relaxes with Betty Jo and Julie after his first NASCAR victory, which came at Valdosta, Georgia, in 1957.

Cale in 1965 in the Banjo
Matthews Ford.

Banjo Matthews discusses
race strategy with Cale.

Cale and Mario Andretti battle it out in late sixties NASCAR action.

A battle-weary Cale Yarborough after winning his first Southern 500 in 1968.

The Ford team of 1969, clockwise from left: Cale, Richard Petty (not many remember Richard as a Ford driver), Lee Roy Yarbrough, Donnie Allison, and David Pearson. Note the size of the carburetor.

Cale and country music great Willie Nelson.

Cale poses with his Junior Johnson Chevrolet in 1976.

When King Juan Carlos of Spain visited the United States in 1976, President Ford asked him who he wanted at his state dinner. "Cale Yarborough," proclaimed the king. So it was.

The Yarboroughs at home on the 1,300-acre Sardis, South Carolina, farm.

Cale in the winner's circle at Michigan International Speedway in 1983.

8

■

It is hard to break my spirit. It always has been. For some reason I always seem to land on my feet. So, when racing had let me down— as I felt it had—I turned back to football. I got an offer to play fullback for the semipro Sumter Generals, and I jumped at the chance. Maybe this would make up, in some way, for the way I had let the folks down in my hometown.

The only problem was that football, like auto racing, was not going to support me. I still needed another job to supplement my income. I could have gone to college, probably on a football scholarship, because both Clemson and the University of South Carolina had shown interest in me, but I let it be known that after high school I wasn't interested in studying anymore.

Instead of studies I went into the logging business. The decision came by accident, when I ran across an old junk truck in the woods one day. I figured that there must be a use for it, and logging was the only thing I could think of. It had been there for so long that it was buried in sand up to its axles. It was a Ford, about a '46 or '47—there wasn't any way of telling—and I was sure it could be salvaged.

I spent a full day digging it out and towing it back to the house with the old tractor. I was real proud of that truck. But I can't say that I got much encouragement from anybody else. In fact, most people who saw it thought I had come unglued.

J.C., who was nine by then, said, "You call that a truck? Why, you'd have to fix it up to get a junkyard to take it."

My brother had become a comedian.

I'll have to admit that it did look a little rough. The truth of the matter is, a junkyard *wouldn't* have taken it. But that didn't matter. I knew that with a little work it would be just the ticket for hauling a lot of logs out of the woods. Or maybe it was a lot of work just to haul a few logs out of the woods.

It turned out to be a bigger job than building a race car. The wheel bearings and the universal joint had to be replaced, and the engine needed a bunch of work, but with the help of some buddies, it was running in a couple of weeks. The engine smoked so much that I put used oil in it, and it made a lot of noise, but none of that was important. This was one of the few vehicles I ever had that I wasn't going to run fast—the *only* one, now that I think of it.

The Cale Yarborough Logging Company was in business. Well, not quite; I didn't have any way to cut down the trees. I shopped around at junk stores and flea markets, and I bought a double-bitted ax and a crosscut saw—and I don't mean the kind with a motor. I mean the kind with a guy on each end of it. It was going to be hard work, but I was used to that. Besides, it would keep me in shape for football. So I hired a couple of black guys who had worked around the gin, and we started to work on the stand of longleaf pines out behind the farm.

It didn't take us too long to cut the trees out of there, so we went from farm to farm, buying what trees we could. Since we were cutting trees for pulp, they didn't have to be too big, and that's probably good, because my equipment—from truck to saw—left a lot to be desired.

I got to the point where I had to upgrade, so I went to Sears, Roebuck and bought a David Bradley chain saw on credit. And, while I was there, I bought a $25 set of tools. Also on credit.

Production almost doubled, and I started making a little money. I bought another old truck, but it was better than the first one; listen, I even used new oil in it. And then I bought a used tractor to haul the logs to the trucks, hoping that I would never again have to work with mules.

After paying my two helpers and buying gasoline and parts—you see, when you work with old equipment, something is always breaking down—and making the time payments, I was clearing about $100 a week. It wasn't bad money for our area. And I was boss.

The only thing I needed was a hobby, something like flying.

Bobby Weatherly was a pilot—that is, if you consider an hour and a half of instruction as being a "pilot." I did. After all, Freddie Huggins, who was a local crop duster, had traded him a couple of lessons for the use of Bobby's motorcycle.

Bobby was the closest thing to a pilot I knew, so I took a copy of *Trade-a-Plane*, the classified-ad airplane newspaper, over to Bobby's and said, "Let's buy an airplane."

"Are you out of your mind?" he asked. "Or did you find gold back there in the woods?"

"No, neither one," I said. "But here's a J4 Piper Cub up in Van Wirt, Ohio, for $600." I held up the paper.

"It must be a winner," he said. "Lemme see that ad."

He was hooked.

He read the ad and said, "I'll meet you over at Vince McDaniel's store tonight. We'll talk about it."

Vince's store was a typical old country store, over in Cartersville. I hung out a lot there, and we always talked football and racing and coon hunting—the same things people talked about in all country stores in South Carolina. Well, that night Bobby, Pete Workman, and I decided to drive up and take a look at that plane.

We left early Saturday morning—Bobby and Pete and I, and Olin Spears, whom we talked into going with us. Olin could really fly a plane, so we figured he could help us get it home, if we bought it.

The trip up was a nightmare. For openers, they wouldn't let me drive because they said I would get us arrested for driving too fast. And then they made me get in the back because I complained about the way Bobby and Pete were driving. "Get back there and go to sleep," they said.

I was fine until we got into the mountains in West Virginia. The winding roads made me sick; that alone would have been bad enough, but I wasn't content just to be sick. I had to get up on my knees and rock back and forth and moan. It was an awful trip. For everybody.

The airplane wasn't much to look at, but Olin said it would fly, so I, for one, had made up my mind that we should buy it. It was worth it to me not to have to ride back in the car. Everybody agreed. We offered the guy $550.

"I'll split the difference," he said. We bought it for $575.

"I'm flyin' back with Olin," I said.

There wasn't any argument about that. They didn't want me in the car any more than I wanted to be in it.

The weather was so bad going back that Olin had to fly way around it. We had to land in Asheville, North Carolina, to wait out the storm. Bobby and Pete beat us back. Naturally I got sick in the plane too. It wasn't one of my better trips.

The weather stayed bad for a couple of days, so all we could do was sit in the country story and *talk* about flying. Around the second day, Bobby's brother, Wib, got to telling how good a pilot he was, and the more he bragged, the more I bragged. It wasn't long before each of us were the best pilots since the Flying Tigers.

"Well, why don't we just go over tomorrow and fly your plane," Wib said.

"Fine with me," I said. "I'll meet you over there at about four o'clock tomorrow afternoon."

We kept the plane in a cow pasture on Bobby's farm. I was there on time; Wib was half an hour late, but when he got there, he was full of enthusiasm. As we walked over to the plane I said to Wib, "You go ahead and get in the left seat. I'll ride on the right side." Of course, the pilot always rides on the left and the copilot on the right. I knew that much.

"Naw, Cale," he said, "it's your plane. You go ahead and ride over there." Swell.

The plane had two sticks, so I wasn't too concerned. If I did have to fly it and I got in trouble, Wib could get me out of it. As usual, I was long on confidence. I had watched everything Olin did, so I didn't think I would have any trouble.

I got it started, and then I taxied it out to the middle of the pasture. And I took off, all by myself. I took that rascal off, just like I knew what I was doing.

"That was real good, Cale," Wib said. "Real good."

If Wib thought it was good, I figured I had a knack for flying. I flew all around, experimenting with this and that and making the plane go up and down and turn and do everything. Of course, Wib didn't know I was experimenting; he thought I really meant to do all those things. I got to know what it took to make it do a lot of things. At one point I even considered trying a loop, but I thought that might be pressing my luck. But I was having a ball.

I kept asking Wib to try it, and he kept saying, "That's okay, Cale, you're doin' just fine. Just fine."

I buzzed everybody I could think of buzzing, and after an hour or so, we both decided it was time to go back. It was going to be dark shortly, and the fuel was starting to get a little on the low side. Getting back was no problem; I just followed the highway. Landing was going to be something of a problem.

"Uh, Wib, I, uh," I said, stammering. "I'd like you to *land* it, just to see how you like the plane. You haven't flown it all day."

"Naw, Cale," he said. "It's your plane. *You* land it."

I was a little more insistent: "Wib, I'd like you to land it."

It went back and forth a couple more times, and finally Wib said, "Cale, uh, there's something I think I have to tell you."

I didn't think I wanted to hear it.

"Well, the truth of the matter is," he said, "I've never flown a plane before."

There was a long silence.

"I never have, either, Wib," I said.

"Oh, hell," he said.

Well, there was nothing to do but land it. There shouldn't be much difference in landing than in taking off; all I had to do was reverse everything I did before. It turned out that landing is a lot harder. For one thing, I couldn't get the plane all the way down. I could get it close, but it was like there was some force pushing it back up. It was like turning two magnets the wrong way, so they repelled each other.

I tried time and time again.

Wib didn't have much to say. He just sat there white-knuckled, staring into space.

"Wib," I said. He didn't answer. "*Wib?*"

"What, Cale?" he finally said. He still had the blank look on his face.

"We're gonna be out of gas after the next try," I said. "So hold on tight. I'm gonna get this thing in one way or another."

"One way or another," he said. "One way or another." He kept repeating it.

I brought it in over the strip and got it as low as I could. And I did the only thing I knew: I cut off the engine. I thought that was called a dead-stick landing, but I wasn't sure. I pushed the stick clear forward, and the plane sort of dropped to the ground. It hit hard and bounced back in the air. The next time it hit, it didn't bounce quite as far. The third time, it stayed on the ground and was rolling down the pasture. We had put up some posts to mark the landing area; I hit one of them with my right landing gear, breaking the landing gear off. The plane skidded to a stop.

"See, that wasn't so tough, was it?" I said. Wib just looked at me. He didn't say a word. He got out of the plane, went straight to his car, and he left.

The next day I started repairing the plane. I went down to Huggins Airport in Timmonsville and got the landing gear off Daddy's old plane. They had taken it back there to use for parts. I found some aluminum tubing and some bolts, and I went back and sawed and cut and bolted until I had the new gear spliced on.

The right landing gear was a few inches shorter than the left one, and from then on, the plane always went down the runway with the right wing tip about a foot closer to the ground than the left one. *Gunsmoke* was popular on television then—you remember, with Dennis Weaver, who walked with a limp—so everybody called our plane "Chester" after that.

I took the plane back up, and I taught myself to fly. I spent the entire day at it, but I mastered it.

Bobby and I flew a lot after that, but Pete Workman wouldn't fly it himself or even fly with us. All he wanted to do was taxi it up and down the pasture by himself. That ended too. One day he was taxiing with the stick all the way back and the elevator up, when a gust of wind picked up the plane and flipped it over on its back. It only broke the prop, but it was the end of Pete's flying career. We bought his share of the plane for $200.

There's only so much you can do with a Piper Cub. It's slow and it doesn't have much range. I mean, you have to get bored after a while. I was bored. It was time for trick stuff. We talked Olin into coming over and flying the plane, so Bobby and I each could get on one of the wing struts. We had seen it in a movie somewhere, and it seemed like a good idea. He tried time and time again to take off, but the weight out there on the wings was too much. It may have been just as well.

We were determined to do something daring. Anything. So we turned to land-based vehicles. I had put a Continental tire kit on my Ford convertible, so I bet Bobby a hamburger that he couldn't stay on the rear bumper, holding on to that kit, while I drove up and down the runway. The bet was on.

I drove as fast as I could, throwing it into broad slides when he least expected it. It took me about five minutes, but I threw him. He went sailing through the air and hit in a kudzu patch. You know how kudzu grows in the South—it's on all the fences and telephone poles. Everywhere. There was so much of the parasite plant along the fence row where he hit that I couldn't even see him. When he pulled himself out, I said, "Bobby, just remember, there's never a horse that couldn't be rode, and there's never a cowboy who couldn't be throwed." Daddy had told me that.

"Okay, buddy boy," he said, "let's see how good you are." He motioned for me to follow him over to his new Ford truck. "I'll just bet you double or nothing that you can't stay on my rear bumper."

"You're on," I said. "There's no way you can throw me off."

"I'll throw you off or I'll turn it over," he said.

I got on the back bumper and got a good hold of the two chains that keep the tailgate closed, you know, the ones with the rubber sleeves on them to keep them from clanging against the truck bed. It would be like waterskiing. He took off and spun it one way and then another. He slid all over the place, tearing up the field, but he couldn't throw me. He kept going faster and faster, until he finally made a mistake. He made a big spin but didn't keep enough power on it. The sod started building up under the right wheels—the direction in which the truck was sliding—and, sure enough, he flipped the truck.

I went flying through the air and hit on my shoulder, but the kudzu broke my fall too. It still hurt like mad, but when I got myself out of the kudzu, the hurt went away. Bobby was out of the truck. He was just standing there, looking at it and shaking his head. It had done a complete flip and landed on its wheels. It didn't look all that bad. Of course, the top was a little flat and there wasn't any windshield or rear window in it, but it could have been a lot worse.

"Well, look at it this way," I said. "At least you won't have to buy me a hamburger."

We were going to kill ourselves on the ground, so I decided to return to the air. It was safer. Aerobatics was the next logical step.

I thought about it for several days before I decided to actually try it. Where do you start when you're teaching yourself? A loop seemed to be as easy as anything. You just pull back on the stick and the plane goes up and over, and when you start back down, you push the stick forward. Simple. There couldn't be much to that. I'd save the snap rolls and hammerhead stalls until a little later, but first I would perfect the loop.

The plane was flying along nicely at about 80 miles an hour. I pulled back on the stick, gradually at first, and then more and more. Sure enough, it went up and over, but there was a problem. I didn't have enough air speed, I guess, and the plane stalled. Upside down. I could tell I was upside down because when I looked up, I saw green. Even with my basic knowledge of flying, I knew that I should see blue when I looked *up*.

There was another problem. The treetops I was flying over kept getting closer and closer to the cockpit. I wasn't even flying level. I was about to crash, if you want to know. "Now, let's see," I said. "I'm upside down, so everything's going to be backward." I talked myself right through it, and I got the plane flying up again, and then I got it right side up.

I knew exactly what I had done wrong, so I tried it again. I wasn't upside down as long that time. After about five tries I had it down perfect. Time to move on to something else.

The something else came in the form of parachuting, and I don't mean emergency-type parachuting—I mean, jumping out of a plane because you *want* to jump out of a plane.

It started with Harold Lyles, who was a sky-diver friend without a plane. It worked out fine: We would fly, and he, in turn, would show us what to do and let us use his chute. The first time I took him up it was a strange feeling. One minute Harold was there, sitting right beside me, and the next we was gone. He opened the door, said, "Byyyeeee . . ." and was gone. It's only strange the first time it happens, but to take off with somebody and land alone is spooky.

First I flew Harold and he explained what to do; then Bobby flew him, and Harold told him. He was doing a lot of jumping and we were doing a lot of flying. But he suggested that we watch for a few times, and we went along with it. He also suggested that we not try to free-fall for a while; just jump out, pull the rip cord, and go on down. He told us how to land, you know, on your feet and sort of spring. He said it might even help to roll after we hit, at least for the first few times.

"One more jump," he said, "and then I'll turn the chute over to you."

It was about time.

I watched from the ground, standing where he said he was going to come down. I saw him jump out of the plane, from about three thousand feet, and I saw the chute open. He was coming right down where he said he would. When he hit, I carefully watched how he landed. It was perfect.

"Nice jump," I said.

"It's nothing you can't do," he said.

I knew that.

He showed us exactly how to pack the army surplus chute and said we could use it over the weekend. "Bring it back over to me," he said, "and if it doesn't work, I'll give you another one."

"Whatta'ya mean, if it doesn't work?" Bobby asked.

"Inside joke," he said.

After he left, Bobby and I got ready to embark on our newest experience.

"Lemme go first," I said.

"Be my guest," Bobby replied.

The toughest part was riding in the little Piper Cub with the chute on. Well, I *thought* that was the toughest part—until I got the door opened and was perched on the threshold, looking down at the patchwork quilt I called home. Bobby circled and I looked. This was going to be the ultimate high dive. "Geronimo," I said to Bobby.

"You say that *after* you jump, Cale," he said.

"Oh," I said. "Well, then, *bye.*" And I jumped.

Wow! What a sensation. The first hundred or so feet was so great that I hated to pull the cord, but I did. When the chute opened, it jerked me so hard that I thought I was going to fly right back up to the plane, like I was on the end of a giant bungy cord.

I was coming down much faster than I had imagined. It looked so slow and easy when I watched it from the ground or from the plane that now I was going like Jack the Bear. The ground was coming up fast, so I got ready for the contact. I hated for it to end, because it was almost the ultimate pit-of-the-stomach sensation.

"You're going to hit hard," Harold had told me, "so let your legs act as shock absorbers." I tried to remember how he had told me to do it. When I hit, it felt like my shock absorbers were up to about my breastbone. Man, I hit hard. I didn't have time to roll because I was too busy trying to stay out of the woods. My aim wasn't as good as Harold's.

I was sure I had broken both my legs. I laid on the ground for a while. I could move my legs and ankles and everything, so I guessed nothing was broken. I got up. Hooray! I could walk. The pain was far overshadowed by the rush I had gotten on the way down.

This was for me.

"Come on down and try it, Bobby," I yelled. I don't know what made me think he could hear me, but that's how anxious I was for him to get the sensation.

Bobby landed and jumped out of the plane. "How was it?" he asked.

"You're not gonna believe it," I said. "Listen, this may be the greatest thing since sliced bread."

We repacked the chute—if you can call jamming all the silk back in the bag repacking—and I helped Bobby strap it on. We were to find out that we didn't know as much about parachuting as we thought he did. I should have brought the two straps around him and up between his legs; instead I brought them *around* his legs. It looked right to us.

"How's it feel?" I asked.

"Real good, Cale," he said, "but are you sure this is right?"

"Of course I'm sure," I said. "You think I'm some beginner or something? I know all there is to know about parachuting."

I figured I had it on him perfect, because it didn't hurt him. When I had it on, it made me feel a lot like a soprano. I thought I was the one who had it on wrong.

We got in the plane with me on the left side and Bobby on the right, riding with his chin about two inches from the instrument panel, because the chute took up that much space, especially because of the way we had it stuffed in there.

When we got to three thousand feet, I said, "Okay, Bobby, anytime you're ready."

"I'm as ready as I'll ever be," he said. And he opened the door and jumped. Just like that. Bobby was all right.

I watched the chute open, and everything looked fine to me. What

I didn't find out until later is that when the chute opened, the whole harness came up and caught under his armpits. It almost came clear off. He was just hanging on for dear life, with his hands clenched together as tight as he could clench them, so the chute wouldn't come off over his shoulders. I guess he hit the ground like a ton of bricks.

When I got to him, he was sitting on the ground with a dazed look on his face. "Well, how'd you like it?" I said.

"I don't know," he said. "I was too busy screaming to pay any attention. You know, Cale, there's a *lot* you don't know about parachuting."

We figured out what we had done wrong, and each of us jumped five or six more times that day. With the chute on right. There was a new dimension to flying. All of a sudden I realized that it was as much fun to get *out* of an airplane as it was to get in one. Maybe more.

We bought our own surplus chute, and from then on we "hit the silk" a lot. That's what the pros say. In fact, I even devised a unique way to get home. On the last pass of the day Bobby would fly over our farm, and I would parachute right into the backyard. Mama never stopped shaking her head and mumbling, "Boy, you're gonna be the death of me yet," when I came in the house. I think she was pleased that Jerry and J.C. weren't the daredevils that I was.

With all the flying the Cub needed constant repairs. We were about to wear it out, so we had to keep working on the engine and the flaps and everything. The bolts finally sheared off in my makeshift landing gear, so I replaced them with twenty penny nails. Our flying circus was a low-budget operation.

I used that term—flying circus—to Bobby one day, and I could see a light bulb light up. I recognized it immediately because my own bulb lit up.

"What are you thinking?" I asked.

"The same thing you are," he said.

"Well, you know, the lumber business isn't all that good," I said, "and I sure could use some extra income. Besides, we gotta pay for gas for the plane and all that, so why don't we—"

He was one step ahead of me. "Start a flying circus," he said.

Bobby was my kind of people.

There wasn't any question in either of our minds that it would work. Every time we jumped there were always half a dozen cars stopped along the road, watching as we came down. On weekends the sides of the road were lined with cars. So we figured that if we put on a real show, we could make some money from it. All we had to do was perfect the plan.

We found a good field near a busy highway over at Cartersville, and we got Bobby's two brothers, Irby and Wib, and Harold Lyles in our scheme. First of all, we had to have some sort of ground show as well. It only stood to reason that it was going to be a little tough to collect the money once we had jumped. We needed to start on the ground, collect the money, and then go upstairs for the aerobatic and parachute show.

"Just let me jump before you start the aerobatics," Bobby said. It suited me fine because it would make the plane lighter.

We bought a couple of old cars for a "thrill show" part of the circus, and then we built a couple of ramps for jumps and rollovers, which, of course, was my department—jumping and rolling.

The show got off to a slow start because we had trouble attracting attention to the action on the ground. The truth is, nobody at all stopped. So the next Sunday we started with a couple of parachute jumps. We had gotten a used PA system, so we were able to announce to the people exactly what they were going to see: "The rest of the show will start in twenty minutes, and one of our people will be going from car to car to collect contributions. We sure would appreciate a dollar a car." Irby did the announcing. And it worked. Before long we had the road lined with cars.

I rolled a car and then made a jump from ramp to ramp. Irby had it down just like a real thrill-show announcer: "And here he comes, ladies and gentlemen, that famous race-car driver, direct from the Southern 500 at Darlington, *Cale Yarborough!* God ride with you, Cale." And then Wib would set off a string of firecrackers as I made the jump. It even impressed me.

Harold and Bobby and I took turns parachuting, and then I did my aerial show. I did rolls and loops and stalls. It was a bargain for a buck a car.

The next week we added a band—country and western—and we got Slim Mims from Florence, who put on a crazy country outfit and did a comedy routine. He was Uncle Ugly.

With the country music and comedy we needed a better, a bigger thrill show; otherwise, I would be playing second fiddle. Show business is no bed of roses. I brought the old race car out of mothballs, and we built bigger ramps. I wasn't going to let Uncle Ugly upstage me. We moved the ramps farther apart.

"You'd better practice a couple of jumps," Wib said.

"Practice?" I said. "What do I need practice for? Listen, all I have to do is get way back there, about as far as that barbed-wire fence, and drive as fast as I can go, and I'll guarantee you, I'll make the other ramp. Easy."

"You'd better practice," he said.

Practice. *Hmph.*

Word had spread about our Sunday thrill show. In fact, the highway patrol came over to help direct traffic. We really packed them in.

I did a couple of rolls with the old cars, the country band played, Uncle Ugly did his routine—using one of the ramps for a stage—and then we took to the air. The parachute jumps and the aerobatic show was the big buildup to the "Jump to Hell."

I got the race car right back against the barbed wire while Irby got the crowd warmed up on the PA. You know, the "here-he-comes" part. I was in the car, buckled up and with my crash helmet on. I got the signal from Bobby and fired up the race car. I took off. I was really moving by the time I got to the ramp; the race car went up the first ramp and went sailing through the air.

Irby was right; I should have practiced.

I looked down and saw the landing ramp way under me. I was flying right over it. It was another aerial show. An unplanned one. The car came down on its nose and flipped three times. It must have been the best show anybody had ever seen because they were still whooping and hollering when I pulled myself out of the car. Or what was left of the car.

Scratch that part of the thrill show. In fact, as far as I was concerned, you could scratch the whole show. There wasn't enough money in it to go through all that.

But it sure did feel good to be back in the race car again.

I guess our fame had spread, because I got a call from the people who organized the Beaufort Water Festival. They wanted to hire Harold and I to do a jump. For fifty dollars each. Man, that's more than we cleared for the whole thrill show. We accepted.

When we got to Beaufort the next week, the Water Festival was under way. There was a parade and a carnival and booths selling everything you can imagine. The bay was filled with boats, and they had set up grandstands where people could watch the boat races and water shows. It was a big thing.

Harold and I were supposed to jump from ten thousand feet, into the bay. I had never even *been* to ten thousand feet, let alone jump from there, but they had boats standing by to pick us up, so why not? They had two Piper Cubs, one for each of us. What could go wrong?

The grandstands were packed when the planes we were in flew over them. It took us a long time to get to the right altitude; in fact, we never did get all the way up. It was taking so long, and the wind was kicking up, so when Harold got my attention and gave me a diving gesture, his two hands together and pointing to the ground, I gave him a thumbs-up sign.

I watched his door open and saw him jump. I followed immediately. I had never jumped in wind that strong. Harold had. He was going straight, working his chute just right. I saw him hit the water within a hundred or so feet from one of the boats. I was drifting away from the bay and toward the center of the city.

As I came down I could see that I was being blown right toward some power lines. I lifted my feet as far as I could. It wasn't enough, so I climbed the chute cords. I missed the power lines, but I came down on top of a dentist's office.

They had to get the hook and ladder truck from the fire department to get me down. Man, you talk about being embarrassed. Oh, not from the landing. That was better—by a whole bunch—than the power lines, but I had to be the only sky diver in history who ever missed an *ocean.*

Something happened the next week that made the Beaufort incident seem like a Sunday-school picnic. As I told you, the thermal drafts over the Pee Dee are real bad; one minute it can be as smooth as glass, and the next you can be bouncing around like a Ping-Pong ball. With no warning. This is what happened: I opened the door of the plane and was perched on the edge, putting on my chute. You see, this particular jump was a spur-of-the-moment thing, and I hadn't gotten ready. I had one arm through the harness when we hit the turbulence.

The next thing I knew, I was falling through the air. When you free-fall, the feeling is one of great exhilaration, but free-fall with a chute on is one thing; free-fall with a chute *half on* is another.

I was fighting like mad to get the chute on all the way, but I could tell that that wasn't going to work, so I started frantically searching for the rip cord. I found it and held on tight, because I was afraid that the force of the chute opening would jerk it clear off. I didn't have to worry much; the chute only got part way open by the time I hit the ground.

I was sure I was broken in two. Everything hurt. I tried to wiggle my toes. They worked. My fingers worked. I was all right.

It turned out that I had hit in a freshly plowed field, and the soft dirt—along with the partially opened chute—had saved my life. I had fallen out of an airplane and survived. Somebody was trying to tell me something.

I figured it was time to give auto racing a try again. I mean, it had to be safer than this. It didn't surprise anybody. But I did have to keep the logging operation going too. I traded my interest in "Chester" to Bobby for two more chain saws and a four-wheeled farm wagon. And I started looking for a good ride. In the meantime I took up waterskiing. It was back to the old swimmin' hole on Lynches River. Bobby, Billy Atkinson, and I got an old Johnson Sea Horse outboard motor and put it on an old flat-bottom boat that had been around my farm for years.

The only problem was that there wasn't much room to water-ski, so we had to cut down cypress trees and make our own course. To say that it was like running a mine field would be an understatement, but we did it. We had to ski between, around, and sometimes over stumps. Again, traffic along the highway stopped to watch. And, again, I loved that. I guess I was a showman at heart. The only thing was that the show had to have some danger attached to it or I wasn't interested.

No race-car rides came along, so to pass the time until one did, I joined the rodeo. It fit right in; it was in Florence, and they needed cowboys. They were going to tour the entire area, and it paid pretty good. Besides, I had ridden bulls when I was a kid and had ridden bareback on horses and mules as long as I could remember. There wasn't any question in my mind that I could ride anything they had.

I joined the American Rodeo Association and trouped around the area with them as they put on shows in every little town. Of course, I got thrown a lot—everybody did—but I figured that was part of the business.

I got to the point that I could ride about as well as some of the regulars. I was doing pretty good, but if you want to know the truth, it was starting to get old. I mean, hitting the ground as often as a rodeo cowboy might be fun to some of them, but it was starting to lose some of its charm for me. But I didn't let anybody know. I guess I appeared a little cocky, because one of the regular cowboys came up to me one day and said, "Don't ever get too cocky about horses and bulls, kid. Just remember, there's never a horse that couldn't be rode—"

"And there's never a cowboy that couldn't be throwed," I said. "I know all about that. Listen, that's my personal motto."

It might have been my motto, but those horses and bulls made a believer out of me. I gave up show business for the last time.

RED CLAY IS THE GREATEST NATURAL

RACING SURFACE IN THE WORLD,

BUT WHITE CLAY WON'T BOND TO ANYTHING.

9

■

There were dirt tracks all around Timmonsville; nearly every town had one, but they weren't good tracks, like the kind you found most everywhere else throughout the South. They were bad tracks, if you really want to know.

For one thing, the tracks everywhere else were a mixture of sand and red clay, and that was a perfect combination for broadsliding into turns and accelerating out of them. Around home we had a kind of white clay that everybody called "bull tallow." That stuff tends to get real hard, and it makes driving on it real difficult. There wasn't much sliding, and the guys who were real power-slide experts, guys like David Pearson and Bobby Isaac, who came down to run them, had a rough time. It took them a while to get used to it.

It was an advantage to me. After all, I'd cut my teeth on bull tallow.

Most of our tracks were fairly flat, and that was something different to a lot of the drivers from other parts of the South. There was one thing that all the tracks had in common: They all looked exactly alike as far as the general appearance was concerned. All of the grandstands were sort of rickety wooden structures. And there was always a concession stand underneath that sold hot dogs and pop and stale popcorn and cigarettes and chewing tobacco. There was a board fence most of the way around the tracks and a wooden guardrail inside of that, right at the edge of the track. The pits were on the inside, and there wasn't much grass anywhere. There were pine trees all around.

Columbia was both the best and the worst track. It was the best because more top drivers came there, so the racing was always good. It had been my favorite track since I was a kid, just because of the good racing. To watch. It was a bad track because it was badly built. Like most of the tracks, including Darlington, there hadn't been any design to Columbia at all. They just found a place, got some road graders, and built it. Then, from time to time, they graded it again, so a lot depended on how good the guy was who was running the grader. They said it was a half mile, but sometimes it was, say, six-tenths of a mile. It was all in how the guy cut it with the motor grader.

It was probably the toughest track to drive in the South. I mean, guys who grew up in the Piedmont Region of the Carolinas, like around Charlotte and Spartanburg, didn't even want to think of driving on a bull-tallow track. Not when they had such good racing in their area. It was all because of their soil. There is a band of red clay that starts up around Richmond, Virginia, and it runs down through Alabama and Georgia, right through Atlanta. So all a guy had to do in those areas was go out into any field and cut a quarter or a half-mile track and water it down with fifty thousand gallons of water and he had a racetrack. Red clay is the greatest natural racing surface in the world. But white clay won't bond with anything. It gets super hard and makes big holes in the track.

A man named Buddy Davenport from Charlotte had built Columbia. He's dead now. But, even if he is, I'll have to say that he didn't know what he was doing. He built four or five tracks around there, and all of them were bad. He really built them to sell hot dogs and not necessarily to race on. But I'll say one thing: They were tough to drive. They had long straights and tight corners, and that made for a lot of wrecks. You had to run hard down the straight and slam on your brakes, and *pow!*

Compared to a track like the one in Hickory, North Carolina, which was wider and much better designed, Columbia just didn't work. I think that's why I loved Columbia. Man, it was a real challenge, and you know me and challenges.

I certainly wasn't the only one. As much as the guys complained about Columbia, there was always a bunch of good drivers there. And I'll bet you that deep down, if those guys admitted it, they were there because of the challenge. All racers are pretty much alike.

Columbia definitely was the toughest track to win a race on, because on any Thursday night you could find Lee Roy Yarbrough, Tiny Lund, Tom Pistone, Ralph Earnhardt, Ned Setra, Bobby Isaac, David Pearson, and a whole motley assortment of guys from down in the hellhole swamps of South Carolina, guys like Rock Raines, J.D. "Junior" Johnson (Slick's daddy), and Wild Bill Brady, who was a crazy guy with a whole lot of money, whose real name was Morgan or DuPont or something. Really. But nobody knew, or cared, for that matter. He drove wild, so they liked him for his driving, not who he was.

Every Thursday night was like *Gunfight at the O.K. Corral, High Noon,* and everything else. In fact, you know, the whole thing was a lot like the Old West. Every driver was a legend. And I've always thought that drivers like that were a special breed. I think all good race-car drivers are; otherwise, there would be a hundred times more of us.

The assortment of drivers was weird. There was even a driver from Charleston, South Carolina, which never produced any race-car drivers, because, well, mainly because they're still too busy fighting the Civil War down there to think much about racing. But they did produce Little Bud Moore.

Little Bud was about my age at the time. He was the first long-haired hippie race-car driver. On the other side of the age ledger you had guys like Ralph Earnhardt, who was probably the best dirt track driver I ever saw, and Ned Setra, both of whom were in their mid-forties. Most of the drivers were older and very experienced, so to throw young drivers like Little Bud and me into a pile of people like that meant you had a fistfight on wheels. Every Thursday night.

And it had the strangest assortment of fans of any track I ever saw: It was a mixture of soldiers from Fort Jackson, the University of South Carolina, students, farmers, and working-type people who worked the first shift in the textile mills. Or the third shift.

If ever there was something built for me, it was the Columbia Speedway.

I went through the pits before every race, asking for rides. I always got one. Look, I'm not going to try to convince you that the rides were good ones, but they were rides, and I was competing against the best on dirt that there ever was. I don't do this too often, but I'll have to admit that I wasn't too terribly impressive in my first few races, although it's a wonder that I didn't get tetanus from some of those old rusty cars I was driving.

I drove anything that had air in the tires. For example, one night I bumped someone in practice and it broke the hood latch on my race car, so I got out and strapped it down with the belt from my jeans. That's the kind of stuff I was running at first. Man, it was fun. You really had to get truckin' down the straightaway. You were going so fast, you had to cross it up halfway down the straight, and you slid all the way through the turns. Of course, it was tough on the car, especially if you ran up front, but I always remember something that Curtis Turner told me at Darlington in 1957. He said, "Kid, if you run up front, you're gonna be hard on equipment. No way around it." And you know, I took it to heart. He knew. Curtis wasn't just a character, he was a great race-car driver. A natural.

Of course, running as hard as everybody did—and you wouldn't believe how hard a lot of those guys ran—there were a lot of crashes. It couldn't be avoided. You always had half a dozen guys heading for the turn in the same groove, and the track was so narrow that you couldn't pass in the corner, and I'll guarantee you that none of those guys would back off, so it was crash city. And then there was a fistfight in the pits after the guys got back there. Standard procedure.

There were many nights that the action in the pits was more frantic than it had been on the track. You might get out of your car and *bam!* some guy would coldcock you. There were times when I came flying out of the car and right on top of some guy. I certainly wasn't going to get a reputation of being a wimp. If you did, they'd run right over you on the racetrack.

One of my best rides came one night in the hundred-lap feature at Columbia. I had wrecked the car I was driving early in the race, and I was standing around in the pits, waiting to see if there was a chance to relief-drive for someone. It didn't happen often, but once in a while a guy would get tired or mad or just plain fed up with the mayhem out there—especially in the long race—and there would be a chance to hop in and finish the race for him. Well, Curtis Crider had gotten fed up with it, so he came in. When he saw me, he motioned for me to come over. "You wanna drive this sucker?" he said. "I mean, it's like World War Three out there."

I didn't say anything. My helmet was already on, and I was pushing him out of the way to get in the car. It was a good ride, and this was my first chance to really show my stuff. I had been holding my own, even with the poor rides I had; in fact, I had taken a lot of bad cars and made them look pretty good. But "pretty good" wouldn't get it with those guys out there.

I gunned Curtis's car out of the pits, and I was really flying when I got to turn one. News flash! There was a big hole in the turn, about the size of a Volkswagen, and I hit it square on. The car went sailing through the air, right over the guardrail, and crashed through the outer fence. It went down through the parking lot, and I was steering like mad to miss all the parked cars. I wound up sitting in the middle of the railroad tracks.

"Oh, yeah," Curtis said when I came walking back, "I forgot to tell you about the hole in turn one."

Some debut to the good cars.

For a long time it was still pick-up-whatever-ride-I-could-get. Bobby had his own car, and we still ran the outlaw tracks. I did right well there, but I was always on the verge of disaster because I drove so hard. One night at Hillsborough, North Carolina, it was so dusty that I just had to follow Bobby, who was in front. He was really charging, and I was right behind him. I couldn't see a thing, but I was running as hard as I possibly could. The track had started to eat out —there were big grooves in it—so Bobby kept going out wider and wider to avoid them. I didn't realize it, but so was I. We went wider and wider and faster and faster.

There was a big old earth-mover tire half buried in the clay to protect the cars from the end of the guardrail posts coming out of turn two. It was so dusty that I couldn't see it, but we were getting closer and closer each lap. I figured it was about time to get past Bobby, so I tried low gear coming out of four. He moved down to keep me from passing. So when we started to come out of two, I swung up high. That would surprise him. Well, I was the one who got surprised. I hit the tire and took the whole right side off the car.

I blamed Bobby for leading me into the tire.

"*Me* lead you into the tire?" he said in disbelief. "You were running within an inch of that thing for the last five laps."

Dust was always a problem. It got so dusty at times that you just couldn't see a thing. All you could do was follow the guy in front of you and hope that he knew what he was doing; or, at least, that he could *see* what he was doing. To this day I still have some eye problems. I mean, anytime I get real tired, my eyes burn, and I'm sure it's from all that dust we used to run in.

One night it was so bad at Sumter that I was following this car in front of me, and I couldn't understand why he kept slowing down. There must be a lot of traffic, I figured, or maybe somebody spun and we had to slow down to get around. But he went slower and slower, and I went slower and slower, right behind him. Finally he completely stopped, and I ran into him. I got out of the car and started to go up and ask him why the hell he had stopped. The dust had settled a little by then, and I could see where we were. I followed that cat right into the pits. And I ran into him. That's dust.

I wasn't making any money at all. There were times when Bobby and Billy Atkinson and I would have to pool our money to get enough gas to just get to the racetrack, and there were lots of times when I coasted into the yard at home at night, completely out of gas.

Some of the tracks were starting to pay appearance money. In other words, they paid the top drivers just to show up. It was in addition to anything they might win. We used to stop on the way and call to see if we could get the money. Bobby or Billy would talk to them and say, "Listen, you guys. I can get Cale Yarborough to drive your race tonight if you'll pay him some appearance money." Most of the time they would say no, but once in a while they said, "Okay, we'll give him ten dollars," or maybe only five dollars. It wasn't much, but it paid for our gasoline.

The first solid break finally came. Marion Cox owned two race cars. Two good race cars—modified '37 Fords with powerful overhead-valve engines. Everybody called Marion "The Preacher," because he wouldn't run any races on Sunday. He was a tad on the religious side. When he asked me to drive one of his cars at Myrtle Beach, South Carolina, I knew this was it. I knew it.

Jimmy Thompson, who was Speedy's brother, and himself a whale of a race-car driver, drove Marion's number-one car. I became his number-two driver. And I was about to learn to drive on asphalt. The half-mile track at Myrtle Beach had originally been dirt, but they paved it. I drove a couple of races on the hard track, and then one night—one beautiful, starry night—I won the feature race. I beat them all, including Jimmy Thompson.

When I won the race the next week, Jimmy got upset. He said my car was faster, and that since he was the number-one driver, he should have the best car. Marion agreed, and he made us switch cars. I won with Jimmy's car the next week.

It was the last time Jimmy said anything about one car or the other being faster.

Just about the time I was getting used to the asphalt at Myrtle Beach, they ripped it all up and went back to dirt. The drivers and car owners complained because the asphalt wore out tires too fast and made it too expensive. And, the increased speeds caused more crashes, which also made it more expensive for everybody. So, to keep the drivers, they went back to dirt.

I still won. I think the confidence the good car gave me was the best thing that ever happened to me. Or maybe it was the asphalt. For some reason, I always felt that I was cut out to drive faster, and the paved track gave me that chance. I was starting to think that maybe I was ready for another try at Darlington.

Why not? I had two more years of driving experience, and at least half of that had been against the big boys. And this time I was only one year under the legal age. There would be no problem at all in faking that.

Bobby Lee of Sumter had a '59 Ford. He was a driver, himself, but he thought I had a better chance, so he offered me the ride. I sent my entry in for the 1959 Southern 500.

When I got up there, I was really accepted this time. Most of the guys had driven against me, and they knew that I was not going to give them any problems on the racetrack. The rookie image was gone for me, even on the track I wanted most to be successful at.

I was so well accepted, in fact, that I even broke into their inner party circle. It's not that they did any wilder things than we did, it's just that they used a little more imagination. Like the night I stopped by Joe Weatherly's room at the Darlington Motel. He had two girls with him, and the first thing he asked me was if I wanted to go for a midnight ride in his plane with them. Flying at night with any of those guys was exactly the last thing in the world I wanted to do. I mean, they all flew, and there's not a one of them that knew the first thing about instruments; not that I did, mind you, but I knew enough not to go up at night with them. It's a wonder any of them survived the flying experiences.

"No thanks, Joe," I said.

"Aw, c'mon, Cale," he said. "We ain't goin' all that far," and he gave me a big wink and motioned with his head for me to come along.

I decided to find out what he had in mind. When we got out to Moore's Airport, where Joe's plane was, it was pitch black. You couldn't see your hand in front of your face. Joe knew where his Aztec was parked, so we loaded in there, the girls in the back and Joe and I in front. I thought that was a little unusual, but then, the whole thing was, so what else was new? He fired it up and told the girls to fasten their seat belts. And then he revved up the engines and the plane bounced around a little, but it didn't move.

"The runway's a little rough, girls, but we'll be off in a second or two, and then it'll get smoother," he said.

I looked at him like he had gone nuts. He winked at me again. And he revved up the engines some more and pulled back on the stick. After a minute or so he cut back on the power and said, "Now that's smoother, isn't it, girls?" They both agreed that it was.

He really worked the controls. He pulled back on the stick and let up on the throttle and smoothed it out for about ten minutes, and then he idled it some and shut it off.

"Well, girls," he said. "How'd you like *that*?"

One of them said, "Oh, Little Joe, it was nice. You know, I didn't want to tell you, but neither of us have ever flown before. It's not a thing like we thought it would be."

It wasn't a thing like I thought it would be, either. We hadn't moved a foot.

As for the race, well, Lady Luck overlooked me again. I blew the engine.

I was back to running Marion's car on the better short tracks, and Bobby and Billy and I ran the other tracks with a car we had built from money we had all saved. Our car was a '37 Plymouth coupe with a 276-cubic-inch DeSoto Firedome engine. It was right hot. We towed it to the races with a tow bar behind the pickup. We did well with that car. But the real speed was on the way to the tracks. We *towed* the car faster than it would run. That wasn't unusual; everybody did.

One night we were towing the car home after winning the feature at Hemingway. I was driving and we were running wide-open—par for the course—when the transmission tore up in the pickup. We worked on it as much as we could, but with no luck. There wasn't any way we could get home. Except—you guessed it—I got in the race car and pushed the truck with Billy steering.

We flew through those little towns wide-open. With no mufflers it must have sounded like the world was coming to an end. It was late at night, and everybody must have been in bed. Until we came through town.

I won a lot of races with that car on those outlaw tracks Bobby had built. My racing life definitely was picking up.

The Marion Cox ride was a blessing. He never had a whole lot of money, but he did have a little old country garage and he knew how to build a race car. He turned out some mighty good modified and sportsman cars, and some of the best early drivers came up through Marion's cars, like the Thompson brothers, Speedy and Jimmy. I considered myself lucky to be on his team.

I was building up a strong friendship at those tracks too. We weren't too friendly when we were out on the track. At least, it didn't look that way. We pounded the hell out of each other, lap after lap, and then we went out and had a hamburger together after the race. We fought a little from time to time, but that, too, was all forgotten after tempers unflared.

The first night I ever ran against Buddy Baker was that kind of night. It was at Columbia. He was as big physically as he is today, which is about the size of Stone Mountain, and he was aggressive on the racetrack. I was leading the race when he knocked me into the infield, and I felt that he had done it on purpose, so when he was going into the pits, I came up behind him in my car and plowed right into the back of his car, knocking the tar out of him. Well, he came flying out of that car, ready to fight. I stuck my hand out to him and said, "I'm Cale Yarborough, you'll *remember* me." He smiled and shook my hand. We've been friends ever since.

The following week I won the race at Columbia, so I had some money in my pocket—three hundred dollars, to be exact. I told the guys that we were going to stop at the Hitching Post for steaks, on me. The Hitching Post was a place where a lot of the race-car drivers stopped on the way home, but it was usually for hot dogs and beer. This night it was going to be different.

There wasn't anyplace to clean up, so when we got there, we were dusty and dirty and greasy. All we could do was wash our hands. But I had money and ordered the best steaks they had—the four-dollar ones—for all our group, which included Bobby and Billy and some guys who helped on Marion's cars. There were ten of us. We waited. And we waited. Almost an hour. But we were talking and drinking beer, and nobody was paying much attention to the time.

A wedding party came in. We could tell that it was a wedding party because everybody had on tuxedos and formal dresses. Besides, the bride and groom were there. There were ten of *them*. *They* ordered steaks. They *got* steaks. "Our steaks," I said to Billy.

"It sure looks like it," he said.

I went over to the guy at the head of their table. "I believe those are our steaks," I said.

"I don't believe they are," he said. "Maybe you're in the wrong place, boy."

It was definitely the wrong thing to say.

I reached down and picked up the steak off his plate and took a big bite out of it. "Tastes like my steak to me," I said.

He got up. Mistake number two. I caught him square on the jaw and knocked him right down the table, sending steaks, bread and butter, and iced tea in every direction.

The place was full of people, and it must have been a full moon or something, because everybody in the place started to fight. It was just like one of those old Western movies: People were flying over tables and into the jukebox and the homemade pie rack and, well, it was fantastic. All of my crew was fighting. Everybody was fighting. Even the women.

I knew it was only a matter of time until the law showed up, so, one by one, I told my guys to get out of there. I took one more punch at the guy who had my steak. Somebody hit me from behind. It must have been with a chair! I know it felt like it. I went down. I figured this was a good way to make my exit. I crawled out through the front door, just as five carloads of state police showed up. I pulled myself up and said to the first one, "You'd better get in there, boys, there's the awfullest fight you ever saw going on." And I held the door open for them.

They rushed in, and we got in our cars and got out of there.

After that, we found another place to stop after the races.

■

If Marion Cox was my first big step up—which he was—Herman Beam was my second, another step closer to where I wanted and needed to get—the Grand National circuit of NASCAR. Herman asked me to drive his car. I accepted. It was that simple. I knew the reputation of his cars, and it was exactly what I wanted. I must have been getting a reputation too.

Herman worked in one bay of an abandoned gas station in Johnson City, Tennessee, but he worked every day at building and preparing a good race car. I hoped that everything I'd heard was true, because if it was, I was on my way.

We had a lot of success with Herman's car, so he decided to go all out and hit the Grand National scene. One of the first big races was the two-hundred-miler on the half-mile asphalt track at Nashville, Tennessee.

About the only thing that happened at Nashville, as far as my career was concerned, was that I qualified well. But I just couldn't get running during the race. I was boxed in time after time, and I wound up running pretty far back in the pack. But Herman was satisfied that I would get it sorted out, so he didn't give up on me.

There's one funny thing that sticks in my mind from that Nashville race. In the drivers' meetings we were told to hold it down on the pace lap; they always told us that, but nobody ever listened. Buck Baker piped up: "Yeah, you guys, don't knock the clown down until they drop the green." He was referring to the big billboard with a clown in the middle of it outside the fence at turn three. I forget what it was advertising. They hadn't any more than dropped the green flag when Buck went flying into three and blew a tire. His race car sailed over the fence, and I swear that it went straight through the clown's mouth. I saw it happen, and I got to laughing so hard that I nearly crashed.

After the race Buck said, "Well, you gotta admit, my aim sure was good."

It seems that in every race something funny happened. A couple of weeks later Tiny Lund got involved in a crash, and his car caught on fire. Tiny was a tremendous man, 6'5", and he must have weighed 260 pounds. He bailed out of that car and was running away from it as fast as he could—before it blew up, I guess. He didn't see me coming down the track, and he ran square into my right-hand door. It didn't hurt Tiny, but it bent the whole door in.

Herman was real upset. "It wouldn't have happened if you hadn't been runnin' so hard," he said.

"I thought that's what I was supposed to do," I said.

Herman was a strange man. He wanted to win, but he also wanted to keep the race car looking just like it did when the race started. I kept telling him that the two thoughts didn't go together. "It's like tellin' someone they can go swimmin' if they don't get wet," I said.

"Well, try to be a little more careful," he said.

Herman was upset a lot that season. I mean, I wasn't out there to be careful. I was out there to win.

The friendships that we all started to build up are the most pleasant memories of that period. I had a lot of race-car driver friends and a lot of press buddies and fans. I was starting to sign a few autographs. That made me feel real good, and I always took the time to sign them, no matter how tired I was. I always figured that if I signed the autograph, the kid might go away and forget about it in ten minutes; but if I refused to sign it, like a lot of the guys did, they never would forget it.

Since Herman lived in Tennessee and I lived in South Carolina, we met at the racetrack, wherever it was. He towed the car there, and all I had to do was show up. It was a good arrangement. But I still wasn't setting the world on fire money-wise, because I wasn't moving up as fast as I had expected. It was a tough circuit. But I was learning, and I knew that I would make it. Soon, I hoped.

To save money Tiny and I drove to the races in his old Pontiac station wagon. We put a mattress in the back and slept there at night. It saved money.

After things got a little better we shared a room at a motel. Most of the guys did because none of us were making a lot of money, except for a select few at the top. The rest of us were just barely keeping our heads above water. Tiny was just a big kid at heart. I'll give you an example: One day we were swimming—or roughhousing—in the motel swimming pool. We were at the six-foot level, which was all right for Tiny. He could stand up and still have a good footing, but it was over my head, so I was losing the battle. He kept pushing my head under water and holding me there. Man, I nearly drowned, but I finally got away, and I told him I'd get him. "When you least expect it" is the way I put it.

Later he was in the shower, and I went around to the ice machine with the wastepaper basket from the room and filled it with ice. Then I put water in it and stirred it around until it was cold—ice-cold. Tiny was singing away when I dumped the ice water over the shower curtain on him.

He came flying out of that shower about like he did out of a burning race car. He looked like a crazed water buffalo, so I hightailed it out the door. I looked around, and Tiny was right behind me, breathing fire—buck-naked. I ran down the steps and around the motel. He was right behind me. I turned another corner and ran through the motel parking lot. It stopped a lot of people, but I guess they figured that it was just a couple of race-car drivers doing their thing. At the other end of the parking lot there was a little old lady just getting out of her car. She was about four feet tall. Tiny slid right up to her. She was looking him straight in the belly button.

" 'Scuse me, ma'am," he said, and he turned and ran back to the motel.

The last time I saw her she was still standing there, motionless, with one hand on the car door and the other over her eyes.

But those friendships were important to me. We shared rooms and rides and helped each other—they would stop working on their cars to help you. Whatever anyone wanted, there was someone there to help. You could borrow anything they had—tools, money, girlfriends, anything. I really feel sorry for some of the drivers today. They missed all that because it doesn't exist anymore.

It was the same way with the sportswriters who were on hand for every race. All of the papers in North and South Carolina covered every race, and the writers got to know the drivers. Of course, they had their favorites, and you could tell it from the stories they wrote. I know that people like Joe Whitlock and Jim Hunter helped my career along, because they became my close friends and wrote a lot about me. It was calling a lot of attention to my career. Besides, they were a lot like me. I wasn't just driving a race car for the money; I was driving a race car because I wanted to drive a race car, and I wanted to drive it better than anybody ever had. They weren't writing stories about stock-car racing just to make money; they wanted to be successful writers. We had a lot in common. They even worked in my pits occasionally.

Hunter and Whitlock shared a room with us at times. The sport of stock-car racing was so young and their papers let the guys cover racing, but they wouldn't pay their expenses. They were in the same boat we were. More than once we took the mattresses off the two beds in the room, and Tiny and I would sleep on them on the floor, and Hunter and Whitlock would sleep on the box springs on the beds. It wasn't bad. It sure beat sleeping in your car.

I guess it's why none of the guys around stock-car racing were cocky. They didn't have a thing to be cocky about. We were all paying our dues.

I'll have to say that dealing with some of the press guys got aggravating at times, especially when I was hot and tired and had been out there all afternoon fighting a bad-handling race car and maybe finished fifth or sixth. It was exactly the last time in the world when I wanted to talk about "how was it out there?" But I always took the time, no matter how tired I was. It was a lot like signing autographs; it was something I felt I had to do if I wanted people to cheer for me. It came with the territory. And I sure did want people to cheer for me. I always did, you know that.

It was Hunter and Whitlock who came up with the first press box at Columbia. They would be the first to admit that it was a little unusual, as press boxes go, but there wasn't one at all at the Columbia Speedway, so anything they did would be an improvement. There was a small, old announcing booth that was up on poles, but it only had room for two or three people in it, so Hunter and Whitlock got a guy named Mike Harkey to bring his flatbed truck over. Actually it was a stake-bodied farm truck, but they took off the wooden racks and it made a good platform.

They parked it over on the pit side of the back straightaway, and the sportswriters sat on it and covered the race. There was always a Styrofoam cooler full of Coke, so it was a good place to go and shoot the bull. I was a regular. In fact, I brought a trunkful of vegetables from our garden every week for anybody who wanted them. I stacked them on the edge of the flatbed, and the guys just helped themselves to the beans and corn and tomatoes, or whatever happened to be ripe when I left home.

Tiny Lund, Buddy Baker, and Lee Roy Yarbrough were among the other regulars who hung out at Harkey's truck. We swapped stories and argued and pointed out good-looking girls and told jokes. Racing may not have been the most profitable profession, but it sure was fun.

Everything was a sort of trial-and-error affair. You had to use your ingenuity to get along, and you made anything work that you had. More than once, when we were building a car, we went to see what size bolt we had before we drilled the hole. That's the kind of operation it was. And, as far as the cars themselves were concerned, most people drove whatever they could get that week. If it was a good car, so much the better; if it wasn't, you did everything you could to make it run and handle like a good car. There wasn't much organization to any of it. As for driving technique, you just went out there and found the place on the track where the car ran best, and that's where you ran it. Simple. And if the track changed during the heat races, which it usually did, you found another place on the track to run.

There were a lot of drivers who could win a race with a car that handled perfectly, but there were only a handful who could do it with the one that didn't handle so well. That hasn't changed. A lot of the superstar racers today couldn't begin to win with the equipment that we had then. By the same token, a lot of the drivers we had then couldn't win with the best of today's equipment. Class will always win out.

I think that a man who is a consistent winner is born with that talent. I really feel that *I* was. Oh, I think I had to develop it over the years to fully bring it out, but I feel it was there from the beginning. Those bad old cars and those bad old tracks just brought it out a little faster and maybe a little better. It was a tough apprenticeship we were serving but a valuable one. We complained about how tough it was at the press-box sessions, which went on well into the night. They usually continued at some roadhouse where they always got noisy and always ended in a fight; nothing on the scale of the Hitching Post war but a brawl of some sort. Lee Roy was the worst of all about starting fights. He couldn't go to the men's room without taking a swing at somebody. I never understood it. He couldn't fight at all, but that never stopped him. He would punch some guy and then wind up on the short end of the horn, getting pulverized every time. Tiny would have to finish the fight for him. It was the same every time: Lee Roy would start it and Tiny would finish it. Of course, Tiny was so big and so tough that if anybody did hit him, he would just laugh. You couldn't hurt him.

Bubba Into was another one of our group who was tough. He wasn't as big as Tiny, but he was as tough as a pine knothole and as mean as he could be when you got him mad. The biggest mistake Lee Roy ever made was the night he got into an argument with Bubba. It wasn't exactly the argument that was the mistake; we all argued all the time, but nobody ever got mad. Lee Roy did that night. He grabbed a Coke bottle and hit Bubba over the head with it. He hit him so hard that it broke the bottle, and you know how heavy those old Coke bottles were. I mean, it wasn't one of those nonreturnable thin ones, it was the old bustle-style bottle. It was like hitting somebody with a lead pipe.

Bubba stood there with his hands on his hips and a look of amazement on his face. He didn't even blink. He just looked at Lee Roy and said in a soft, easy voice, "You really shouldn't have done that, Lee Roy."

"Oh, Lord," I said.

Lee Roy knew he had done something real bad.

Bubba picked up Lee Roy and threw him through the window, which, unfortunately, was closed. We all grabbed Bubba and calmed him down, because he was ready to go through the window after Lee Roy. He might have killed him. In a few minutes Lee Roy peeked around the front door and said, "Listen, Bubba, I'm, uh, I'm, well . . . I'm sorry 'bout the Coke bottle."

"Aw, that's okay, Lee Roy," he said. "You can pay for the window."

"Sure, Bubba," Lee Roy said. "Can you help me pick the glass out of my hair?"

I always took a carload of guys home at night, and when I dropped them off, there was usually a battle with their wives too. They just couldn't understand why we were out raising cane half the night. Didn't they know that we were talking racing? I guess not, because one of the guy's wives chased me off with a broom one night. Racing was getting dangerous.

■

A lot of people helped me—people like Pete Keller, who was the Southern field manager for NASCAR. Any time he could, he got me a ride, right from the start, and I'll never forget him for it. Other drivers and track promoters helped me. It was a good feeling. And, even if the good ride with Herman hadn't come along, they would have continued to look for rides for me. I owe a lot to all of those people. They kept me in racing.

Pete was the one who lectured the drivers before every race. It was always the same lecture. We all listened quietly, nodded our heads, and promised that we would follow the rules to the letter. "Honest, Pete." Well, one night at Columbia, Pete was going through his lecture again, but he was being a little more specific this time. The driving had begun to turn to mayhem out there. If you got in somebody's way, why, he would just run over you. You had to do the same thing or you wouldn't even make the first lap, so it was dog-eat-dog, even before the green flag dropped. More than once there was a pileup in four, while the starter still had the green flag behind his back.

Well, this particular night Pete said, "Lee Roy, if you as much as touch Little Bud's car—I mean, *touch* it—I'm gonna fine you fifty dollars. Do you understand?"

"Sure, Pete," Lee Roy said, "but that was an accident last time. I really didn't mean to knock Little Bud out of the track."

"Sure," Pete said. "And that goes for every one of you. We're not gonna stand for it."

Everybody said, "Okay, Pete, no problem," or "Aw, sure, Pete, we'll behave," or something like that. But Buck Baker said, "Pete, you go through this lecture every week, the very same talk. I mean, we listen to this bull crap every week. Let's just all chugalug a pint of whiskey and start the race."

I suppose Pete had to try, but it didn't do any good. The minute they dropped the green flag, everybody was out there beating each other to death. And Lee Roy had slammed into Little Bud before they got to the back straight.

Of course, the main reason Pete had singled out Little Bud as the one to stay away from that night is that he had won the race the week before. The guys always tried to get the driver who won the last race. That night was no exception.

Lee Roy won, and after the race he said, "Well, boys, I guess it's my turn in the barrel next week.

He was right.

Bobby and I went to Daytona in 1960, just to watch the Second Annual Daytona 500. The year before, Lee Petty had beaten Johnny Beauchamp in a photo finish. That 1959 race had gotten so much publicity that I had to see it in 1960. Besides, I wanted to see what a two-and-a-half-mile track looked like. Two and a half miles! I figured a man could really run on that. And there might be a slight chance that, well, you know, somebody might want me to drive for them. I always had hope.

We got there early because we wanted to see the practice sessions as well as the modified-sportsman race the day before the 500. It turned out to be one of the best moves I ever made, because I did get a ride in the modified race. A fellow named Roger Odom from Charleston, South Carolina, had converted a 1955 Chevy drag racer to a modified, and after driving it on that big track, he decided that it wasn't for him. He didn't want any part of it. He had seen me drive, so he asked me if I wanted to try it. I don't know why people kept *asking* me; why didn't they just point me in the direction of the car and stand back? Everybody should have known that I would drive anything that had wheels on it.

The first time I went out on the big Daytona track, I couldn't believe it. I thought Darlington was big, and it is, but this place—man, this place was about the size of Georgia. I got disoriented the first time around; I mean, it seemed like I was never going to get back to the start/finish line. But you would be surprised at how quickly I adapted to it. After half a day of practice the track felt as natural to me as Route 403 in Sardis.

It felt so good that I qualified way up in the pack. It was a real break. There were fifty thousand people there for the modified-sportsman race. Everybody had come to town for the 500, of course, but they came to this race as well. After all, they *were* race fans. And there I was, sitting up near the front where they would notice. I figured that it was a real shot in the arm to my career.

I'll have to admit that I was nervous as I sat in the Chevy and waited for the pace car to come out. I had qualified at over 140 miles an hour and had been running 170 plus in the straightaways, and, I'll tell you, that was fast, especially for somebody who was used to mostly quarter- and half-mile tracks, and most of them dirt, at that. The two races at Darlington had been brief, and the speeds were nowhere near what I had turned at Daytona. Also, I knew that a lot of the drivers were in the same boat as I was—they were sort of local heroes who were driving their first really big race. If they were half as nervous as I was, this could be a wild and woolly race. But I knew that I would calm down when they dropped the green; I just hoped they would.

The butterflies always go away the minute the green flag drops. That's one of the nice things about it. And they never come back until the next race. But I must have liked the butterfly feeling, because I kept going back for more. When the green flag dropped, I shot up high, near the wall in the front straightaway, and nailed it hard. That surge of power you feel when the green comes out is maybe the best feeling in all of racing. It rocks you back in your seat as far as you can go, and you feel the blood rush to your shoulders and arms. There's a light-headed feeling for a second while your eyes catch up with the speed at which the car is suddenly traveling.

By the time I got to the first turn, all of my reflexes had caught up, and I brought the car down off the bank a little and right into the turn. I swept through turn one and took dead aim on the leader of the race. I went up high, near the wall, as I came out of turn two and ran wheel-to-wheel with the lead car down the back straightaway. Just before we got to turn three I pulled slightly ahead of him and we ran that way through three and into four. As we came down off the high bank in turn four, I tucked my car down in front of him. I was leading the race.

Lap after lap I led, and the feeling got better with every lap. I had a groove that was working perfectly for me. The high banks started to feel very natural. And I mean they were high. They didn't look like it from the infield when I first saw them, but once you were out there, they seemed like mountains. And they are. Listen, they are four stories high and so steep that you can't walk up them. But I sure had that Chevy walking up them. I was going like Jack the Bear around that monster track.

Automobile racing is like dancing with a chain saw. You never know. There wasn't any question in my mind that I had that race won —in front of fifty thousand racing fans from all over the country. Until about twenty laps from the finish. I went sailing through three and four, just as smoothly as anybody could have done it. Anybody. When I came out at the top end of the front straightaway, I was on the gas hard. Suddenly there was a familiar rumble, and the car began to fill up with smoke. I looked at my oil-pressure gauge, and it was sitting, lifeless, at zero. I had blown my engine. The dream was over.

I held on tight, but the car didn't spin. I brought it down to the apron and coasted into the pits. Bubba Farr won in a Ford.

I had been in that position before. Every real race-car driver has. I mean, there are times when the whole picture changes. It can be a blown engine or a blown tire, or maybe somebody else blows and spins and takes you with them. But it happens, and you have to learn to live with it. But why, I asked myself, did it have to happen that day? I had that race won. I really did.

It was the first time I felt like crying since my first Soap Box Derby.

I stayed for the Daytona 500 and watched Junior Johnson win in a Chevrolet. But as I watched him in the winner's circle I couldn't help but wonder what the view was like from there.

That night we stopped in at a place called Robinson's, which is on South Atlantic Avenue in Daytona. Everybody went there, every night, until all hours. All of the drivers and the guys from the tire companies and the pit crews went there, as well as a lot of racing fans. Curtis Turner and Little Joe Weatherly were there. Curtis said, "Listen, kid, me and Little Joe here, we got us a pad right across the street there. Right there. You'll have to come over and party with us. Any night." He pointed to a slightly shabby-looking two-story frame-and-stucco place, directly across the street. "It's our party pad," he said proudly.

I couldn't understand why two guys who were as successful in racing as Curtis and Little Joe would stay in a place like that. I said, "Why do you stay there? I mean, it isn't exactly the best place in town."

Curtis said, "Well, kid, when I get ready to go home at night, I figure the worst thing that can happen to me is that someone might step on my fingers."

It made sense.

■

It took a while to come back to reality after Daytona. I mean, the real world I actually lived in—logging and short tracks. But I settled back into my natural environment. I had to. After all, I had led that big one for a long time. It actually gave me more confidence and loosened me up—on and off the track.

For example, a bunch of us were coming home in my Ford convertible one night from Columbia when we saw an old guy stopped by the side of the road with the hood up on his beat-up old pickup. Good Samaritan time. I pulled up behind him and asked if I could help. The guy said that his battery was dead and that if I wanted to give him a push, he sure would be obliged to me.

As he got in his truck and I lined my bumper up to his, he said, "It'll take thirty-five or forty miles an hour to get 'er to run. I'll wave my arm out the window when it's runnin', and you can back off. Thank you, boys."

"Okay," I said, "you just wave."

We got him up to thirty-five, and sure enough, his arm went out the window. "Guess he's started," I said.

"I don't see no arm wavin'," Lee Roy said.

"Me, neither," Bobby said.

When I got him up to sixty, he had both arms out the window. At eighty he was waving arms and legs and his hat. Everything. I backed off and pulled around him. We all waved. He was still going about eighty, and he was holding on to the wheel with all his might. He was as white as a ghost.

■

The next week Lee Roy tried to stay out of everybody's way, but it didn't do a bit of good. Little Bud caught him going into three, and he knocked him right through the guardrail. While everybody else was working on each other I won the feature. And I could hardly wait for the next week.

There was so much that could affect the outcome of a race on those old dirt tracks around home. For one thing, the way you qualified had so much to do with who won the race, because it was so hard to pass on the tracks, so if you started out front, you had a much better chance to finish in front. It was why everybody tried so hard to qualify well. But there were times when you simply didn't have your car set up yet when it came time to qualify. And the condition of the track was important. If it had rained recently, that changed it, or if they got too much water on it, that made a difference. But most of the time it was too dusty. Junior Johnson said one night at Columbia, "It's so dusty out there that if you threw a bucket up in the air, it wouldn't come down."

And Buck Baker found out at the old dirt track at Charlotte, North Carolina, that dust can be a real problem. He was following the car in front of him, just like we all did when, all of a sudden, he was upside down in the parking lot. The guy in front had run through the fence, and Buck followed him right through the hole.

And one time at Hillsborough, North Carolina, I had a flat tire and had to make four laps before I could find the entrance to the pits.

But none of us would have changed much at all, even if we could.

I knew I was on my way when I got twenty five dollars in deal money at the Columbia Speedway. That was what they paid the top drivers, so it put me in fast company. It wasn't much, but it was what it meant that was important to me. I was considered to be one of the top drivers. I didn't think until later that I would now be a regular *target,* too. But that didn't matter. By then I could hold my own with the best of them.

"LISTEN, IF YOU DON'T LIKE

THIS PARTY, THERE'S ANOTHER ONE

STARTING IN FIVE MINUTES."

—CURTIS TURNER

10

■

Curtis Turner took a liking to me, and he sort of took me under his wing for a while. I used to stay with him anytime I went up to race near Charlotte, and I'll tell you, that was always an experience. For one thing, the man was made out of cast iron. I guess there never has been a race-car driver like Curtis; he was tough on the racetrack and tougher off it. He used to go out and party all night and lots of times would come straight to the racetrack with a two-hundred-dollar silk suit on. He'd put on his helmet and race in the suit, and he was always competitive. Nobody ever understood how he did it. I mean, even starting up one of those loud race cars when you have a hangover had to be brutal. But it never seemed to bother old Pops.

There was always a party going on at Pops's place, no matter if he was at home or on the road. And sometime during the evening he always said, "Listen, if you don't like this party, just wait; there's another one starting in five minutes." What a place to stay.

One time I was staying with Curtis and he got a call from a couple of girls who wanted him to drive them in a parade. "Sure," Pops said, "I'll pick you up tomorrow and haul you little sweeties in that rascal."

When he told me what he was going to do, I asked, "How you gonna do it, Pops? You don't even have a convertible."

"Aw, that's no problem, kid," he said. "Just hang loose, we'll figure something out."

Can you believe it?—he took the hood off his new Cadillac and hooked the hood with a chain to his Farmall 140 tractor. Then he dragged those girls along in that in the parade. After the parade he went out and bought another hood for his Cadillac. The man was a legend.

Or there was the time when I was up there in the early spring and he was telling me how to qualify at Darlington—I mean, *really* qualify. He said, "Now, kid, you have to . . . aw, hell, lemme *show* you." There had been a late snow, and everything was covered, so he went out and got the Farmall tractor again and drove it right up the three or four steps to his patio, which was a great big thing off the kitchen of his house; it had to be big for his parties.

He made lap after lap around the patio, explaining to me as he went along how he drove each turn. He finally ended up knocking down the railing, but he really did teach me something. Turns three and four at Darlington were a lot flatter than one and two, and Curtis showed me exactly how to get in there and get out. The fact that it cost him a patio railing didn't mean a thing to him.

The only thing better than watching Curtis party was watching Curtis drive. He was a natural. He had the ability to control a car— whether it was sideways or straight or on dirt or asphalt—better than anybody I ever saw. I mean, it was a sort of sixth sense. He seemed to be able to pick up the car and *set* it over where he wanted it. The car didn't even seem to turn, it just seemed to wind up over there where he wanted it.

You could always tell when Curtis was driving a car. I remembered that from watching him when I was a kid. If you saw a whole pack of cars coming, and there was one a little bit more sideways and kicking up a lot more dust than the rest, you didn't even have to look at the number on the door to know that it was Curtis Turner.

I watched him one night when he went into a turn at Columbia, behind three cars. Well, he must have weaved right between all of them, because when the dust had lifted and he came out the other side of the turn, he had passed them all.

He drove deeper than anybody else into the turns before he backed off; that was one of the only flaws he had—maybe the only one. He drove in so deep at times that it actually slowed him down. He spent more time going sideways in some races than he did going straight, and you just naturally go faster when you're going straight. But he sure put on a show.

I heard this story once about Curtis and his airplane—well, the truth of the matter is that there were lots of stories about Curtis and his airplane, but this one in particular sticks in my mind: Curtis and a friend were up flying over Gaffney, South Carolina, when they ran out of booze. That's right, booze. Curtis didn't think a thing about flying and drinking.

"No problem," he said. "I've got a friend down there in Gaffney who runs a bootleg business, so we'll just land this rascal on the highway and get us a bottle and take right off. Nobody'll even see us."

It sounded good to his buddy. After all, it was Saturday and it was outside of town, so why not? The only problem was that there was a Little League baseball game just letting out when Curtis was about to touch down on the highway in his twin-engine Aero Commander. There was traffic coming at him, so he pulled back on the stick and they decided to get out of there. He was afraid that someone might have gotten the number on his plane and might report it to the FAA.

Curtis flew all the way back to Charlotte, North Carolina, at about fifty feet off the ground so they wouldn't pick him up on radar, and when he got back, he decided to land at Concord, just a few miles northeast of Charlotte. He picked that airport because they didn't have radar. In fact, they just had a little old shack and one man who answered radio calls.

144

As he went in he said, "This is N muff-humpf-rumpf, requesting permission to land," purposely garbling his number, so they wouldn't pick it up elsewhere on the radio.

The voice at the shack at the edge of the little landing strip said, "It's no use, Curtis, they're looking for you all over the South."

The incident cost him his flying license, but it didn't stop him from flying. "I never could find that damn license, anyway," he said.

Curtis was an original. And he was some race-car driver. I know you can't substitute the word *nerve* for courage—they're two different things—but Curtis had more nerve than anybody I knew. As for courage, well, he had a lot of that, too, but I've always felt that courage, after all, is nothing more than controlled fear. I know it is for me. And I'm sure it was for Curtis, too, although he probably wouldn't have admitted it.

■

Let me tell you this: There's more to life than racing cars. For one thing, there's girls. I had been so completely engulfed with racing that I hadn't taken nearly enough time to improve my social life. If you want to know, it didn't exist.

I had taken a job milking cows for a cousin of mine, a farmer on the other side of Olanta, because the logging business had about gone belly-up. I mean, I had about three part-time jobs because racing wasn't doing much more than paying for the good times we were having after the race. I would have been ahead financially to stay at home. So, you see, I had to have other sources of income. Racing has always been like that. For every Curtis Turner or Fireball Roberts who makes a pretty good living, there's always a hundred others who are on the way to the poor farm. But there are always a handful on their way up to big money; that's the category I always put myself in.

In spite of my confidence I needed something more, namely female companionship. The drugstore in Olanta was a good starting place, because I had heard that there was a cute little gal working there. I went to town one day, after one of my jobs, to see for myself. Man, were they right. She was prettier than any race car I had ever seen, and that included Darlington *and* Daytona.

I made the drugstore a regular stop after that. It was milk shakes and Betty Jo Thigpen from then on. And race cars, too, of course. But when I wasn't racing, I was taking Betty Jo to the local drive-ins and to the movies in Timmonsville. For a big night we went to Florence to the movies. There wasn't a whole lot more to do around there, but it really didn't matter. I was in love.

Suddenly I had another interest that was almost as important as racing. I wish that I could say that her parents were as excited about our romance as we were. But I suppose they had good reason to tell her how wild race-car drivers were; after all, they were right. "It doesn't matter," she told them, "Cale is a perfect gentleman."

The only problem was that everything I did seemed to disprove what she tried to tell them. For example, one night, when I was on my way to see her, a cow walked out in front of my car. I was running flat out, as usual, and I swerved to miss the cow and ran my brand-new Pontiac in the ditch. The very next trip over there, I was driving my brother Jerry's car, and you won't believe it, but a mule walked out in front of me. The only difference in the outcome this time was that I hit the mule before I hit the ditch. Livestock, 2; Cale, 0. This was getting old, not to mention expensive. It seemed like I was showing up on foot every time I went to see her.

Fortunately my luck was improving on the racetrack. We were running a lot of Grand National races, and although I hadn't won one yet, I was starting to finish pretty far up, and I qualified even better. In fact, the better I ran, the more I noticed a well-dressed man hanging around our pit.

"Who is that guy?" I asked Joe Whitlock.

"That's just Jacque Passino," he said, "That's all."

"No kidding," I said. "Who's Jacque Passino?"

"Jacque Passino," he said, "*is* Ford racing as far as I'm concerned."

"You mean like Ford *factory?*" I asked.

"Exactly," he said.

I started being very friendly to Jacque Passino. And he, in turn, started giving us a lot of parts for Herman's Ford race car. Everything was falling into place. Well, for a while. We ran at the Richmond fairgrounds on the dirt. It was a good, fast track, and I was really running well. I had started back at about the middle of the pack, and I had worked my way up to third place when Little Joe Weatherly blew an engine right in front of me. I saw the oil from his freshly ventilated engine. It was right in the groove. I knew what was going to happen, so I held on tight. In a case like that, it doesn't do any good to hit the brakes. It's too late for that. You can do one of two things: keep everything running as smoothly as you possibly can, hoping that you sail right through it; or pray. You also need to tune your senses as finely as you can, trying to feel the slightest hint of a spin. If you catch it right at the start, you might be able to avoid it. You almost never do.

I didn't.

The car hit the oil and spun to the right. It sort of hooked, caught a bite on the other side of the oil, and that sent it right through the guardrail. I hit hard, but I had done it before, so I knew pretty well what the results of a wreck like that were. It usually meant a new car. I climbed out the driver's window and surveyed the damage. New-car time. It was totaled.

I drove all the way home from Richmond that night, and I had a lot of time to think. Every thought began and ended with Jacque Passino. Was it the end of the Ford parts? Worse than that, was it the end of what I thought was a trip to the Ford factory team? There was only one way to find out. I wasn't one to sit back and wait for an answer. So, first thing the next morning, I took the bull by the horns and called Jacque in Dearborn, Michigan.

He already knew about the crash. "How were you doing before you hit the oil?" he asked.

"I was runnin' third," I said.

"That's good, Cale," he said. "Don't worry, I'll help you. Just as long as you don't mess up. But if you do something stupid, that's the end of the help."

I breathed a sigh of relief. He told me to have Herman go over to Charlotte and pick up a new body from Holman and Moody, and he said that he would authorize it. You see, Holman and Moody represented the Ford factory operation in Grand National racing. They built the cars and ran the operation, and they had some of the best drivers in all of stock-car racing. It was where I wanted to end up. It was, as far as I was concerned, the end of the rainbow. Ford was going to supply us with the major parts. It was up to us to get the minor ones. It was a terrific deal.

There never had been a time, even after Darlington in 1957, when, deep down, I didn't feel like I was going to make it as a top race-car driver. But now I had something concrete to support it—help from the top. I wasn't exactly driving for Holman and Moody, but as far as I was concerned, I wasn't too far from it. If it had been baseball, I would have been in the Triple A league.

Maybe it was time to take another big step in my life. Sure it was. I asked Betty Jo to marry me. She said yes. But she also asked if I really thought I was going to make enough money in racing to support a wife and, hopefully, a family. I told her, "I'm going to make it big in racing." She knew that I was serious. And then I added, "And while I'm waiting to make it big I'm going into the turkey business."

"The turkey business?" she asked. "Are you sure, Cale? I mean, *turkeys?*"

I told her that I had done a lot of studying about the turkey business, and I was sure it would pay off. I must have been very positive because she bought the whole package—me and the turkeys.

We decided to wait until I had things a little more in order before we broke the news to her parents, because, well, if you must know, they weren't going to be too excited about her marrying someone who was only a race-car driver. It was going to take something far more than that.

I spent the next several weeks building a turkey house. First I made some plans and figured out how much material I needed, and then I built that rascal. I covered the floor with wood shavings I had gotten from one of the lumber mills, because I read that this made a good, cheap bed for the birds.

And then I bought a used ten- by fifty-foot house trailer and put it over on the back of the farm, near the turkey house.

It was time to make the announcement to her parents. We already had the license and everything.

"You tell them, Betty Jo," I said, "and I'll pick you up tonight, and we'll go down to the preacher's house and get married."

"Just like that?" she said. "You want me to just say, 'Oh, by the way, Cale and I are getting married tonight'?"

"Believe me, it will be better that way. It'll be easier if I'm not there," I said.

She had to agree with that.

Betty Jo lived down in the country near Hebron, and when I went to pick her up that evening, I could tell that she was upset. Things had not gone so well.

"What went wrong?" I asked.

She told me that *we* were going to have to talk to them about it. Oh, boy. They weren't too excited about us getting married in the first place, but if we were going to do it, the least we could do is have a church wedding, you know, with *guests* and everything.

"We don't want a big wedding," I said to them.

"Well, *we* do," they said.

"I don't know what I want," Betty Jo said.

The whole thing made me so mad that I said, "Well, I know what I want. I want to leave." So I left. On the way out I said to Betty Jo, "We'll wait a while, or maybe we won't even get married at all."

I drove around for two hours. I was mad, and then I was hurt. And then I was mad again. And then I thought, "Why the hell do I have to put up with what her parents want? This is what I want, and I'm going to have it."

I wheeled the car around and headed for Betty Jo's. I was going back there to get her, and I didn't care what anybody said. I was twenty-two and she was eighteen. It was our decision. All the way back to her house I dreaded the scene that I was sure was going to take place, but as I turned in the drive to her farm, the headlights picked up something. There, right beside the drive, was Betty Jo, sitting on her suitcase. This definitely was the girl for me. She reminded me of me.

By the time we got to the preacher's house in Sardis, he was gone, so we sat there in the car in his yard and waited for him. He got home at about a quarter to twelve, so I'm not real sure to this day whether we were married on April 7, 1961, or April 8. It may have been after midnight, but we celebrate it on April 7.

We drove to Charleston for our honeymoon—if you can call it a honeymoon. We stopped at a motel just outside the city, because it was already about three in the morning, and the next day we drove around Charleston until I couldn't stand all the one-way streets and all the traffic, and we came home. That was it. But I had to get back, because my first load of baby turkeys was supposed to arrive late that afternoon. All in all, it had been some twenty-four hours.

By the time we got back to our new home, the truck with the turkeys was waiting there for us. We unloaded them into the turkey house, and I said, "Well, that oughta hold 'em until tomorrow, honey. Tonight we can get a good night's sleep. In our own home."

"I hate to be the one to tell you this," said the guy who brought the turkeys, "but one of you is gonna have to stay with the birds tonight."

"What do you *mean,* one of us is going to have to stay with the birds?" Betty Jo asked. I can still see her, standing there with her hands on her hips.

"You can't leave 'em alone," he said. "The temperature has to be just right, and if it goes down too much, you'll have to close the doors and windows. It it gets too hot, you'll have to open them. Somebody'll have to stay here."

We were going to spend our first full night of marriage sleeping with five thousand turkeys? It was our future we were protecting. Why was there never anything simple about my life?

■

Betty Jo had never been to a race. Can you believe that? We had dated for over a year and I had never even taken her. To tell you the truth, I didn't think that the racetrack was anyplace for her, but I could see that she wasn't going to buy that after we were married. I put it off for six months, but she wanted to see what this racing thing was all about—this thing that had such a hold on her husband. I took her to Columbia. She liked it, but I could tell that she didn't fully understand it, either.

"At least I'm glad you don't go any faster," she said. "I wouldn't want you to get hurt."

She definitely wasn't ready for Darlington or Daytona yet. Maybe I wasn't, either, because at the very next race at Darlington, we screwed up the Ford deal. Wouldn't you know that it would be at Darlington. Jacque Passino had told us that we had to supply the small parts and that he expected us to use the best. He didn't want some fifty-cent part to take us out of a race. That's exactly what happened. I was running well, up near the front, when a wheel bearing went out. I only brushed the wall, but I was out of the race.

After the race Jacque came over to where Herman and I were leaning against the race car.

"What happened?" he asked.

"Wheel bearing," I said.

"Was it a *new* wheel bearing or a *used* wheel bearing?" he asked.

"Used," Herman said sheepishly.

"Well, you messed up," he said. "That was uncalled-for."

It was the end of the Ford deal for Herman. And for me.

The turkey business was all I had to turn to, and I'll have to admit that I had my doubts about it, right from the start. Anybody would. Turkeys are the dumbest creatures in the world. They are so dumb that I lost several of them from drowning. In rainstorms. That's right, they would look up, with their mouths open, and literally drown themselves. I wouldn't have believed it, either, if I hadn't seen it for myself.

There had to be something better than this. Once again, racing was at rock bottom, the logging business was worse, and I was surrounded with five thousand of the dumbest birds in captivity. My life wasn't turning out at all like I had expected. I really thought we were going to starve to death. I needed a real job.

I was out feeding the turkeys one day a few weeks later when I heard Betty Jo calling me from the trailer: "Telephone, Cale!" It sounded important, because she had that certain tone in her voice.

It was. The call was from a man in Charleston who wanted me to drive his race car in an important race in Savannah on Friday night. I can't tell you how happy I was. He said it was a good race car. That was enough for me. I accepted, and once again my hopes soared. This was going to be a big race, and if I could win it, it would mean three or four hundred dollars. That would buy a lot of food. For us and the turkeys.

I remember this particular incident very clearly, because I think I was lower at that point, both financially and mentally, than at any time in my life.

Betty Jo made sandwiches for us to eat on the way down there— and enough to eat while we were there. We stopped by the store and filled up the car with gas. On credit. I had exactly ten dollars in the bank—it was all I had to my name—so I got a ten-dollar check cashed at the store, and we were on our way. Of course, we forgot the sandwiches on the kitchen table, but I promised Betty Jo that we would eat along the way. We had ten dollars, I told her.

It started raining, but the weather forecast on the car radio said that it would clear, particularly on the Georgia coast. It meant a slippery track, but that suited me fine. I knew that I could outdrive most of them on a slick track.

Just about the time my daydreams were leading me into the winner's circle, I heard a siren. I looked in the rearview mirror and saw the flashing red lights. A cop. I had been doing 50 miles an hour. The sign at the side of the road read, "45-mile-per-hour zone. Welcome to Walterboro, South Carolina." Surely he would give me a break. Wrong. I seemed to be real short on breaks along about then.

He looked at my license. "Well, Mr. Yarborough," he said, "you can pay me or you can take it up with the judge."

There wasn't any question. I didn't have time to "take it up with the judge." I handed over the crisp, new ten-dollar bill.

Betty Jo was crying when we pulled away.

"Easy come, easy go," I said. Inside, I felt as bad as she did.

There is a toll bridge just before you get to Savannah; as we got close to it, it dawned on me that toll means money—fifty cents, to be exact, and I didn't have a cent in my jeans.

"You got any money, sweetie?" I asked.

"None," she said, weeping. "Not a penny."

I kept driving. "Well, we're gonna have to have fifty cents for the toll bridge," I said. Then she really started crying.

"Stop crying, honey," I said. "Get in the backseat and pull the bottom cushion out. There's always some coins under the backseat of a car. It's an unwritten rule."

She looked at me like I was crazy, but she climbed over the seat and took out the bottom cushion. She found thirty-seven cents. She started crying again. Between sobs she said, "You aren't going to make the race because of thirteen cents."

"I'm gonna make that race, Betty Jo," I said.

We were at the tollbooth. The man had his hand out.

"Fifty cents, please," he said.

Fortunately there was no traffic behind me because my story took a while. I told him exactly what had happened, beginning with Darlington and ending in the 45-mile-an-hour zone in Walterboro. We were on a first-name basis by then.

"If you'll take the thirty-seven cents," I said, "I promise you I'll pay you on the way back. I'm gonna win that race."

"Cale," he said, "you're the only one who's come through this bridge in a week with a story that I believe. Good luck, boy."

"Thank you, Buford," I said.

I dropped the thirty-seven cents in his hand, and he became a part of my real-life soap opera.

Pit passes cost a dollar each. The guy at the pit gate recognized me, thank God, so I didn't have to tell him anything but, "I gotta find the guy who owns the car, and I'll bring the money back over to you." This was one man who was used to dealing with people who were broke. Believe me.

I had no trouble finding the race car. My deal started with a two-dollar loan. Betty Jo went back over and paid for our pit passes while I watched them get the car ready. You see, I was a driver, I wasn't a mechanic, so I never got involved with anything mechanical. After the first race car I stayed away from all that stuff. It really never interested me in the first place. I mean, the only reason I made my own modifications to my street cars when I was a kid was because I couldn't afford to have anyone else do it. Once I started driving someone else's cars, I always figured that he had his job and I had mine.

It was a good car. I could tell that after only a few laps of practice. I brought it back in before qualifying. Betty Jo had gone over to sit with Lee Roy's wife. In fact, there were several of the wives over there. She told me later that she really had a miserable time because they were constantly going to get something to eat, and they kept asking her to come along, but she told them that she had just eaten and that she was "stuffed." Actually she was about to starve, but she didn't have any money, and she didn't want them to know. The world of racing was a whole lot less glamorous to her than it was to me.

In warming up for the first heat race, I blew the engine on the race car.

It was the night Murphy's Law was invented.

To this day I don't know why, but I still had hope that things were going to turn around. I went to the track promoter and told him my story, and he let me have twenty dollars "until the next race."

I could tell that Betty Jo was about ready to burst into tears again when I went over to the grandstands to get her. But she was putting up a good front because of the other wives. When we were in the car, I said, "How 'bout a hamburger?" She started crying.

"That's mean, Cale," she said, sobbing. "You know we don't have any money. We can't even get back across the bridge," and then she really started crying. "You can't even pay that nice man his thirteen cents."

"What about this?" I said, holding up the twenty-dollar bill.

"Where did you get that?" she asked. Her eyes were as big as saucers.

"Well, we'll call it an advance," I said.

We stopped at the first hamburger joint we came to. And then I filled the car with gas and we headed for the toll bridge. When we got there, traffic was backed way up because of the race crowd. I gave the man at the tollbooth on that side fifty cents and said, "Here's thirteen cents I owe that man over there; you know, Buford."

"Okay, I'll see that he gets it," he said.

"No," I said, "I want to make *sure* he gets it. I'll wait'll you go over and give it to him."

"You can't wait," he said. "Look at all that traffic."

I turned the motor off. "I'm waitin'," I said.

He could tell that it would be a whole lot simpler to just go over and give Buford the thirteen cents, so he did. Buford waved to me.

I've been over that toll bridge a lot of times over the years—even on the way to Daytona—and I always have to stop and talk for a while. I've even buzzed it a couple of times with my airplane, and when I tip the wings, somehow I know that Buford knows who it is.

I had an immediate problem. I had to make a decision. Was I going to continue raising turkeys part-time, racing part-time, logging part-time, and playing semipro football part-time, or was I going to concentrate on one job? There was only one logical answer. I announced my retirement from racing. The sports pages all over the South picked it up, and I got calls from all over, from people trying to talk me out of it. I thanked them as nicely as I could, but it didn't change my mind. I had to quit racing.

There wasn't a thing in the world that could change my mind. Betty Jo was pregnant, and I had to get my life in order. I had to make a decent living. It would take some real effort in the logging business during the day, and extra work taking care of the turkeys in the evening when I came home. I might even get more turkeys.

I was feeding the turkeys one evening when Betty Jo called me to the phone again. "It's Mr. Passino," she said.

Well, maybe there was *one* thing that would change my mind.

Jacque asked, "What are you *really* going to do, Cale?"

"I'm going to log and raise turkeys," I said. And then I added, "I'd really like to race, but I don't have a car, and I've got a family started and, well, Jacque, I'm about to starve to death racin' cars."

"Well, I want you to go up to Holman and Moody in Charlotte and get yourself a seat fitted. We want to work with you some more; only this time we want to make sure it's done right."

Was I hearing right? "Do you mean that I've got a Holman and Moody ride?" I asked.

"It only means that we're looking for a new driver," he said. "We're bringing in another driver, and the two of you are going to try out."

It is a little over one hundred miles from Sardis to Charlotte. I was at Holman and Moody when they opened at seven-thirty the next morning. I found out that the other driver they were bringing in was Benny Parsons from Detroit. We each were going to have a car for the next race, which was at Asheville, North Carolina. The one who did best in the race would get the ride and would join Freddy Lorenzen on the Holman and Moody team. The Ford factory team. Another challenge.

Man, that was some operation. They had guys like Waddell Wilson there building engines, and, well, they had the best there was in every department, so it was easy to see why they turned out the kind of cars and the caliber of drivers they did. It was the West Point of stock cars. It was where Fireball Roberts and Ned Jarrett and David Pearson and Freddy Lorenzen went to school.

They molded a seat to fit me and told me when to be at Asheville.

I could tell you qualifying and race stories from here to Monday, but they all get to sounding alike. And I could tell you how I felt each time, but let me just say that this was another in a long list of bright hopes I had in my early years. And I'll just say that I qualified well and ran most of that race like a Holman and Moody pro. *Most* is the key word. I was leading the race when somebody ran over something on the track and kicked it through my radiator.

You don't have as much hard luck as I was having without developing a pretty tough skin. I mean, you get used to about anything, even bad luck. And that's exactly what I said to John Holman after the race: "If it wasn't for bad luck, I wouldn't have any luck at all, John."

"It's not as bad as you think, Cale," he said. "You did a damn fine job out there, and it wasn't any fault of yours that you didn't win that race. We're giving you the ride."

People who wake up at the Pearly Gates must feel a lot like I felt at that moment.

It was near the end of the season, and I only got to drive a few races, but it sure was different than anything I had ever been around. There was a real pit crew, and the car was hauled to the track on a truck. Second, there were all kinds of new parts. And the best part was that it said, in big letters, clear across the front fender of the car, COMPETITION PROVEN. HOLMAN–MOODY. It definitely was, as Ford advertised, "Total Performance."

■

Lots of times I drove to the races by myself, particularly in the late stages of Betty Jo's pregnancy. One particular night sticks in my mind. I had raced up near Norfolk, Virginia, which was a long drive, but I had to be home the next morning because I had a big turkey deal and it was important that I be there, so I drove all night.

The way the turkey business worked in those days was that a lot of people like me raised the birds and big companies either bought them or they brokered them. Maybe it's the same today, I don't even want to know. I had a lot of dealings with General Mills, who acted as a broker; they sold the birds to someone who, I assume, did something with them, and they wound up in the grocery stores as General Mills turkey rolls or something. I really don't know. All I know is that I wanted to sell as many turkeys as possible.

This time they had a buyer for five thousand turkeys, which was about half my entire flock. I had more than that, but they were in different stages; there were that many ready for the market. Well, the trucks showed up an hour or so after I got home, and we started loading the five thousand turkeys for their trip to New York.

We hadn't any more than gotten started when Betty Jo called me. This time it wasn't the telephone. I could tell by looking at her that the time had come. I must have had a look of panic on my face, because she said, "Honey, I know you can't leave. I'm all right. I can drive myself to the hospital, so you go on and finish and then come on down."

Betty Jo is the best thing that ever happened to me. Not only has she stuck by me, right by my side, through the toughest times anyone could ever have, but she has done it with courage and a whole lot of understanding. And class.

She went to the hospital, and we loaded the turkeys. One of the drivers gave me a receipt and said that I would get the money as soon as the birds were delivered to New York. It was standard procedure. I had done it many times, so I wasn't concerned. Besides, I was dealing with a pretty big outfit.

When I got to the hospital a couple of hours later, I had a daughter. We named her Julie Ann, and I had never been as proud in my life as I was that day. It was better than winning Darlington.

Betty Jo and Julie came home three days later. So did the five thousand turkeys. By the time they had gotten the birds to New York, the bottom had dropped out of the turkey market and they refused to accept them, so they brought them back. They hadn't been fed or watered for three days, and they were about half dead.

I worked as hard as I could to save them, but most of them died. It was awful. I tried to get them buried as fast as I could, by digging out big trenches with the tractor and pushing all the carcasses in it, but it was mid-September, and that's one of the hottest times we have in South Carolina. The odor was terrible.

I quit the turkey business.

I must have had a lot of faith; otherwise, I don't think I could have taken all the ups and downs of my life. And the downs always seemed to come in pairs. It was only one week later that John Holman told me that they had decided, after all, not to put the extra car on the track the next season.

"I'm really sorry, Cale," he said. "I'll guarantee you, it's nothing you did. You did a real good job for us. Ford has just decided not to race the extra car next year and, well, you understand, my other drivers have been with me for a long time."

"I know, John," I said. I was crushed, and I guess it showed because John put one of his big arms around my shoulder and he said,

"I'll tell you what. You come up and work in the shop for me, you know, just doing odd jobs, and maybe something will turn up for you. You know, it's not the worst place in the world for a race-car driver to hang around. If something does turn up, you'll be the first one to know about it. We won't have to look for you."

It did make sense. "I'll go home and talk it over with Betty Jo," I said. "I'll let you know tomorrow, John."

Betty Jo said exactly what I expected her to say: "You know best, Cale. You do what you think's right."

"Well, honey," I said, "it's not much money. In fact, it only pays a dollar and a quarter an hour, but it's the only way I'm going to be able to get any kind of break at all in racing."

She knew I was right. The life of picking up a ride whenever I could was driving us both crazy. At least, this way, I would be where the action was. So I decided to give it a try. But it would be my *last* try; I promised myself that. I know, I had said that many times before, but this time I meant it. I couldn't go on like this forever.

The first thing I did when I got to Charlotte was to look for a place to stay. I bought a *Charlotte Observer* and read the classified ads. An apartment was out of the question. I went to look at several, and there wasn't a thing I could afford, not even in the worst sections of town. A dollar and a quarter an hour figures out to fifty dollars a week. Out of that I had to send money to Betty Jo and Julie Ann. And I had to eat. And I wanted to save some, even if it was only a dollar a week.

I moved into a two-dollar-a-night motel, out near the Holman and Moody garage, near the Charlotte Airport. And the next day I started my job of sweeping floors and running the forklift and anything else they needed done.

It wasn't an unpleasant job; I was around race cars, and almost everybody I knew in racing came through those doors at one time or another—the drivers and mechanics and sportswriters and car owners. If you want to know the truth, I really liked the job because of the people and the cars that revolved around it. But I did try to hide my broom when somebody important came in. Once again I was a little duck in a big pond.

Little by little I saved enough money to rent an apartment so I could move Betty Jo and Julie to Charlotte. I had worked overtime every chance I got and picked up a ride here and there in sportsman cars, so it didn't take long.

I did get to drive Daytona again too. Bernard Alvarez had a new Ford that he was going to put in the 1964 Daytona 500, and I talked him into letting me give it a try. I figured that if I did well, it wouldn't hurt my image a bit at Holman and Moody. And it *was* a Ford.

I'm not sure how much it did for my image, but I'll guarantee you, it gave me a good story for the book. I was running in one of the qualifying races. You see, at Daytona they had qualifying, and then, in addition to that, they had two 100-mile qualifying races. All of this, of course, is before the 500, so you get to race a lot down there. Well, I was in the first 100-miler, and I was running well, I might add, when a car hit the wall coming out of four. He was right beside me, I saw him hit, and the car almost came apart. There were parts flying everywhere. I spun my car on purpose, because there were parts all over the track in front of me. As I was sliding sideways I was trying to keep it headed toward the grass inside the track. I knew I could get it stopped down there without hitting anything, and then I could get back in the race, unscratched.

Scratch that. There was an explosion in my car. I thought it was a tire or maybe both right tires. I mean, it sounded like dynamite. But my car did slide down into the infield, and when it stopped, I saw, for the first time, what had happened. The entire tire, wheel, and part of the front suspension of the other car had come through my right window, and it had taken out my entire dashboard, steering wheel, and steering column. There wasn't anything in front of me. It shows you how involved you get with a crash. I didn't even realize that the steering wheel had been torn from my hands. If it had come through at a little different angle, it would have taken my head with it. It was another time when I wasn't too unhappy about an accident. I had a head. And I was ready to take it back to Charlotte.

When I got back to Charlotte, I found a nice little one-bedroom furnished apartment for sixty dollars a month. The move up there wasn't difficult. I mean, it certainly didn't take a truck. The only thing we had was a stereo I had given Betty Jo for Christmas a couple of years before, and an old black-and-white television and Julie's bed and a few clothes, so I just drove down and picked them up and we moved. All in the same day.

My life was complete again. I had my family with me, and things were starting to pick up a little at Holman and Moody. In fact, I was getting to take some of the race cars they built and shake them down at the airport. And I was racing a lot of sportsman races. Some of them were as far away as Georgia and Alabama, so I took Betty Jo and Julie with me and we slept in the car. Why not?

"I'm just about back where I started," I said to Betty Jo one night in Georgia when the mosquitoes were about to eat us alive in the car. "It doesn't look like I'm going to make it, does it?"

"Now, Cale Yarborough," she said—you know, she sounded just like Mama—"I don't want to hear any more talk like that. You're the best race-car driver there is, and folks are going to find it out right soon. Now you get to sleep. You have to race tomorrow." And she waved the back of her hands through the car, driving away some of the mosquitoes.

"Shoosh," she said.

**MAYBE THE WAY TO TEACH SOMEONE
TO FLY A 747 IS JUST TO PUT THEM IN A 747
AND FORGET ABOUT THE PIPER CUB.**

John Holman had an old shack on the Catawba River that he had
once used as a sort of fishing camp, and I guess he felt sorry for the
bleak existence we were leading, so he offered to let us stay there for
nothing.

"It's going to take a little fixing up, but it'll save you some money,"
he said. "It's yours if you want to live there."

It was a deal. And he was right; it *did* need some fixing up. The
roof leaked, it needed painting inside, some windows were broken,
and the screens were out, but we could see that it could be made
into something real nice. And the price certainly was right. We
could put the sixty dollars we were paying in rent toward food and
gasoline.

I used to go grocery shopping with Betty Jo because I liked to look for bargains. I always thought I was beating the system if I found a good buy, like the black-eyed peas. They had a special at Winn–Dixie. I'll never forget it: two cans for fourteen cents. I bought every can they had in the store, which was several cases. Let me tell you, we lived on black-eyed peas for a long time. To this day neither of us is real fond of them, even though they might be the traditional dish of the South. We eat them on New Year's Day, of course, because that brings you good luck, but that's about the only time. I never order them when I'm out.

It was fun fixing up that old place. We bought paint and window glass and screens for the doors, and when we were finished, it was as cute a place as you could find, and it was right there on the river, which actually was a lake because it had been dammed up. It was like a vacation house.

No Grand National rides came along, so Holman and Moody decided to take a year-old race car they had been thinking of selling and put me in it. They hired Red Mylar to maintain the car out of his own shop, and Holman and Moody supplied the parts. It might have been a left-handed Holman and Moody ride, but it was a ride in a relatively competitive car, and I knew that if I drove it well, I could work my way back to a really first-class ride. But I would have to drive well, maybe even over my head.

I ran every race on the Grand National circuit in 1965, fifty-four of them, so if you count it as experience, it may well have been the year I got started for real. And it was high time, because some of my buddies were getting ahead of me. Lee Roy had won two races the year before and had finished in the top five eleven times. Tiny had won the Daytona 500 in 1963, and was doing real well. But I had been known to catch up before, so this made me that much more determined.

I was helping to test a Holman and Moody car in Charlotte the day before the Valdosta, Georgia, race, so I planned to fly down there with Ralph Moody on the day of the race, get qualified, run the car, and fly back to Charlotte with Ralph. It was the only way I could do both things. But the weather turned real bad and we couldn't fly. Red got Sam McQuagg to qualify the car, and he had it in about the middle of the pack. There was no way I could get there in time for the race.

The rain moved south, and the Valdosta race was postponed until the next day, so I loaded up Betty Jo and Julie and we drove all night to get there.

Valdosta was a half-mile dirt track, just the kind I had cut my teeth on, so I didn't have much trouble getting to the front, in spite of the fact that most of the top Grand National drivers were in the race. While I was out front I didn't even let myself think of winning. There had been too many disappointments before, so I just concentrated on driving as smooth and as fast as I could. With ten laps to go a car spun in front of me and I nicked his bumper. My car careened sideways, but I was ready for it, and I turned the steering wheel back the other way, got off the gas for a second, and when it started to come back around, I hit the gas again. I went right on through the turn in good shape. Sideways but in good shape.

With two laps to go Buddy Baker and I started through turn one, side by side. Two cars can't go through the turn at one time that fast. Everybody said that. He didn't back off, and I sure didn't either. We were scraping the sides of our cars together. Sparks were flying, but we *did* go through the corner together, and we both made it. Coming down the back straightaway, I pulled ahead and was able to get past Buddy before we got to three. I crossed it up and shut the door on him. The starter had the white flag up as I went by, indicating that there was one lap to go. Four turns. Half a mile. As I went into one, it seemed like every car on the track was loose and was going to hit me. I stayed on it hard, passing them up high. The dirt was flying. So was I. As I went into three, I could see the starter with the checkered flag up. I was yards from my first Grand National victory. I could feel my heart pumping. I took a deep breath and sailed through three and four and down the front straightaway. As I roared across the start/finish line, the starter waved the checkered flag frantically. I had won my first Grand National race.

The feeling I had as I drove the victory lap around the track, waving the checkered flag out the window, is almost impossible to describe. I wanted to stop the car and get out and jump up and down. I wanted to run up into the stands and kiss Betty Jo and Julie. I wanted to kiss

Buddy. Well, maybe I wasn't that carried away, but I *was* happy. I felt that my long, tough apprenticeship was over. And, you know, I think it was.

Daytona was next—the Firecracker 400. It was probably the race that brought me into the national racing picture. It was just like it had been when I ran the modified-sportsman race there in 1960: I led it early. The only difference was that this time I was leading drivers like A. J. Foyt and Junior Johnson, and Freddy Lorenzen, who had the number-one Holman and Moody car.

Lap after lap I led. I was really excited about running in front of A. J., because I had always thought of him as the most versatile driver in the world. There wasn't a thing he couldn't drive, and he had proven it—from Indy to sports cars to stockers. A strange thing popped into my mind: "I wonder if I should try Indy?" Driving the world's premiere race course is no time to daydream, particularly when you're leading, so I brought my thoughts back to the situation at hand.

When my engine blew, the world of reality came crashing down again. But this time I wasn't dejected. I had led that race for a long time, in front of a hundred thousand fans. They wouldn't forget Cale Yarborough. Neither would Ford. I knew that.

And that didn't take long. Ford arranged for me to get a Banjo Matthews ride. That was something like getting traded to the Cowboys after playing a season with the Saints. Banjo Matthews had been a good race-car driver himself, mostly in modifieds, but he won a lot of races, and when he turned to car building, he knew what he needed. You might say that landing a ride with Banjo was my first top-shelf ride.

I think that I started becoming a real race-car driver while I was driving for Banjo. He took the time to tell me a lot of things, and he was a good teacher. It helped tremendously to be in one of his cars, too, because they were among the best in all of stock-car racing. I made real progress with him.

Here's the way the Banjo ride came about: Bobby Johns had been driving Banjo's car, but he decided to give the Indianapolis 500 a try, so they came to me. I ran the World 600 at Charlotte, and for a first try in a new car, everybody thought that I did a good job. So Bobby came back and ran the Atlanta 500 for Banjo, and apparently he thought I had done a better job in the car, so he offered me the ride on a permanent basis. As permanent as anything ever is in racing, which means that you drive it until somebody better comes along. It's part of the game.

Keep in mind that in those mid-sixties days of Grand National I was driving against some of the greats like Richard Petty and Ned Jarrett and Junior Johnson and Fireball Roberts and Curtis Turner. I could go on. There were a lot of great drivers, some just coming up, and others who had been around for a long time. It was just like it had been when I broke into racing at the Columbia Speedway in Columbia, only on a much bigger scale.

It was time to move back home too. The heavy racing schedule had taken me away so much that Betty Jo took Julie and went back to Sardis anytime I was going to be away for a long time. There were times when I was gone for two weeks at a time, if we had two races in a row that were far away from Charlotte. She got lonely.

I never did feel comfortable taking them to too many races, because, well, if you want the truth, I still didn't feel that auto racing was the place to take your family. It was all right for a bunch of us guys, but all the hootin' and hollerin' that went on around a racetrack wasn't for women and children. You're talking about a pretty wild and woolly sport in those days.

We had bought a much nicer house out on Lake Wylie and were happy out there, but it still wasn't home. It wasn't the Pee Dee region both of us loved. I remember one time Richard Petty said, "A man can't forget his upbringings," and that's exactly how I felt. I think most of us drivers felt that way. I also think it's why drivers in NASCAR were a little more humble than most athletes. So I bought a big white house with great big columns in Timmonsville, and we went home. I knew all of us would be happier there. Another thing I did was start investing my money. I was doing a whole lot better, so I started buying land. Someday I wanted to be in the middle of a thousand-acre farm near Sardis. That was my dream. I bought five hundred acres. I figured that land was better to invest in than most

166

things. Somebody told me once, "Buy land, boy. They're not makin' any more of it." Made sense to me.

Timmonsville was about a central a place as any, so it worked out just fine for everybody.

■

Little Joe Weatherly was always called the Clown Prince of Racing, so he tried hard to live up to it. He and Curtis Turner borrowed the Darlington pace car one night and ended up in a contest to see which one could drive closest to the telephone poles. The closer Curtis got, the more Joe was agitated. "You call that close?" he would say. So Curtis got closer. Far too close most of the time. When Joe took over, it was the same thing.

When they brought the car back, Bob Colvin, the general manager of the track, who in a weak moment had let them borrow the car, stopped pacing the floor to look out his office window at his pace car. They had parked the left side toward the office.

"Wow," he said, "I'm sure glad to see it in one piece. I'll have to tell you, boys, I thought you might tear it up."

"Aw, Bob," Curtis said. "We wouldn't do that, it's the *pace car.*"

It wasn't until Bob got in the car that night that he noticed the broken glass in the right windows. He got out and ran around the car. The whole right side was gone—the side the fans in the grandstands see.

Little Joe always had some practical joke to pull on people. That year at Darlington he tossed a rubber snake into everybody's car just as they were ready to pull out of the pits to practice. Some of the drivers came right out of their cars, and then Joe laughed like mad. He did it to me. I didn't leave the car, but it scared me.

When I went home that night, I went snake hunting, and sure enough, I found myself a four- or five-foot rattlesnake. So I got the forked stick on its head and caught it, and then I took it back to the house and pulled its fangs out with a pair of pliers. It's something you have to be pretty careful about doing. I put it in a burlap bag, tied it up right, and took it to the track with me the next day.

I was in luck: Little Joe was in his race car. I went up to the car, leaned down, picked the snake out of the bag, and tossed it right into Joe's lap. He looked down at it, and then he looked at me with an are-you-kidding? smile on his face. And then the snake started to rattle. Joe froze. Then he let out a war whoop, and I've never seen anybody get a seat belt off and get out of a car so fast.

He was as white as a ghost. As soon as he stopped shaking he turned red. You could just see him reach the boiling point. Everybody was falling down on the ground laughing. Joe ran over to his toolbox, got a ball peen hammer, and took off after me. He chased me clear out of the pits, and I'll tell you, I was running like I had never run in football, because I knew he would have killed me if he had caught me.

I don't think he ever showed up at the track again with a rubber snake. In fact, I don't think he ever touched a rubber snake again.

It was a wild bunch. Fireball Roberts was a funny man. He wasn't much on practical jokes, but he was funny if you got to know him. It's just that he was a private person and didn't let too many people ever get to know him. It didn't do a whole lot for his popularity because people didn't understand that he was pretty much of a loner. But he was the best at one-liners of anybody in racing. He crashed one time, and while he was walking back to the pits, a guy ran up to him and stuck a microphone in his face—they do it all the time—and, I'll tell you, nobody wants to talk at a time like that. But this guy said, "What happened out there, Fireball?"

Fireball glared at him. "I *crashed*. It is possible to crash out there, you know."

And one time, when he was flying his plane back from Mexico, he stopped at the Texas border for fuel and the usual customs check. The official looked over his papers and said, "Everything seems to be in order, Mr. Roberts. Did you bring anything back with you?"

"Christ, I hope not," Fireball said.

And I'll have to say that Banjo wasn't far behind them in the hell-raising department. I'll also have to admit that I was part of it, from time to time. Here's a good example.

We were running a Firestone tire test at the Charlotte Speedway one week and had gone to a little barbecue place for lunch, a few miles from the track. Banjo drove one car—a Ford—and one of the Firestone tire engineers drove the Chevy. I was in Banjo's car.

We raced all the way to the place and back, which is what we did every day. Everywhere. I mean, they *were* rental cars. We always raced clear back to the double tunnel, at the track, and that's where the race ended. The first one there was the winner. This time we were side by side. A tie? Not yet. The Chevy went through the right side of the tunnel, and Banjo went through the other side—the exit side.

"Sure hope there's nobody coming," I said.

"There's nobody comin', Cale," Banjo said. Thank God there wasn't.

There's a high bank, about sixty feet up, on the other side of the tunnel, which definitely is not wide enough for two cars. To make matters worse you have to make a hard right turn to get to the road. Both cars made the right turn. They slammed together time after time as they raced up the hill. Banjo was on the cliff side. At the top of the road there was a telephone pole, and we were headed straight for it.

"You're gonna hit that pole, Banjo," I said.

He didn't say a word. He was still going wide-open.

"*Banjo,* you're gonna hit that pole," I yelled.

Nothing. Full speed.

"*Banjo!*" That's all I got out. *Blam!* He centered the pole. The crash threw us both out of the car. The accelerator stuck on our car and we hit the Chevy, sending both cars into a hurricane fence. I got up and felt around a little to see if everything was there, and I looked at Banjo, who was sitting in the dust. His glasses were hanging off one ear, and he was bleeding all over.

"I *told* you we were going to hit that pole," I said.

He looked at me with a completely dazed expression. His eyes were spinning in his head. "What pole?" he said.

After we got him all patched up he called Hertz and told them that he needed another rental car.

"What's wrong with the one you have?" the girl asked.

"The radiator's leaking," he said.

"What happened?" she asked.

"I don't know. It just stopped," he said.

I'm surprised anybody ever rented cars to us again.

■

The sixties ushered in the era of the superspeedway, and somehow I think it's appropriate that I came along at the same time. From the first time I ever drove Darlington and Daytona, even in less than impressive equipment, I always felt that this was where I belonged. I think if they had had Charlotte and Atlanta and Rockingham and Daytona right from the start, it might have done more for my career than anything. I've never been totally convinced that all the time I spent on those short tracks did anything but slow down my career.

Maybe the way to teach someone to fly a 747 is just to put them in a 747 and forget about the Piper Cub in the beginning. That way you don't have any bad habits to break. This is pretty much what Banjo did with me. Nobody knew a whole lot about running a super-speedway in those days, so Banjo just had me driving them about like I drove the short tracks. I charged hard when everybody else, like Freddy Lorenzen and David Pearson and Richard Petty, had a much more conservative style.

I mean, I had never been your typical great, unbeatable Saturday-night hero, like so many guys were, in the first place. Little Bud Moore was more of that type, but oddly enough, he never made it on the superspeedway. Maybe he needed a Banjo.

But I made mistakes on the superspeedway, too, just like everyone else. One of the biggest ones I made was at Darlington. I went sailing out of turn one as fast as the car would stick on the track, and Sam McQuagg was there in the orange number 27 Ford. I figured I could pass him no matter what anybody said about passing there. I went down under him and we touched. From there on it was like a dream sequence. I felt the car raise up off the track and remember seeing it go up over Sam's car. Everything got real quiet, and I thought, "This

170

is just like being one of those astronauts." You have strange thoughts at times in a race car. And then I looked down. Everything was green under me, and I knew that wasn't right. If I was on a racetrack, it should be black down there. I knew that I had to be sailing over the parking lot. I also knew that it was about a fifty-foot drop, just from the top of the track in two, so from where I was, I knew that I was going to hit hard. "Oh, Lord," I thought, "I hope Banjo's cars are as strong as everybody says they are."

I was doing everything I could to land that car. You always do. It doesn't do any good to mash the brakes when you're in the air, but I did. Listen, I still keep steering when I'm upside down.

The car started down. I braced myself as well as I could. When the car hit, pain shot through my entire body. I saw all colors of the rainbow, and I could hear the sound of the crash, like it was coming from over in the palmetto grove across the highway. It rumbled like summer thunder for a few seconds and then went away. And the colors went away. All I could hear was the cracking and popping of the hot, twisted metal. My teeth hurt, and there was a dull pain in my temples and in my shoulders and neck.

I reached down and ripped open the seat belt, and I pulled myself up and out the driver's window. I didn't know if it was going to catch on fire or not. I fell to the ground and crawled a few yards away, and I sat down and looked at the car. "Boy, is Banjo gonna be teed off," I said.

Joe Whitlock was the first one to get to me. He saw me sitting there half dazed, and he started laughing a nervous, crackling laugh. He squeezed my shoulder.

"Man, what a ride," I said.

Everybody said it was the most spectacular aerial show they had ever seen at Darlington. Banjo? Well, Humpy Wheeler had been beside him, and he told me that Banjo never said a word. He kept looking out there between one and two where the car no longer was, a lot like a ship captain would have looked at the dock in old Charleston after he dropped off a load of silk. Somehow he knew that I was all right, Humpy said, but he also knew that I would never try that again.

When I came back to the pits, he said, "Glad you didn't get hurt, Cale. Let's move on to the next one." He never did say a word about the car or about my mistake. But he started working with me, giving me little tips all the time, things that would make me smooth.

I think the thing he taught me was that I had to channel my desire. I learned that there was a time to use it and a time not to use it. Banjo taught me to go fifteen rounds instead of three.

Banjo had seen a quality in me that nobody else had, and he worked to bring it out.

Driving a superspeedway was something that was hard to do, even if you did it well. It took a lot of things to make a winner there.

I still have a clipping of what Fireball had to say about driving. Here's what he said: "People seem to think that race-car drivers have special courage. It's not so. It doesn't take any more guts to be a race-car driver than it does to be a jet pilot or a steeplejack or a lot of things. There's a lot of difference between having guts in racing and being plain foolish. Guts is experience. You learn the hard way what you can do to a car. You know how much punishment the car can stand and how much you can stand and how you react.

"Doing something you have no idea that you can do or that your car can do is plain stupid. It takes good thinking to win a race—preparation by expert mechanics and a good ride by the driver—and even if you get all that together just right, you aren't going to see that checkered flag wave for you unless Lady Luck smiles a lot on your side."

It made a lot of sense, because Fireball was one of the great superspeedway drivers. He was one of the few who ever fared better in switching from short tracks to long ones. There were some who didn't make the switch all that well. And there was Herb Thomas, who had gotten hurt on a half-mile track and never even got to try Daytona, and that's a shame because he was so good. But, by the same token, Fireball had never done well on the old beach course. He tried to be like Curtis, but he wound up upside down a lot.

There were a lot of drivers who made the switch with no problem at all, guys like Buck Baker and Joe Weatherly and Curtis Turner and

Junior Johnson. Although Buck always said he liked the short tracks better.

For one thing, racing on a superspeedway takes a lot of strength and concentration, and I think this is where I had an edge. My arms and shoulders have always been big, and I have always kept in good physical condition. I could start to tell what a difference it was making, because I noticed that I was as strong and running just as fast in the last hundred miles of a five-hundred-mile race as I was in the first hundred miles. A lot of the other drivers, even the top ones, would start to lose a little of their edge late in the race, particularly if it was super hot, like Darlington on Labor Day or Daytona on the Fourth of July.

It's a whole lot like taking an entire NFL season and wrapping it up into a single afternoon. There aren't two teams in auto racing, no rest between plays, no substitutions. You can't let down for a minute. Running bumper-to-bumper with a guy, wide-open, takes total commitment; the whole race does, every inch of the way. If you're not beaming in on the guy directly in front of you, you're checking your gauges. You can't take your mind off it for a split second. And when the race is over, my ears ring for a couple of days, and at times I have a headache for as long.

Sometimes it gets so hot on the steering wheel that it will burn your hands if you move them, and you have to put them back where they were. Your lips blister, and the floorboard gets so hot that the heels of your shoes melt and you have to keep lifting them so they won't stick. It gets up to 140 degrees in there. I've known drivers who have lost as much as fifteen pounds in a five-hundred-mile race.

I was determined that I was going to be one of the great superspeedway drivers. And I can tell you, the only problem at all that I was having was in what Banjo told me. I had to channel my desire, because there was only one place I wanted to be—out front. I mean, I was a charger, and there wasn't any way I could change. A lot of drivers, like Richard Petty and David Pearson, would hold back until late in the race, and you never did know what they had until maybe in the last few laps, then they would blow by you like you weren't there.

Some days your car works better than others; some days you work better. But there was one thing they always knew about me: If I was running back in the pack, that's as fast as I could run; otherwise, I would have been in *front* of them.

There's something to be said about holding back until later when attrition and fatigue have taken over, but in those days, at least, I felt that I had to be out front. It's where I thought my sponsor wanted me, and my fans. That sure suited me fine.

I could tell that there was a world of difference to how I was running too. I was beginning to learn how to drive against each driver on the circuit, and that helped a lot. I learned that you really have to know who you're following or who you're passing. I mean, if something happens two or three hundred feet in front of you, if a car spins or hits the wall, or two or three cars get together, it's important to know what the guy in front of you is going to do.

If you're so close that you can't see for yourself what's up there, you might follow him right through the hole—if he's a David Pearson or a Junior Johnson—because you have that much faith in his ability. It might not be the same if you're following some unknown driver. But if you're back a little farther, maybe you can see better and might take a different route, no matter who went through the hole.

One of the toughest guys to run against late in the race was Bobby Isaac, particularly on a tight superspeedway like Atlanta or Charlotte. And I guess he must have thought I was, too, because he told reporters one time, "Cale Yarborough is tough. I don't have any fear of him spinning out, but I do have a fear of him taking me places on a racetrack where I've never been."

I guess it's the first time I ever realized that I was taking the race car in some pretty unusual places, but I could hold it, so I kept right at it. And I kept looking for the best and the fastest place to run, no matter where it was.

It was a good time for me to break into the superspeedways because there was so much happening in the mid-sixties. For one thing, the automobile manufacturers were in racing right up to their camshafts, all of the Big Three, so there was a lot of money to build and test and develop new and faster race cars.

Another big factor was the Tire Wars. Both Goodyear and Firestone were spending millions on race-car tire development and design, and not only were the cars getting better, but also they were getting faster and safer because of the wider, stickier tires.

Firestone had all of racing to itself until Goodyear came along in the late fifties at Darlington. But Goodyear got serious around 1962, and they started testing new tires at every major track before each race. Firestone did the same thing, so at one race Goodyear would be the answer and maybe at the next race it would be Firestone. The drivers were switching back and forth, depending on which tire company was on top at the moment. And in some cases, which offered better deals. The tire guys became almost part of your crew. They also didn't miss any of the parties.

The only problem with the higher speeds was that it caused a lot more serious crashes. So if coming along when I did was a good time on one side of the ledger, it was also a bad time on the other. Some of the crashes were bad. I mean, a lot of them took away some old friends.

The first in a long line of really tragic accidents happened at Riverside on the road course. Joe Weatherly came roaring into turn six, a right-hander, coming up hill, and he lost it for some reason. His familiar number 8 slammed into the wall. It didn't seem like the kind of wreck that would particularly hurt anybody, but I guess his body came part way out of the car and his head was crushed. When I heard the news later, it really hurt me. Little Joe was gone, and he took a lot of the fun around a racetrack with him.

It's hard to block out a thing like that, but the next time you get into a race car, you have to do it. It's not that it isn't a concern; it is, it's grief, but you just can't let it play on your mind or it will ruin you.

When I ran the World 600 at Charlotte, after the Riverside tragedy, I was able to get out there and run the faster speeds and not worry about it. I had enough confidence in my own ability to get me through.

The race started well, all the cars got through the high banks for the first few laps without an incident. That's always the toughest time, the first few laps, when all the cars are still bunched up and the faster cars that might be farther back because of qualifying problems are streaking up through the pack. I always breathe a sigh of relief when the first few laps are over. The cars have stretched out some, and the faster cars have moved past many of the crazies. But on lap seven Junior Johnson spun coming out of two. His car slid sideways, right into the path of Fireball and Ned Jarrett. They both hit Junior, and Fireball's car was sent across the track, down into the concrete abutment along the inner wall. It drove the gas tank up into the driver's compartment and the car exploded. There were flames everywhere. Fireball was trapped inside. Ned got out of his car and tried to get Fireball out, but he couldn't do it.

When I came by, I could see Fireball inside. The next time I came around, the safety crew had gotten the fire out and were taking Fireball out of the window of the car. He was lifeless.

I tried not to look at the remains of Fireball's car the next few times I came around under the yellow flag, and finally, thank God, it was gone. I didn't have to look at it anymore. Once the car was gone, I was able to put the crash out of my mind. I had a job to do, and I went on to drive the best race I could. But after the race it all came back. Again I could see Fireball, trapped in all those flames, and I could see the burned car.

"How's Fireball?" I asked, the minute I got out of the car.

"Not good," someone said. "He was burned real bad. They don't think he's going to make it."

Fireball later died.

■

When Lee Roy and I came up to Grand National, it was like going to Vietnam. We were learning to drive the superspeedway with blood all around us. But it was everywhere in racing. Davey MacDonald and Eddie Sachs were killed at Indianapolis, but it's one thing to hear of a death at Indy; you can insulate yourself from that. When it happens around you, it's hard to ignore.

It didn't stop in NASCAR, either. Jimmy Pardue and Billy Wade were killed. All of us moved from one state of shock to another, and people started talking about race-car drivers having a death wish. Well, I can tell you that we don't have a death wish,—at least the ones I know don't. We all were stunned by our friends getting killed.

If anything, I've got a *life* wish. I don't want to die, I never have. I really don't know why everything I have ever done leans to the dangerous side; I don't even want to know. I really don't *care* why. All I know is that I don't want to die. I might want to *test* fate, but I don't want to meet it.

Jimmy Pardue and Billy Wade were killed in tire tests, and I wasn't there. And I know when I heard about it that I was shocked and sad, but I could feel my defense mechanisms going up. It's like I swallowed it and then immediately threw it up. I told myself, "I didn't see it, I wasn't there. It happened a million miles away." I think that's one of the things a good race-car driver has to do; you have to have the ability to wipe fear away like you wipe water from a windshield. You have to say, "It'll never happen to me." And you have to make yourself believe it.

I think it's why it's so difficult to get anybody in the racing business to go to a funeral. They may express genuine concern, but inside they're saying, "Look, I'm sorry. Just don't make me go to the funeral." I know race-car drivers, some top ones, who have never been to a single funeral. I have been, but I'll tell you, I'm the exception to the rule. But I have always been able to deal with death. Maybe it's because I learned at such an early age what it feels like to lose someone who means so much to you. I know that life goes on and you still have the memories. Whatever I felt, I know that it helped me get through the most brutal period of racing.

It's hard to say for sure, but maybe it really helped me to avoid crashes. Maybe it's how I learned to concentrate as well as I can, because that's what makes the difference—concentration.

■

There were other things happening in NASCAR that would change the lives of a lot of us. The Chrysler products were starting to blow our doors off, if you really want to know. Nobody is sure how it all happened, but the hemi engine they had was so superior to anything Ford or GM had that none of the rest of us had much of a chance. Unless one of the MoPar—that's racing talk for Chrysler, it comes from their Motor Parts Division—broke or crashed, they won everything. It was a mistake on everybody's part to ever let them get that far ahead. Nobody knew how it happened.

Ford argued with NASCAR that something should be done about the hemi advantage. By 1966, Plymouths and Dodges were winning everything. NASCAR did nothing that pleased Ford, so Ford pulled out of Grand National racing. With it, of course, went my ride with Banjo.

It was time to try Indianapolis.

THE FIRECRACKER 400 WAS
ANOTHER CALE AND LEE ROY SHOW.

12

■

For a stock-car driver to go to Indianapolis is pretty much like a pro football player signing up with a baseball team. The only thing they have in common is the fact that they are athletes and they both use balls. But it's the kind of balls they use that makes the difference.

The same is true with stock-car racing as compared to Indianapolis racing. A stock car is just what its name implies; it is a big car that looks just like the one you drive to work. It isn't, of course, but it's that big and looks like you could drive it to work. In the sixties they weighed four thousand pounds. An Indianapolis race car is a single-seat, open-wheeled car that has been designed and built just for the racetrack. It weighs about sixteen hundred pounds. Both have ferocious engines.

In 1966, when I decided to give Indy a shot, there had only been two drivers who had successfully made the crossover from one form of the racing to the other: A. J. Foyt and Paul Goldsmith. That is if you don't count Dan Gurney, who came from Indy cars to NASCAR, but he mainly raced at Riverside on the road course, and that's the kind of thing he had been doing before he went to Indy. So I don't count him.

A lot of drivers had tried the switch, but none of them were too successful. Bobby Johns had done well by finishing seventh in the 1965 race, but he came back to NASCAR after one year, so nobody ever knew how well he would have done. Marshall Teague had tried it three or four times and was killed in an Indy-type car while testing at Daytona. Curtis and Junior and Lee Roy had tried but didn't even make the race.

It didn't matter what the odds were, I was going to try it. I had come too far in racing to give up now. I had made $25,000 in 1965, and that was a good bit of money back then, even in racing. Besides, I really felt like I could drive anything that had wheels on it.

The first thing I noticed about Indy was the difference in the drivers. Oh, they were friendly to me and I liked them, but it wasn't the same thing as it was back home. I guess it's the difference in the number of races each year. There are only a handful of Indy car races each year, and only one at Indianapolis, and a lot of them only drive that big one. They just don't get too close to each other. In NASCAR everybody drove every race, which was forty-five or fifty races a year. We spent every weekend together, and man, you really get to know somebody when you spend that much time with somebody. Most of them didn't spend that much time with their wives.

We were like a family in NASCAR. We traveled together, helped each other when we could, raced together, partied together. I felt a lot like an outsider at Indianapolis, until I realized that *everybody* was sort of an outsider. Still, they were fun to be with, and they were race-car drivers. That part doesn't change.

Lloyd Ruby became a friend from the Indy experience and he helped me a lot. A.J. helped me too. In fact, he's the one who took me out on the track the first time. I had never even seen the track. We walked out to the pits and onto the track, and I looked up and down. Everything was so flat. I mean, this track, of course, had been built in 1909, so they didn't think of banked turns then, but somehow I expected it to look a lot different.

"Where's the front straightaway?" I asked.

"You're standin' on it, Cale," he said.

How did I know? The track was so much narrower than I had expected that we walked right through the pits and onto the track before I realized it. I thought we were standing on pit road.

"Are you sure this is safe?" I asked.

"It's as safe as any track," he said. That was easy for him to say, —he had won the 500 twice. But he had won at Daytona, too, so he should know what he was talking about. He took me around the track in the pace car and showed me exactly what groove to drive. When we came back, Rolla Vollstedt was standing at the entrance to Gasoline Alley. Rolla is the one who supplied the car for me to drive, the red-and-yellow number 66 Jim Robbins Special. It was a rear-engined Ford V-8.

"Think you can handle this track?" he said.

"Yes, sir," I said. And I really thought I could. In fact, I knew I could.

There's some sort of honor to being the first one out to practice at Indy each year, and I wanted it. When they opened the gates to the pits, I made a dash for it. So did A.J. We ran together, and Lloyd Ruby beat us both to the track. Oh, well, Ruby was a nice guy.

They have a very strict driver's test at Indianapolis. You have to go out there and run a few laps at, say, 120 miles an hour, and then up it to 130 and then 140 and so on, and you're observed by United Auto Club officials all the time. It looked like the qualifying speed was going to be well over 160 miles per hour that year, so it meant the cars would be doing about 200 on the straightaways. They had to make sure that any driver out there belonged there. I made an almost perfect score on my driver's test.

I really enjoyed driving the Indy car because I always loved the sensation of wind in my face, and with the open cockpit you got plenty of that, so I thought that maybe I had found a home in racing. At least until NASCAR got its act together. I qualified at over 159 miles an hour, which was good for twenty-fourth spot.

Driving an Indy car was a completely different sensation. They are so much more responsive, mainly because there is so much more horsepower, compared to the weight of the car, and because the steering is so sensitive. All you have to do is move the steering wheel an inch and it will go right through any corner. So it's very easy to oversteer the car. You have to drive it like you are on ice.

The big difference is *where* you drive the car. I mean, rule one is that you stay completely away from anybody, at almost any cost, because of the open wheels. If you run up on someone, the rotation of his wheels might just pull your car right up like a gear. And if that happens, it's bye-bye time, right through the air. It's a whole 'nother ball game up there.

You should never touch your brakes in an Indy car, unless it's an absolute emergency, and then you're better off trying to steer around something, even if you have to slide, because touching your brakes is sure to send you into a wild spin. What you do is run like the hammers of hell down the front straightaway, back off the throttle just a little as you get to the turn, and when the car starts turning, you get back on it and power it through the turn. You can do the same thing in the back straightaway. Of course, you do just about the same thing in a stock car, but the Indy cars are much more precise and much more delicate. It's nerve-racking.

You get more of a sensation of speed at Indy because of the open cockpit. I liked the whole thing.

The tire wars had spread to Indianapolis too. Goodyear had invaded Firestone's hallowed ground in 1964, and by 1966, they were starting to attract some good drivers. A.J. had been the one who talked them into coming down there, because he was mad at Firestone. A.J. is not one to fool with. So Goodyear decided to give "the big race" a shot. The only problem was that in trying to get a jump on each other, both Goodyear and Firestone developed some tire compounds that were revolutionary. *They* said. They stuck like glue, but in some cases, they stuck too well. They got so hot that big chunks of rubber came off, and there were days when it sounded like the Fourth of July.

The tire companies got gun-shy, if you'll pardon the expression. On one occasion Lloyd Ruby blew a Firestone.

"What happened, Lloyd?" asked Bill Pittman of the *Indianapolis News.*

"Blew a tire," he said. The Firestone people flinched.

"Next time," they told Lloyd, "don't say 'blew' a tire, say the tire equalized pressure." What that meant was that all of a sudden there was the same air pressure on the inside as there was on the outside of the tire. It was a nicer way of saying it. The PR way.

When it happened to some Goodyear drivers, they also said we "equalized pressure on a tire." The newspapers were saying "blew a tire," just like always. The Firestone PR guys told Ruby and the others to "say *anything* else. Say you ran over something on the track, say something broke, but don't even mention the word *tire."*

The next day in practice, Ruby blew another tire. Again Pittman asked, "What happened, Lloyd?"

"I blew a wheel," he said.

■

On race day I couldn't believe the scene. I thought I was used to crowds, but this was something else. There were three hundred thousand people there, and bands and hot air baloons, and, well, you name it, it was there. I had never seen anything like that before. I was a little nervous before I got to the track, but *after* I got there and saw all those people and felt all that tradition, the butterflies were doing a square dance in my stomach.

When I got in the race car and settled way down in that thing, I thought, "Man, you've really got yourself into something this time." Once more I realized what a different feeling it was to sit down so low and to look out and see the open wheels. But I felt good about it and had a lot of confidence that I could actually win the race. Mario

183

Andretti and Jimmy Clark were in the front row. But I had run laps almost as fast as their best qualifying times when I practiced, so I really felt that I had the track figured out.

That's one thing about Indy: You're there for the whole month, and by race time you have a lot of running under your belt. I was ready.

Unfortunately I never got the chance to show my stuff. We made the parade lap and the pace lap, and then the pace car pulled off. The butterflies went away when I jammed down on the gas. But, for some unknown reason, Billy Foster got sideways and hit the outside wall in the front straightaway. He bounced back into the middle of the pack, setting off the damnedest chain reaction I had ever seen. Cars were spinning everywhere, and the air was full of tires and wheels. A car hit me from the side, and another plowed into the back of me.

One of the things you have to watch for at Indy is the wheels. They're on spindly little axles and break off easy. The cars are delicate, compared to what I was used to. A wheel came down on my windshield. My car was so badly damaged that I was out of the race. Ten other cars were out with me, including A. J. Foyt and Dan Gurney. In fact, Foyt's fuel tank ripped open, and his driving uniform was soaked with alcohol. He pulled himself out of the car, and he climbed the ten-foot high chain-link fence like a monkey, to get off the track and into the grandstands, just in case there was a fire.

I didn't make a single lap at Indianapolis because the crash happened just after the green flag dropped. I didn't even make it to the first turn.

Some new life I had picked out for myself.

I went back home, where I figured I belonged. By then NASCAR had worked out some of its problems with Ford, and I landed another good ride. This one was with the Wood Brothers Racing Team, one of the legendary teams in all of racing.

The Wood Brothers had perfected the pit stop into a form of the ballet. When everybody else was hurrying through pit stops and looking a lot like it was a Chinese fire drill, the Wood Brothers decided that it needed some order. So they started practicing every maneuver until they had it down pat. Each member of the crew could do it in his sleep. It made such a difference in their pit-stop times that nobody could believe it. For the first time people fully understood that races could be won and lost in the pits as well as out there on the track.

The Wood Brothers became so well known that they were asked by Ford to go to Indianapolis to help get the Lotus Ford team straightened out. The first thing they did up there was work on the race car. They made sure that everything that should come off or go in did, like the wheels and fuel. The car wasn't to their liking, so they honed everything until it worked like a well-oiled clock. Then they worked on their own act, adapting it to that particular car. They beat every record in the Indianapolis book.

In addition to fast pit work, the Wood Brothers built fine cars. It was a dream team, and I was their driver. The first race I drove for them was Darlington, the Southern 500. Man, it felt so good to be back in those big old taxicabs again—that's what they felt like after Indy. A feeling of real security. It was like eating your mother's cooking.

I finished second in that race, just a whisker away from winning the race that meant more to me than any one in the world. It was so hot inside the car that day that they had to pour cold water on my accelerator foot every time I came in because the heel of my shoe was melting and sticking to the steel floorboard.

Driving for the Wood Brothers was the start of my *winning* career in NASCAR. I had learned a little with each step up to that point. Marion Cox had made me a good driver on short tracks; Herman Beam had made me a winner on them; the Holman and Moody connection had given me a Grand National ride, and Banjo Matthews had taught me how to drive it. Now the Wood Brothers had added their contribution. For one thing, they worked on slowing me down a little. They never had to tell me to go faster because I was always going as fast as the car would run; they kept after me to save a little of the car for the end of the race. It worked. A little.

I won my first superspeedway race at Atlanta in the five-hundred-miler in 1967. I would like to be able to tell you that I felt like I was on top of the world—I should have been—but for some reason the victory didn't feel any better than my very first Grand National win on a short track at Valdosta. Maybe it was because I had become so competitive that I *expected* to win. If you want to know the truth, I expected to win every race after that. I always felt that way for that matter, right from the start; otherwise, I wouldn't have raced. But now I *knew* that I could win.

The Atlanta win was great, particularly the way I had to win it. Mario Andretti was a lap down, but he kept right in the groove. He wouldn't pull over and let me pass. That may have been the way he drove at Indianapolis, but it wasn't the way *we* drove. I tried high and low, so I finally went right up beside him in one, and we went through one and two side by side; I finally got by him and went on to win. I collected $20,000 that day; half of it was mine and half belonged to the Wood Brothers. It was the deal we had made, which was pretty much of a standard deal in NASCAR. I invested part of mine in a dry-cleaning business in Hartsville, South Carolina, and I bought another five hundred acres of land.

My racing career had reached the point where I felt exactly like I did the day I finally moved the five-hundred-pound bale of cotton after trying day after day. Son Ham would have been proud of me. I knew that I was on my way.

The Firecracker 400 at Daytona was a real milestone for more reasons than one. For one thing, I won. It was a wonderful feeling after leading there twice before. But I really thought at one point during the race that the Daytona jinx was going to get me again. We were trying to conserve fuel as much as possible, so I was told to stay out there as long as I could, hoping for a yellow flag, so I could pit under caution and not lose so much time. But the yellow didn't come, and they kept me out there one lap too long. As I got back on the throttle coming off turn one, the car sputtered. I knew what had happened. It died completely coming off two, and I coasted down the back straight and got lined up for an entrance into the pits, still going very fast. The Wood Brothers didn't know I was coming in, so the customary man with the pit board wasn't out there to guide me to my pit. You see, you come into the pits so fast and they all look alike at that speed, so you need a gauge. I ran right by my pit. But Junior Johnson, who was a car builder by then—he had built Lee Roy's car, in fact—saw what was happening. He knew I was out of fuel because he had been there, and he picked up on it immediately. The "family instinct" rose up. He grabbed *his* pit board and jumped out into the pit road. I slid to a stop in his pit. His crew refueled my car. Of course, that's highly against NASCAR rules, so when I roared away, the NASCAR guys ran over to Junior and screamed, "You can't do *that!*"

"Whatta'ya mean," he said in mock amazement. "I just put gas in my race car."

"That wasn't Lee Roy," the guy said, "That was *Cale.*"

Junior looked shocked. "It *was?* Well, I'll be damned."

They went away, shaking their heads. The next year, the rule had teeth in it. But that year I won the race, and Junior's driver, Lee Roy, finished second. I never forgot that. And it had always stood as the benchmark on NASCAR loyalty and friendship as far as I'm concerned.

I made $56,000 in racing in 1967. Maybe that's all I need to say about it. Oh, there is one other thing: I gave Indy one more try. But I didn't give up my NASCAR ride. In fact, I drove both the Indy 500 and the World 600 at Charlotte. On the same weekend. One was on Friday and the other one was on Sunday, so I raced eleven hundred miles in forty-eight hours.

Lee Roy also drove Indy that year. I finished seventeenth and he finished twenty-seventh, but I will have to say that I sort of took Lee Roy out of the race—not on purpose, of course. I spun on lap ninety-nine, and Lloyd Ruby and Lee Roy tangled, trying to avoid my car. Lee Roy hit the wall, and Ruby hit the inside retaining fence. I gathered up my car and continued until late in the race, when I equalized the pressure of a tire and crashed.

I jumped in my airplane, which had been upgraded to a Beechcraft Bonanza by then (listen, I had even gotten a pilot's license), and I high-tailed it to Charlotte, where I also had mechanical woes. But I did set a track record in qualifying. All in all, it was a busy weekend.

My big year with the Wood Brothers was 1968, and it was one of the biggest years anybody ever had, for that matter. I won $136,000 and six races, including the Daytona 500. And that's when purses were about a quarter of what they are today.

And what a race that Daytona 500 was. The car was running letter-perfect for the first twenty or thirty laps, but it started cutting out. I would run fine for half a lap, and then it would miss like mad, especially when I got back on the gas hard. I pitted and told the Wood Brothers what it was doing.

"Ignition," said Glen.

"Right," agreed Leonard.

Leonard dived through the passenger side window, and his head disappeared up under the dash. In a minute he had a part in his hand from up under there. In another minute he had a new one in. "Go get 'em, boy," he said.

The crew had new tires and a full load of fuel, and I roared onto the track, three laps behind the leaders. I put that red-and-white number 21 Mercury in a groove that most people didn't even know existed. I was turning record laps, and I guess the crowd was going wild.

People told me that the radio account of what I was doing was unbelievable. Nobody had ever seen anything like it before, but I was determined.

I caught Lee Roy by the eighty-ninth lap, and from there on it was dog-eat-dog. He led one lap and I led the next. But at the checkered flag I was out in front.

We did that a lot that year. In the Firecracker it was another Cale and Lee Roy show, and between us, we led all but nine laps, but again, I led the last one.

But after the 500, everybody used the Wood Brothers as the standard of pit excellence. Somebody said, in one of the papers, "The Pettys are like Boy Scouts, they come 'prepared.' Their cars are right, but if anything happens during the race, that's usually it. But the Wood Brothers, that's different: If it happens during the race, they can get it going again."

That means a lot to a driver.

Of course, everybody started practicing their pit stops, and within a few years there wasn't all that much difference in how long it took to get tires and fuel in the pits—a good pit stop when nothing goes wrong takes about eighteen seconds. But it was the pit stop when something was needed other than tires and fuel where the Wood Brothers shined.

Every one of the six crew members—and that's all that's allowed over the pit wall at one time—has a job. One jacks the car up, one refuels, one cleans the windshield and talks to the driver, and the rest work on tires and wheels. Like I said before, when it's done right, it's like a ballet. By the time the wheels stop turning, each man is at work.

With the Wood Brothers, there was almost never a mistake. You couldn't say that about many of the other teams. It's very important because you can drive like mad out there and then come into the pits and easily lose all the advantage you've gained.

So with work like Glen and Leonard did on my ignition at the Daytona 500 in 1968, I have to credit them with winning the race every bit as much as I do with the determination I had out there on the track—that will to catch up.

Throughout the whole racing world the Daytona 500 is considered second only to the Indianapolis 500 in terms of prestige. Sure, there are people who will argue that LeMans or some of the formula-one races are more important, but for the most part, everybody agrees that the Daytona race is second. You just can't argue the fact that Indy is number one, just because it's been around since the beginning of time, and Daytona didn't come along until 1959. And there's the three hundred thousand people. I think it's mostly tradition, and I also think that Daytona is a better and tougher race, but that's just my opinion. Most people don't agree with me. I had been on the pole at a record 189 plus—nine miles an hour faster than Curtis Turner had run the year before. That and winning Daytona immediately moved me to the top rung of the racing ladder. I was up there with all the greats I had always admired so much. The $47,000 in prize money didn't make me unhappy, either.

The fact that Lee Roy was right behind me made me feel even better about it. But it confused a lot of other people. Because of the instant publicity, a lot thought that Lee Roy and I were brothers. I guess they didn't notice the difference in the spelling of our names—I've got one more o—but our careers had been very similar, and now we both were right up there.

Many of the newspapers and magazines referred to Lee Roy and I as "overnight successes." All I could say was that it sure was a long night.

I had flown not only Betty Jo and Julie down to Daytona with me, but I had taken Mama along too. After the race Mama kept asking me, "When are we going to leave, Cale?" And I kept telling her, "Soon." But it wasn't real soon because there were so many people there to interview me, and everybody wanted autographs. I was some kind of celebrity, I guess. I'll have to admit that I was enjoying it, so I wasn't in any hurry to leave.

Mama kept after me. I couldn't understand why in the world she was so eager to get home. I didn't want to leave all that, but I finally gave in. We left a couple of hours later than I had planned, but to tell you the truth, I would have stayed longer if it hadn't been for Mama.

When we flew over the toll bridge at Savannah, I wondered if Buford had heard the news. I hoped he had, because he helped me get to where I was, in his own little way.

I was keeping my plane in a hangar at M. B. Huggins Airport, the little grass strip in Timmonsville, and when I got within sight of the runway, I could see cars parked everywhere. They were all over the place, up and down the highway, along both sides of the runway. Everywhere. I got worried. "I wonder if anything's happened down there?" I said. "Just look at all those cars. I sure hope it's not M.B."

"I don't know what it is, Cale," Mama said.

"Neither do I," Betty Jo said.

I landed and started to taxi over to my hangar on the other side of the field, and I saw M.B. out at the edge of the runway. He was motioning for me to come over where he was.

"What in the world is going on?" I said.

"My, oh my, I don't know," Mama said.

Why did I get the feeling that she wasn't telling the truth?

I taxied up to where M.B. was and he motioned for me to cut the motor. When the propeller stopped, I reached over and opened the door. The Timmonsville High School band marched out from behind the hangar, playing the high-school song. And they rolled out a big old red carpet. The mayor was standing there with a wreath of roses.

I don't mind telling you that there were tears in my eyes when I walked down that red carpet. Everybody was cheering and throwing confetti. Right then I felt that everything I had done to get to the winner's circle at Daytona had been worth it—every blown engine, every crash, and every day of hard work. Even the turkeys. Well, maybe not the turkeys. But everything else.

That's the reason Mama was so insistent that we leave. All those people had been waiting hours for me. They had a parade for me all the way from the airport, right through Timmonsville. It was along the same route that I had towed the original race car so many times when I was a kid. And it was the same road that I had driven up and down to work. I'd even done a little late-night racing on that road. A lot, in fact. We went by the old theatre and by my high school. And on that day, that very day, I was king of the walk.

I feel sorry for people who didn't grow up in small towns, especially that one.

On Monday morning I called the school in Timmonsville, and I did something that I had promised myself I would do the minute I could afford it. I told the principal, "Listen, I want all the kids in the whole school who can't afford to eat the hot lunch to be fed, and I want you to send me the bill every month. From now on."

I'll tell you why I did it: I always had money for the hot lunch program when I was a kid, and I always remember how hungry I was when the lunch bell rang. I used to fly down there to eat. But there were always a few kids who stayed in the classroom. I knew they didn't have the money. And I knew that they were just as hungry as I was. I didn't ever want a kid to be hungry in that school again. I paid for their lunches until a government program took it over a few years later.

■

They remodeled the Darlington Raceway in 1969, improving the third and fourth turns. There would never be a Darlington Stripe again. Of course, it made it a whole lot easier and safer to drive, but some of us hated to see the change. They had always referred to Darlington as "the track nobody could tame." And you know that it was the track where I really wanted to win. I had one more shot at it in the 1968 Southern 500.

You can imagine how much I wanted to win that race. We had already been told that the day after the race they were going to start tearing up the track to improve three and four. It was my last chance to win a race on the original track, the track where superspeedway stock-car racing had been born. As far as a lot of people were concerned, stock-car racing, period, had been born there. I know it had been for me.

As I practiced that year I kept thinking of the time when I saw my first race there at twelve years old. And about the time when I thought I was such a hot-shot driver at seventeen. This was my last chance at taming that old track.

I can't say that I "tamed" it, but I sure got its attention. I ran so well in practice and qualifying that all of the papers were listing me as one of the favorites. They also picked David Pearson and Richard Petty, a tough pair to beat—the old guess-what-we've-got duet.

It had been eleven years since John Bruner and Norris Freil had personally escorted me out of the track.

On race day I used my same old strategy: I got out front as soon as I could and stayed there as long as I could. Pearson and Buddy Baker chased me all day, but Petty wasn't up to speed most of the time, so he wasn't any problem. Paul Goldsmith was. His Dodge was running well. In fact, all of the Dodges and Plymouths were. Pearson and I had the only Ford products that were in contention.

Late in the race I was leading Pearson by a few seconds. I had made my last pit stop, and it had been a perfect one. Pearson had made his final stop. All I had to do was drive the groove that was working for me, not brush the wall too hard coming out of four, and keep Pearson back there. All three were hard to do, especially the last part, because Pearson was "The Fox."

With ten laps to go, the car was running as well as it had at the start of the race, maybe better. But it didn't sound like it. Every time I touched the wall in four, it sounded louder. There were cracks and creaks and gurgles that I didn't hear earlier in the straightaways. When you're leading a race, you notice noises that you never heard before. They were there all along, of course. You just didn't hear them.

My Mercury sounded like it was going to self-destruct at every turn. I kept checking the gauges; everything was all right. Keep in mind, a stock car doesn't have too many gauges. You don't have time to look at them, except a quick glance, and they're turned so that the needle of each one points straight up when it's reading what you want it to read. That way all you have to do is look at the needle. You don't have to read the numbers. There is oil pressure, oil temperature, water temperature, fuel pressure, ampmeter, and tachometer. There isn't any speedometer. Your pit crew keeps you informed of how fast you're going.

Everything was perfect in the gauge department, but I still tapped them from time to time, just to make sure none of them had stuck. How could everything be so good if the car was making so much noise? I looked, time after time, in the rearview mirror to see if the car was smoking. No smoke, but a lot of Pearson.

It came down to the white-flag lap. If I could keep him back there for one more lap, I would have my job done. Coming out of four, I hit the wall hard. The car groaned, and so did I. It got a little sideways, but I was right on it to gather it up, as we say. I looked in the rearview mirror. Pearson did the same thing. I knew I had him.

The checkered flag was a beautiful sight. I won the 1968 Southern 500. I got it in under the wire and under the bulldozer's nose.

I'll have to give a big chunk of the credit to the Wood Brothers because they not only had that Mercury running perfectly, but also their pit stops were better than usual, if that was possible. It was one of those days when everything came together just right. But I'll also have to give part of the credit to "desire," because I wanted to win that race more than any race I had ever run.

And, you know, the car didn't make any of those noises when I drove it around for my victory lap.

I've won at Darlington four more times since then, but none of them meant as much as it did to win on the old Darlington track.

We raced at Martinsville, Virginia, the next week, and I'll tell you one thing, the track there has to be the prettiest racetrack in the world. Clay Earles and Dick Thompson keep that track as neat as a pin, with flowers and grass and a little lake with ducks on it. It's beautiful. It's also a tough track to drive. It's a half-mile, flat oval with tight turns. They start about the same number of cars there as at Daytona. It makes it interesting on that short track. But I was on a roll.

I was leading the five-hundred-lap race when somebody hit me and knocked me into the fence, but I bounced down into the infield, and the car seemed to be all right. What I didn't know was that the right rear fender was bent in so far that it was cutting into the tire. Petty came around again, and he actually stopped to tell me. It saved me from blowing the tire and having a bad crash. I went in and got a new tire and went back out to finish second. Behind Petty. If anybody but me had to win that day, I was glad it was him.

But again, that's the kind of family we were. I did the same kind of thing many times. All of us did. I mean, every one of us wanted to win, and we drove as hard as we could to do it. If we had to bang somebody to get past, we did it. But if anybody got in trouble or needed help, we were always there, too, just as anxious to help him as we were to beat him on the track. You just don't find that in any other kind of racing.

I was flying back and forth to most of the races in my Bonanza, and I'll tell you, the trips home were long. Can you imagine racing for five hundred miles and then having to fly another two or three hours? At times I was so tired that I could hardly get in the plane, and my ears were ringing so much that I had to turn up the radio as loud as it would go, just to hear what the guy in the control tower was telling me.

There were times when I even dozed off while I was flying. But I wasn't alone; many of the other drivers were doing the same thing.

I took Betty Jo and Julie along with me to Rockingham, North Carolina, for one race, and it got rained out, so I went over to the driver's lounge to see if Lee Roy or any of the other guys had called the airport for the weather. They had. Lee Roy said, "It looks okay for us, Cale. I checked Florence. The storm is moving away from us, so we're all right." Well, it would have been all right if we had left then, but you know us—we stayed there for another hour, talking racing.

When I took off, I expected to climb out of the weather by the time I got to five thousand feet, but instead, I climbed right into the worst rainstorm I had ever been in. The weather had changed drastically in the hour we had shot the bull. I kept climbing, trying to get out of it, but there seemed to be no ceiling to it.

I turned south because the weather had been better there, according to the Florence tower. The higher I got, the harder it rained. It was raining so hard, I couldn't see the prop. I was at thirteen thousand feet, and the lightning was flashing all around us. I hadn't said a word. I looked at Betty Jo, and she was holding Julie tight. She also hadn't said a word.

The engine started missing. It was being drowned out. I leveled off and cut back on the power. I knew that it would miss more if I pushed it too hard. I knew I was in real trouble. It was by far the worst weather I had ever flown in. I put the landing gear down because I was afraid that I would be too busy later. And because I was sure that we were going down.

The engine finally quit completely. We were at 13,500 feet. I banked the plane and turned it around, keeping as level a glide path as I could. I didn't want to go south anymore because I knew we were headed for the Great Pee Dee River Swamp. I knew that if we went down in there, they would never find us.

The turbulence was so bad that sometimes we were going straight up and at other times we were going straight down. All of the needles were locked on the instruments. I kept pulling back on the stick when we were headed straight down, trying to save it, but it didn't help. It didn't help to work the stick when we were going straight up, either. The plane was in someone else's hands. It would fly straight up until it finally stalled out, and then it would fall, sometimes backward, for a couple thousand feet. Once I was upside down. With no power.

There wasn't a thing I hadn't tried to save the plane, but it was useless at that point. I looked over at Betty Jo and Julie. I didn't gave a damn how bad it was, I *had* to save that plane. If I had been there by myself, I think I would have given up, but I couldn't let them die.

Sweat was popping out all over me. I don't even know what I did, but the plane turned right side up. It was still being tossed around like it was a toy. I looked at Betty Jo again, and she put her hand on my arm. She didn't say a word, but she was telling me that she had faith in me.

I held on and did everything I could think of. I still couldn't see the prop. And it was stopped.

Wait! What was that? Through the rain and lightning I thought I saw a yellow streak down there. But it went away. I was able to get the plane headed for whatever it was I had seen. I leveled it up, and the lightning lit up the sky again. There it was! I had come out of the clouds right over an old country dirt road. It had been cut out of the thick piny forest, probably by loggers. And I was right over it, not ten feet over the treetops. It looked as long as Kennedy Airport. I made a perfect dead-stick landing; well, it was as perfect as it could be under the circumstances. The mud and water was flying as we bumped down the road. It finally sank to a stop in the mud. We were safe.

We sat there in silence for a while. I know we were both thanking the good Lord.

"I've got to go find help," I said. "You all stay here and I'll be back soon."

When I got out of the plane, my knees were so weak that I almost dropped to the mud. Betty Jo handed me an umbrella. "I don't need it," I said. "I just want to stand out here in this beautiful rain and this beautiful mud."

I started walking. It *was* a logging road, so there were no houses anywhere. I walked for miles. Then I turned around and went back to the plane. "I'm going the other way," I told Betty Jo. There was nothing the other way, so I went back to the plane and told her that we would have to spend the night in the plane. "I'll get help when it gets daylight," I said. "I'm not going to leave you alone in the dark anymore."

"I'm not afraid, Cale," she said.

"Neither am I, Daddy," said Julie.

I had some family.

We covered up with a couple of blankets I had in the back of the plane. Just after daylight I was awakened by somebody pounding on the door of the plane. I jumped up and opened the door. It was three Marines who were out on maneuvers in a jeep. They had been coming down the logging road when they suddenly saw the plane in the middle of the road. They told me that it was a ten-square-mile wooded area and that we were right in the middle of it.

The plane had broken out of the clouds right over the road, just at treetop level, and all I had to do was drop it in.

The good Lord had put us there. I didn't have a thing to do with it.

The Marines took us in to a country store where I made a phone call. I knew where James Garner and Dickie Smothers were staying in Rockingham. They had come from Hollywood for the race, and they were the only ones I knew who had stayed over in Rockingham. They came after us and took us home.

I called a fellow I knew at Pinehurst, which was near where the plane was, and told him where the plane was. I asked him if he could go get it and fly it out of there. They had to wait until the weather cleared and the road dried up, and then they dug it out and cut the tops out of the pine trees so they could fly it out. And even then they had to get a crop duster to do it. Nobody else could.

When I went to look at the plane, every bit of paint was off the wings. They looked like polished aluminum. In fact, they were. I sold it and bought a twin-engine plane.

I never took my family along in the airplane after that because, well, if you must know, it scared the wits out of me. I've never been afraid to do anything; oh, there have been butterflies a lot and there have been times when I've been scared for a minute, but the airplane incident was something completely different. It didn't just involve me, it involved my family, and I'll tell you, that's a whole different thing.

There was another reason. Betty Jo gave birth to our second daughter, Kelly, on April 11, 1969 and, once more, I was on cloud nine. Julie was seven years old, so it was wonderful having a tiny girl around the house again.

When B.J., which is short for Betty Jo, came along on June 21,

1971, it was the same thrill. I didn't know exactly what it was going to be like, living with a whole houseful of women, but I was sure I could make it. And, I'll tell you, it's been wonderful.

Over the years I'll bet I've been asked a thousand times if I missed not having a son, and I can honestly say that I have never even given it a thought. Well, maybe that's going a little too far, because it's impossible not to give it a thought when every reporter you ever talk to says, "If you had a son, would you want him to race?" I *have* given it a thought in that respect, but I've always had the same answer: "If I had a son and he wanted to drive a race car, I'd help him, but I'd never try to talk him into it."

Once and for all I'd like to say that I've never missed not having a son. With three wonderful daughters what more could a man ask for? Except maybe a wonderful wife, and I've got that, too. It's been a perfect family life.

■

Lee Roy and I had careers that were almost identical. We both lived in South Carolina, our driving styles were similar, and we came up through exactly the same tough apprenticeship at exactly the same time. We even drove the same tracks. And we partied together. At that point, in 1970, we both had the same number of Grand National victories: fourteen. I didn't get into quite as many fights as he did, but that's about the only difference between us.

You get to know a guy when you do all those things together. It's why I was concerned when I heard that while testing tires in Texas, Lee Roy had had a really bad crash. I heard he hit the wall, head-on, at full speed. That's the worst kind of crash. No matter what, when you see the wall coming straight at you, you try everything you can to hit it with either side of the car or, at least, at a slight angle. Head-on or straight from behind is what has killed more drivers than anything else.

I guess Lee Roy couldn't get it sideways in time. It happens at times, as much as we try to avoid it. He was hurt bad. I went to see him in the hospital and he had the strangest look on his face I've ever seen on anybody. He was as white as a ghost, and he had a far-out look in his eyes. I wasn't even real sure that he recognized me. He didn't talk much, and when I left, I was really worried about him.

A couple of weeks later we were supposed to race at Rockingham, so I called him and asked if he was planning to fly his own plane up there. He said he was, so I asked him if he wanted to fly up with me. I didn't think he should be flying, so I arranged to fly over to the Columbia Airport and pick him up. And we arranged to have his wife, Gloria, come over to our place after we got back from the race and meet us.

He still had the dazed look in his eyes when I met him at the airport, but he seemed all right physically.

There wasn't anything unusual about his driving at Rockingham, except that he didn't charge hard at all. We started out close together, and I quickly got right up front. He stayed back in the pack, running a conservative race. I finished second to Richard Petty, and Lee Roy ran way back. It wasn't the old Lee Roy.

On the way back in the plane, he didn't say a word. He just stared straight ahead. I talked to him, and all he did was nod his head yes or shake it no.

I saw him the next week, and you know, he didn't remember a thing about going up to Rockingham with me. In fact, he really didn't remember running the race. Oh, he said he did, but I could tell he was making it up. He didn't *remember* that race.

Lee Roy never did anything outstanding on the track after that, and pretty soon Junior had to let him go. He did get a ride with someone in the Firecracker 400 at Daytona the next year—I don't even remember who it was—but Jim Hunter told me that he went to the airport to pick him up. He knew what time Lee Roy was supposed to get in, and he had arranged to meet him out front. Jim drove around the circle three times before he recognized Lee Roy. The reason he didn't know him was that the guy standing there had on a bizarre outfit, plaid slacks, and a dirty old striped sport coat. He was unshaven, and he had a big beer belly that hung over his trousers. And his hair had turned white.

Jim pulled up to the curb and rolled down the window. "Lee Roy?" he asked.

"Yeah," Lee Roy said. "You s'posed to pick me up?" He didn't seem to be real sure who Jim was, and they had been friends for years.

The next thing we heard about Lee Roy was that he had tried to kill his mother and they had him locked up in a mental institution. We took up a collection around the track and raised a whole bunch of money to help with treatment for him. Junior even went to see him because he felt particularly bad. He felt somehow responsible, since it was his car that Lee Roy had crashed in. He wasn't responsible, of course, but Junior is just that softhearted. He's a fine man.

We did everything we could for Lee Roy because we weren't just going to turn him loose. He was one of us and one of our oldest friends.

I was really upset when I talked with Junior after he got back from seeing Lee Roy. He said Lee Roy not only didn't know him, but he didn't remember a thing about ever driving a race car. The whole thing was such a tragedy, but I think the worst part is that he didn't even remember what a great race-car driver he had been.

In his prime, which was in the late sixties, he was real hard to beat on a superspeedway. In 1969 alone, he won races at Darlington, Atlanta, the Firecracker 400, the Daytona 500, and the World 600s at Charlotte and Rockingham. He was named Driver of the Year by everybody. Nobody has matched all that since.

Over the next few years a lot of people from racing visited with Lee Roy, and he never did remember anything. He kept getting worse and worse until he finally became a vegetable. He wasn't on top long—but he would have been—and that's a shame because there aren't many people around today who even remember him. His name never got too high on the record books, and it won't be too many years, when all the rest of us are gone, that nobody at all will remember that Lee Roy Yarbrough was one of the all-time greats.

Lee Roy died of a massive brain hemorrhage while Bill Neely and I were writing this book. It had been fourteen years since his bad crash. We heard it early one morning. We didn't work anymore that day.

"MY BIKE IS BROKEN, DADDY."

13

■

Mose Nowland was with the Ford factory group when the company was in racing in the sixties and seventies, and he's still with Ford. He's the one who recently told me the exact date that my life changed again —December 4, 1970. It wasn't the birthdate of another daughter. It was the date Ford pulled out of racing. He could pinpoint the date because that's the day he went to the Ford Racing Division in Dearborn, Michigan, and found the door padlocked.

I guess Ford felt that it had proved everything it needed to prove in racing; it had several great years in Grand National, had dominated Indianapolis for a number of years, and had won LeMans a couple of times, so what more could they ask for? Their Pantera sports car program was rolling along, and the feds were beginning to hone in on them on damage control and emissions on passenger cars, so they decided to use their racing talents to solve the problems the government was climbing on all the auto manufacturers about.

It left me without a ride or, at least, without a Ford ride. This time I felt that Ford's move was a permanent decision. They hadn't left angry like they did in the mid-sixties; this time it was a calculated decision, and a simple thing like rules changes wouldn't bring them back.

I dug out my road maps to Indianapolis again.

You know, it's odd, a lot of drivers spend their racing lives working toward Indianapolis. It's Mecca for most race-car drivers. I was using it as a refuge when I didn't have a serious ride in Grand National. It's not that I didn't think Indy was important. I did; it was just always number two on my priority list.

Gene White, who was a Firestone racing tire distributor from Atlanta, offered me a chance to get in the Indianapolis 500 in 1971. I will have to say one thing: I was always able to get rides when I wanted them. That was a comforting feeling.

Lloyd Ruby was the number-one driver for the team, and I wasn't sure how he was going to take this hotshot NASCAR guy coming up there, particularly since I was getting so much publicity. When I had been there in 1966 and 1967, I hadn't built quite the reputation I had by the time I returned. But Ruby wasn't the least bit upset. He helped me all he could, and I really developed a liking for him.

Lloyd had the worst luck of any driver in Indianapolis history. For one thing, he was a great driver, and he had led the race so many times, he stopped counting. He didn't even want to know, because it was the kiss of death every time he got out front. Some fifty-cent car part broke or somebody ran into him or something bizarre happened. Every time.

I've always wanted to win every race I entered, but right after me, I was cheering for Ruby in the 1971 race.

This time both Ruby and I had bad luck. He had qualified seventh and was leading, but he developed gear problems with only twenty-six laps to go. I went out with sixty laps left when a valve cover came loose and sprayed out all the oil.

One thing I can say about Lloyd, he could make an ill-handling car handle well if it was at all possible. He was driving one of the wedge-shaped cars, and he said, "You couldn't steer this thing down the beach. I mean, I'm scaring myself to death out there." I like Lloyd Ruby.

The following year, I started the race in thirty-second position—one place from last—and I finished tenth. I would have done even better if I hadn't run out of gas midway through the race. It cost me at least two laps, but I wouldn't have won, no matter what. There would have to have been the awfullest crash in Indianapolis history to get me to the winner's circle. I was having so much trouble handling the car that it's a wonder I even finished.

I wasn't happy at Indianapolis, mostly because I wasn't doing as well there as I had in NASCAR. With all due respect to Gene White, his cars just weren't the best, and I didn't know enough about Indy cars to tell them what was wrong. It was a case of the blind leading the blind.

Lord, how I missed Grand National.

There was no question that I could get a ride, and a good one if I went back, even though it wouldn't be a Ford, because they really were out of racing. I never dreamed, not for one minute, that I would be lucky enough to land a ride with Junior Johnson. But Bobby Allison had decided to run his own car, and that left the ride in Junior's Chevy wide-open. He offered it to me. I took it.

It began a friendship that will last forever. Junior had been one of the driving greats and one of the great characters in all of NASCAR. He also kept Chevrolet in the winner's circle for a long time. He was a master car builder.

To understand and appreciate Junior you have to know something about his background.

Junior was one of many NASCAR drivers who got his start by running moonshine. You've read all the stories, and I'll be the first to admit that they sound like something some writer would make up —fiction—but I assure you, they are all true. These guys really did run white liquor, and they ended up in real cops-and-robbers chases on back roads. Junior even served some time in the federal prison in Chillicothe, Ohio. But he wasn't a desperado. He was just the opposite; he was one of the kindest and most honest men I ever met.

A lot of men like Junior came from Southern families who had been in the moonshine business for generations. They were hill people, and they felt like they had a God-given right to make white lightning. There is a belief in the Southern mountains that there are two forms of lightning, white and red. A fire started by the strike of white lightning, they say, can't be put out; it has to burn itself out. But a red lightning fire is easily put out. So you can see where they got the name. And if you ever tasted it, there would be no doubt.

But there are a lot of people, particularly down South, that still prefer white liquor. And men like Junior and Bob Flock and Buddy Shuman and Curtis Turner hauled it long before they became stock-car racing greats. In fact, some of their wildest and certainly bravest deeds were done on the dark back roads of the Virginias and the Carolinas, running wide-open, often with their headlights off, a Fed hot on their tail.

It's no wonder that they were immediate successes when they turned to NASCAR. Junior told me a lot of wild tales about those early days. My favorite was one about Bob Flock, who was one of three successful brothers from the earliest days of NASCAR—Bob, Tim, and Fonty. Well, Bob is the one who ran liquor.

"At Lakewood [a racetrack in Atlanta], they had a ban on anybody racing that had ever been arrested," he said. That made for some pretty funny episodes. Once the cops tried to stop the races, and the fans ran off the cops. And they wouldn't let Bob Flock race at Lakewood because he had been arrested for hauling moonshine. So one night he waited until the race had already started—they were already running—and he just came onto the track in the back straightaway. Well, when the cops found out that he was in the race, they started chasing him. On the track. It was like an episode of the Keystone Kops; the race cars came sliding around that old dirt track, pushing and bumping, with dust flying, and here came the cops, right in the middle of the action.

After several laps Bob gave the high sign to his buddies in the pits, Junior continued, and the next time around, Bob came right down through the pits and right out the back gate the guys had opened for him. He went right out onto the street with the cops hot in pursuit. Right through downtown Atlanta. He finally gave himself up because he was running out of gas. "Well, hell, what did I do wrong?" he asked as he got out of his race car.

■

Junior was a great race-car driver and one of the best car builders who ever hit NASCAR. He is also a very colorful man. They tell the story of the year he came out of the hills near Ronda, North Carolina, to drive a few Grand National races. It must have been around 1953. Well, he looked so good that Bill France, who dreamed up NASCAR in the first place and ran it until he retired in the late seventies—to tell you the truth, he still may be running it—but, anyway, France went to Junior after one of his good races and said, "Junior, you're really doing well."

"Thank you," Junior said.

"In fact," said Bill, "you're doing so well that we expect you to drive all thirty races on the schedule this year."

"Naw, Bill, I'm only gonna run a few of them, just to see if I like it or not," replied Junior.

"But you're committed, Junior."

"Naw, Bill, what it is, is I'm *involved*," Junior said.

"You're *committed*, Junior," Bill said, a little more sternly.

Junior looked at him for a minute, and then he drawled, "Bill, you've got the words all wrong. Now, listen: If you sit down to breakfast tomorrow to bacon and eggs, the chicken is *involved*. The pig is *committed*."

Junior ran the races he wanted to.

Driving for Junior made me feel like I was really a part of the NASCAR past. Racing was already starting to change. Many of the original hell-raisers were gone, and the sponsorship money was getting bigger, so the companies demanded a better image of their drivers. That took care of a lot of the parties. I felt sorry for the guys who were coming into Grand National then. I mean, guys such as Darrell Waltrip and Dale Earnhardt and Neil Bonnett, who came into racing in the seventies, missed a lot by not being around for the wild carryings-on of people like Little Joe Weatherly and Curtis Turner and Soapy Castles and Darel Dieringer and the rest. Well, I had always felt like maybe I missed some by not coming along a little sooner myself. But by being with Junior I had a bridge to the earliest days, the time when stock-car racing was really stock-car racing. Those guys raced cars right out of the parking lot.

I was having a great time driving for Junior, and I was having an even better time listening to his stories and eating his wife Flossie's fried chicken at the racetrack. We were family.

There was a sequence of pictures, showing Junior flipping a car in one of the old beach races at Daytona. That part wasn't too unusual; everybody flipped cars in the sand when it got rough late in the race, particularly coming out of the south turn where you left the mile-long pavement section and turned to start back up the beach in the sand. But the last photo in this series showed Junior climbing out of the back window of the '53 Pontiac, even before the car had come to a complete stop. He never would tell anyone how he got in the backseat in the first place.

Well, I don't know, either, but I can tell you how quick he was at getting out of a tight place. The story starts in a private airplane, and Junior really doesn't like to fly. But we had a friend in a parts warehouse in Charleston, and he wanted Junior and I to fly down there for a store opening. He said he would have his pilot come over to Ronda, North Carolina, and pick up Junior and then come down to Timmonsville and pick me up. It took a lot of talking, but I got Junior to agree to it.

The guy who owned the parts place was Gwinn McNeill, who was an ex–Piedmont Airlines pilot. It was his twin-engine plane. That made Junior feel a little bit better, but he was still nervous. He rode in the back, and I rode on the right side in front. It was the same seating coming back.

When we got close to Timmonsville on the way back, it was night.

Gwinn radioed in, they turned on the marker lights for the field, and he started his final approach.

"You're a little high for this old grass strip, Gwinn," I said. I hated to tell a former airline pilot how to land, but he *was* too high.

"I'm all right," he said.

Junior was leaning forward. Gwinn kept coming in too high.

"Gwinn, I hate to tell a man how to fly his own airplane, but you're too high," I said.

"No, we'll make it," he said.

"Gwinn," I said, "you're not gonna make it. You're too damn high and you're too damn fast."

Junior was almost in the front seat.

"We're okay," he said.

"Listen, it's easy to go around and try it again," I said. "I mean, I've landed here a thousand times. You need to line up again. Get lower and slower."

"No," he said. We were over the end of the runway by then, and he dropped it in.

When we hit the grass, we were still doing about 120 miles an hour. The grass was wet. He put on his brakes and the plane started to slide. He had his brakes locked up, and we were still going as fast as we had been in the air.

Here's what was around us: There was a big ditch at the end of the runway; there were hangars on one side; and they were doing some construction on the other side, so there were bulldozers parked there. None of them very good choices for stopping. We were going sideways, still doing 120 miles an hour, when we went by the bulldozers. They looked like hotels. We were headed straight for the hangar. But just before we hit the landing gear collapsed and the fuselage hit the ground. The right wing dug in, and the force tore it completely off. The plane was ripped to pieces.

When the plane came to a stop about five feet from the hangars, I was still in the right seat beside where the only door had been, but Gwinn was sitting on my lap. We looked outside, and there was Junior standing in the middle of the runway. The door by me was the only door, and how or when he got past me and out of it, I'll never know. Junior was an escape artist. I don't know how they ever kept him in Chillicothe.

I didn't know if the plane was going to catch on fire or not, and Gwinn is a big man, but I picked him up and I sat him back on his own seat and got out of there.

The plane had been brand-new, but it was totaled. I got my plane out to fly Gwinn home, and he started to get in the right seat—you remember, that's the one usually reserved for the copilot. Junior tapped him on the shoulder and said, "Mac, you get in the back. I can do that good."

■

My years with Junior were the best ones I ever had. Up until then I always ran hard; in fact, I guess I ran too hard, because I didn't always finish the race. I used up a lot of cars if you want to know the truth. I learned a lot from Banjo and from the Wood Brothers, but with Junior I calmed down a little.

In my very first year with Junior I not only won four races, but I finished in the top ten nineteen times out of twenty-eight races. It was a result of Junior calming me down and Herb Nab building strong, fast engines. The key word, of course, is *finished.* The next year I won ten races and a quarter of a million dollars.

This all began during the period I was talking about way back there in the part Bill Neely calls the prologue; you remember where I said that I wasn't going to spend too much time with the winning years? Well, the years with Junior are that period. It sure changed my image, though, I'll tell you that. Why, they even put up a sign just as you come into Timmonsville that says: TIMMONSVILLE, SOUTH CARO-LINA, HOME OF CALE YARBOROUGH, NASCAR CHAMPION.

People around home expected me to change, but I tried hard not to. I still went coon hunting and fishing with my old buddies, and I hung out in exactly the same places. I didn't feel any different than I ever had. I mean, I was still the same Cale Yarborough who had grown up on a farm in Sardis. There wasn't a thing I was ever ashamed of, so why should I change?

I remember one day when we were getting ready to go hunting and I was putting on the old overalls I always hunted in. The knees were worn through, and a fastener on one of the bibs had broken years before, so I was twisting a piece of wire around the metal button, and saw my buddies looking at me like I was crazy. I guess they figured that I could afford a new pair of overalls.

I said, "If I win Daytona again this year, I'm gonna get me a new pair of overalls."

I still haven't gotten them, even though I've won ten races at Daytona since then.

■

As good as racing can be to you, you're never immune from heartache in automobile racing. In 1975, at Talladega, Alabama, I had qualified well and was in good shape to win the race. I was confident. Before the race, Tiny Lund and I were talking about how much things had changed,—for the best, we agreed. He asked me if he could fly home with me after the race. His wife would drive up from their fishing camp in Cross, South Carolina, and get him. It sounded good to me; it would be a nice break because flying home after a race is not only tiring, it's also boring.

It didn't work out that way. During the race Tiny got sideways and hit the wall. His car bounced back across the track and stalled right in the middle of the backstretch, with the driver's side facing oncoming race traffic. A car hit him broadside at about 200 miles an hour.

When I came by, I could see him slumped forward in the car. I knew that nobody could survive a blow like that. I knew he was dead.

It took them a long time to get his body out of the car, and I looked somewhere else every time I came around under the yellow flag. I tried with everything that was in me to put it out of my mind, but there was no way. I remembered all of the times we had slept in the car, and I remembered how we always traveled together when both of us were coming up through the dirt-track ranks of the Pee Dee. I remembered how he used to come over to my car and help me work on it. Tiny was the closest to me of any of them.

For the first time I wondered why he did it.

I was able to put it in the back of my mind when they dropped the green flag again, but it took me a long time to stop thinking about it. I still do when I think of the old days. But, like all the other times, I knew that life had to go on. And I still felt like it could never happen to me. You have to think that; otherwise, it would be all over.

I suppose a lot of us did some wild things off the track to take our minds off what might happen on the track. I can't say why, but I know strange things were always happening to me: like the time Junior gave me a bear cub. I flew up to get her, and we just put her in a cardboard box in the back of the plane. It was easy.

I was flying alone, but that was no problem; the bear was only half grown. It wasn't that simple. About fifteen minutes before I got back to Timmonsville I looked around, and the bear was just getting out of the box. She had eaten through the side of it. She was almost loose in the plane. I reached back and turned the box over with the hole on the bottom side, trying to hold it down with one hand and fly the plane with the other. It wasn't one of my best landings.

Suzie was around for a long time. I kept her in an old cage I had gotten from a friend who worked for the Department of Highways— a small four-by-four cage they once used to keep a prisoner in. We won't even get into that.

But the bear story is far overshadowed by the lion story. I guess it was my zoo period. A friend who knew how much I loved animals, and how much they loved me, gave me a lion cub. It was only a few days old and its mother had died, so Betty Jo and I raised it on a baby bottle, and it was as tame as any dog I ever had. It was never shut up a day in its life.

We gave him the original name of Leo, and we raised him with a Springer spaniel puppy, so Leo really thought he was a dog. It was fun to watch the two of them roll and play. As Leo got older some funny stories developed: We were having our new house built out on the farm near Sardis, and the electrician was under the house, working. No problem, except that Leo heard him under there and went under to see what was going on. The electrician heard a noise and looked over one of the heating ducts to see what it was. When he saw Leo, he almost tore out all of the ducting getting out of there. He sent his assistant back to finish the job and pick up his truck.

Leo was as tame as a house cat; it's just that when he got to weigh about five hundred pounds, he knocked people flat when he jumped up on them. He was just trying to be friendly, doing just what the Springer did. The only difference was that the dog only weighed about thirty-five pounds.

Leo and the dog had full range of the farm, so they played in the woods a lot, because I guess it was cool in there. One day a couple of little black boys who lived on a neighboring farm used the woods for a shortcut. Betty Jo heard their screams and she went running. There they were, up in a tree, yelling their heads off, and at the base of the tree were Leo and the dog, sitting there, looking up. They wanted to play. The boys didn't.

It was the last time they ever came through the woods. It may have been the last time they ever went through *any* woods.

By the time Leo got to be full-grown, I knew that I had to get rid of him. He still wasn't the least bit mean, but he was just too big, so I gave him to the Spartanburg Zoo.

They put Leo in the cage with the other lions, and that didn't work at all. He cowered in the corner of the cage, looking at the lions in fear. He didn't know what they were or, at that point, even what he was, but he was sure he wasn't one of *them.*

They finally realized that Leo was as tame as I said, so they let him roam the grounds. Leo went from cage to cage and finally took up with the wolves. That was a lot more like it. But the full roaming privileges didn't work there, either, because zoo officials became afraid that he would hurt somebody, so they decided to have him declawed. They had him put to sleep.

For a long time after Leo left, we all looked around before we opened any door. It was hard to break the habit. We had always looked, because, you see, Leo would come in the house or get in the car, just like a cat or a dog. He sat up in the car, and I'll tell you one thing, it sure turned a few heads when you were driving down the highway.

While we're talking about those days in the seventies, I guess we have to bring up Curtis again. I mean, I don't suppose anybody will ever write a book about stock-car racing without talking a lot about Curtis Turner. People will be writing books fifty years from now and still be talking about Ol' Pops because he was such a rare character and such a great race-car driver.

Curtis's years of driving for the Wood Brothers must have given the guy the idea for *The Odd Couple*, because that's how different Curtis and Glen and Leonard were. The Wood Brothers are soft-spoken, hardworking Christian gentlemen; Curtis, well, you've already heard a lot of Curtis Turner stories, so you know what he was like.

Leonard told me once that he got to the racetrack on race morning and there was a body in the race car. It was Curtis sleeping it off. He got up, rubbed his eyes, and said, "Mornin', boss. You ready to go racin'?"

Leonard just shook his head. He must have thought Curtis was a scoundrel. But Curtis, as bad a shape as he was in that morning, went out there and won the race.

"He was an iron man," Leonard said. "I don't suppose there's anybody in the world who could do what Curtis did—every week."

As much as they disapproved of his conduct, the Wood Brothers had to admire the man's driving. Everybody did.

Curtis may have been hard on equipment—he had to be, as hard as he drove—but he won a lot of races. You know, he isn't credited with winning too many Grand National races, but there's a reason for that. He tried to organize the race-car drivers—into a union, believe it or not—in the sixties, and Bill France, who ruled NASCAR with an iron hand, exiled Curtis from running in his circuit for a number of years. During that time Curtis was running every outlaw track he could find. It's hard to tell just how many races he did win, because nobody ever heard much about those races.

Bill finally gave in and let Curtis come back to NASCAR, and he won some more races, but he wasn't around long enough to really get back into the swing of things.

Curtis loved flying his airplane about as much as he did driving a race car. And he was about as wild in it too.

Curtis and Fireball were out one night flying over Daytona Beach.

"Hey, Balls," he said, "let's buzz the beach, you know, out there around Ormond where all the lovers are."

It sounded fine to Fireball, so they flew up north of Ormond and came in over the beach at about twenty feet off the sand, the power cut on their engines. When they got just about to the spot where all the guys and gals did whatever they did on the beach, Curtis flipped on the wingtip landing lights and revved up the engines, full-bore. Well, to the people lying on the beach it must have looked and sounded like the world's biggest semi coming down the beach. The truck that came out of nowhere.

I guess there were people running and diving into the bushes and the ocean in all stages of undress.

"It was the damnedest thing you ever saw," Fireball said. "Why, I bet a lot of those people never did go back, even to get their clothes."

Curtis started flying when he first went into the timber business. He wasn't in the business on the small scale like I was; he was in it in a *big* way up in Virginia. I guess he made a million dollars in timber, but he dribbled most of it away. People said he could estimate a forest better than any man who ever lived. He could fly over and, in one pass, tell you with unbelievable accuracy how many board feet of lumber was in there.

It's how he learned to fly so well, zooming in here and buzzing there. He was a good pilot. I knew how well he could fly an airplane; that's why it was hard for me to believe it when I heard the news.

Curtis Turner died in a plane crash in North Carolina.

He had been teaching a friend of his how to fly, and they just flew into the side of a mountain. The other guy had a history of heart problems, so the CAA officials who investigated the crash determined that the guy had a heart attack and collapsed over the controls, jamming them. Apparently Pops couldn't pull the plane out of it.

It was a big loss to everybody. But, you know, it was almost like there was a plan to it. Racing was changing so much; it was no longer the rough-and-tumble world that it has been in the fifties and sixties.

It was almost like there wasn't a place left for Curtis anymore.

It certainly wasn't that he couldn't do it; it seemed like he didn't *want* to do it anymore. It wasn't any fun for him. Little Joe and Fireball and most of his buddies were gone. I'm almost glad that he didn't see how much the sport was going to change. But I still miss him. Everybody does.

■

The Daytona 500 in 1979 may have been my wildest finish. But to understand that one, and how drafting is used, you have to know about the 1976 Daytona 500. Drafting doesn't always work the way you hope it will.

Here's what happened.

"I guess it had to happen," Richard Petty said after the race. "Me and David have been running side by side so many times at the finish line that it was inevitable."

And inevitable it was. I had problems, and A.J. and Buddy Baker and even Darrell Waltrip were long gone from the leaders. It was Petty and Pearson, running nose-to-tail at the end. Petty was in the lead, and Pearson was running in the vacuum right behind him. They roared through the thirty-one-degree banks at the east end of the track, down the eighteen-degree slope of the tri-oval, through turn one and two and down the three-thousand-foot backstretch. It was the last lap, and everybody instinctively knew that it was coming. Pearson pulled out of the draft and shot in front of Petty as they went into the third turn. The hundred thousand fans hunkered up their shoulders just a bit, unconsciously trying to give him a little more room to tuck in the Mercury.

The crowd wasn't over the effect of the first slingshot when Petty pulled out from behind Pearson and made *his* move. He cranked the Dodge left, dropping down under Pearson as they blasted into the fourth turn. They were running side by side coming off the high bank. It was a move few would even try. I thought it was cool. Petty edged forward as they entered the tri-oval. Pearson was a foot from the wall.

Petty was almost clear of Pearson when he hit the dip. His car moved to the right, clipping Pearson's left front fender. The Mercury slammed into the wall, rebounded across the track, and spun into the infield, demolishing the entire front end. Petty crashed into the wall two hundred feet in front of the spot where Pearson had made contact. His car, too, spun into the infield, badly damaged.

The first thing Pearson did was get on his two-way radio to the pits. "Where's Petty? Where's Petty? Did he get across the finish line?"

"No, no," shouted someone in his pit crew, "Stand on it."

Pearson had the foresight to push in his clutch when the car hit the wall, throwing the car into neutral. His engine was still running, so he dumped it into first and stood on it. Grass and dirt flew from behind his rear wheels, and the car sloshed back and forth, heading for the track. Petty's Dodge was dead. He had slid backward, stopping one hundred yards short of the finish line. Had he spun past the line, even off in the grass, he would have been the winner. But he hadn't, and Pearson gunned the Mercury toward the starter, who held the checkered flag over his head. There was a look of total disbelief on Petty's face as the Wood Brothers' car limped past him.

It looked as if Pearson should be rolling into a junkyard instead of Victory Lane, but Pearson pulled himself from the car, flashing a smile at his sponsors, the Purolator people.

Later Petty went to Pearson and said, "I'm really sorry I hit you, David." Pearson replied, "Aw, that's okay, Richard, you didn't do it on purpose."

What else could they have said?

That's what happened in 1976. Here's the way it went in 1979.

It had been a hectic day. It had rained for a while and everything was a mess. We had to wait until the track dried off, and then everything got hot and sticky. Not long into the race, Bobby Allison and his brother, Donnie, tangled between one and two. I was right behind them. I had to spin to keep from plowing into them, and when I went into the infield, there was so much mud that the car bogged down. They had to bring a wrecker over, and I was two laps behind by the time I got back in the race.

Donnie's car had gotten right back in the race, so he was leading, but I made up a lot of time—I mean, I was really trucking—and in about fifty laps I got right up behind Donnie, in his draft. I knew I had more horses than he did, so I just stayed back there, waiting until the last lap, when I planned to pull out and pass him before we got to the start/finish line. It couldn't miss.

It doesn't always go like you plan; that's racing. I decided to pass him coming down the back straightaway on the last lap, rather than wait until I got to four, because I saw Bobby way up there, slowing down. He was two or three laps down, so I knew he had to be slowing down so he could block for Donnie when we got to three. It would have kept me from getting past. I told Junior on the radio: "I'm gonna have a problem up there, so I'm makin' my move now."

"Stand on it," Junior said.

I pulled out of the draft and down under Donnie as we started into the back straightaway. He moved down to the left, forcing me down low on the track. He kept coming down on me. I kept moving toward the infield. Finally there wasn't any room left. In fact, I was off in the wet grass, but I was still going 200 miles an hour, so I didn't bog down. There was only one place to go, back on the track. I turned the wheel hard to the right, and our cars hit. I could feel the grinding metal. Both cars slid up across the track. They bounced together again, but I held my ground. They hit a third time, but I kept steering to the right. Donnie was one surprised cat. There was no stopping it; the cars crashed into the concrete retaining wall on the outside edge of the track, and then they both spun into the infield.

Behind us, Richard Petty went by. He had been way back in third place, but now he was going to win the 500. I didn't care at that point. I was too mad.

Bobby had pulled his race car into the grass. He was running back to see if his brother was all right. I flew out of that car and decked Bobby. And then I went over and punched Donnie. I mean, it was the worst thing I had ever seen in racing. I'd do the same thing if it happened again.

■

During my eight years with Junior—from 1973 through 1980—I won three NASCAR Grand National Championships. One year I finished all thirty of the races on the schedule, and nobody ever had done that. Another one of those years I finished in the top ten twenty-seven times out of thirty. It was a real tribute to the Holly Farms team of Junior and Herb, and it gave me real confidence in my equipment. All I had to do was push the button and aim it.

One of the things that made me feel good was my superspeedway record with Junior. I won twenty-four races. But I think my short track record was even better than that. When I started with Junior, I heard some of the drivers talking one day in the pits. One of them said, "Well, we won't have to worry about Cale on the short tracks, anyway. He can't handle them." It bothered me at first, and then it made me mad. I was determined to show them. I guess they didn't remember where I had learned to drive a race car. In my years with Junior I won more short track races—twenty-nine—than any other driver. And I won three times as many as the guy who made the remark. I won't even mention his name because I don't want to embarrass him.

In 1978, I won more than half a million dollars in Junior Johnson's Oldsmobile. And in the years I was with Junior, I won three million dollars. You can see why I was so happy with Junior.

Like I said, sponsorship was getting real big by the end of the seventies. Sponsors were important to all of us because the cost of building a race car had gone up to probably $100,000, and all of the expenses had skyrocketed. Winning races wouldn't hack it anymore, so you had to depend on more than purses; you had to depend on sponsors. It's why you see so many decals and names on the sides of race cars today. *That's* what's paying the bills.

Well, I had a meeting scheduled with Junior and the people from Mountain Dew—as in the soda pop. They were going to sponsor Junior's car in 1981. I was all dressed up with a suit and tie on, and I went out the back door of our new house—the big, sprawling brick one that sits on my 1,300 acres of land near Sardis—the place I always wanted. My private twin-engine plane with my own personal pilot was waiting for me at the Florence Airport. I'm not bragging, I'm just showing you what racing and sponsors and car owners like Junior can do for you, even for a kid from a little old farm in South Carolina. In fact, I might still be driving for him if it hadn't been for a casual conversation with my girls.

My daughter B.J. and some of her friends were sitting on the back steps, looking bored to death.

"Why are you all sittin' around?" I asked. "I mean, why aren't you out riding your bikes or something?"

"My bike is broken, Daddy," B.J. said.

"Well, why didn't you tell me?"

"I *did*, Daddy," B.J. said. "I told you three times."

"You mean to tell me that you told me three times that your bike was broken," I said, "and I didn't do anything about it?"

"That's right," they said in unison.

"You all wait right here," I said. I went into the house and called the sponsor. "Something's come up at home," I said. "We'll have to reschedule the meeting."

I took off my suit and put on a pair of jeans and a work shirt. I spent the next two days fixing all the kids' bicycles. They were a mess. It took me three trips to the store to get parts, but I got all of them in perfect shape.

The next week I told Junior that I wanted to cut back on my racing schedule. I figured that I had enough money to live on comfortably the rest of my life, so I wanted to spend some time with my family for a change. I guess I hadn't realized how much time I had been away from them over the years, but because of some broken bikes, I learned that my kids were growing up without knowing their daddy. That was going to change.

I knew that Junior was committed as far as the sponsor was concerned and that he would have to put the car in every race of the 1981 season, so I told him that I was going to have to quit and find a ride with someone who only wanted to run the superspeedways, which was about half the races. I told him why. Junior understood, but then I knew he would.

I gave up a lot, but I gained a lot more.

I still had racing, even though it was on a limited schedule, but I needed *some* of it, and I had a Honda/Mazda dealership in Florence and some dry-cleaning places and a Goodyear tire dealership with Billy Atkinson, as well as some rental property. Besides, I had saved a lot of my winnings, so I sure wasn't going to starve. What I was going to do was give equal billing to my family. For a change. I got the ride I wanted, with M. C. Anderson. I drove a good Buick race car for two years and won $350,000, driving half the number of races that I had been driving. And I can say that I felt I had the best of both worlds.

THERE ARE ONLY TWO PARTS TO RACING:

WINNING AND LOSING.

THERE'S NO SECOND OR THIRD OR FOURTH.

YOU WIN OR YOU LOSE.

14

■

There is more to driving a stock car at 200 miles an hour than it looks to someone sitting in the grandstands watching somebody else do it, especially if you're going to drive one well. And there certainly is more to building one than just stuffing a big motor in it and pointing the driver toward the racetrack. It's important to have a top engine man and car builder and a good pit crew. You have to stay on top of everything. If one team goes particularly fast one week, you can bet that by the next week there will be half a dozen teams that have found out the formula.

The secret of going faster is often discovered by accident. One guy will stumble across something that works, and he wins for a while until everybody else breaks his code. But there have been times— many times, in fact—when the secret isn't exactly legal. Cheating was a lot more common in the early days than it is today, and I could write a book on that subject alone, but I'll just give you a couple examples.

One year at Daytona, Smokey Yunick's Chevelle was getting more miles out of a tank of gas than anybody else's race car, even the other Chevys. The car could stay out there four or five laps longer than anybody else, which meant maybe one pit stop less. It was enough of an advantage to win the race. It made NASCAR officials suspicious, so they checked Smokey's car. I mean, they checked every place for a fuel reserve, even in the roll bars, which had been used on cars for hidden fuel before. They checked the fire extinguisher, which also had turned up fuel in another car once. Nothing. As a matter of fact, they took out the fuel tank and checked for anything unusual.

Smokey put up with it as long as he could, and then he got mad. "That's it!" he said. "You guys have checked everything three times. I'm takin' the car back to my garage." He got in it and drove away. After he left, somebody noticed that he had forgotten his gas tank. It was still lying there. They never did find out where the extra fuel was, but it obviously was somewhere; otherwise, he couldn't have driven the car without a gas tank.

The other incident involved Cotton Owens, who showed up at Atlanta one year with one of his usually fast Dodges. This one was so much faster than any of the other Dodges that NASCAR inspectors watched it closely. There was something about the car that just didn't seem right, but they couldn't put their fingers on it. They called it in and checked everything. Again, there seemed to be nothing. Still, there was something about the car. In desperation they hauled out the templates, which were full-scale forms—gauges built from stock-bodied production cars. Placed over a car, they could tell if any alterations had been made to the body of the car. It was supposed to be a snug fit all around.

Cotton's car could have driven through the templates at 200 miles an hour.

What he had done was build a perfect seven-eighths-scale reproduction of a Dodge body. It was slightly smaller in all dimensions than a stock-bodied car, and that gave it less overall area, thus cutting down on wind resistance. It went faster. It must have taken weeks to create it, and the workmanship was perfect. It gives you some idea how creative cheating can be.

But when NASCAR was much younger, cheating used to be commonplace. It had to happen. They started with strictly stock cars, which obviously didn't handle at all on a racetrack, so they had to improve them. It was against the rules to change suspension parts, so little by little they managed to sneak on stronger shocks and springs and spindles; and when everybody was doing it, NASCAR had to change their rules to make those parts legal. Race cars have to be much stiffer, suspension-wise, than passenger cars; otherwise, they couldn't take the turns as well or as fast as they do, or they would never last an entire race. The same is true with all the parts.

As the car builders modified things on their own, NASCAR kept changing the rules. As a result the cars got better and faster and a lot safer. A lot. Today a race car is not any more "stock" than an Indy car is something you drive to work. A Grand National stock car is a sophisticated race car.

And the drivers have to be just as sophisticated to be competitive. When you have a combination of driver and crew and mechanic who have their act together, you've got a combination that's hard to beat. That's why it's so tough to answer the question I get so often: "Who's the best driver you've ever had to drive against?" Well, I can't answer that. One week it might be Richard Petty, and the next week it might be Buddy Baker or Bobby Allison or Dale Earnhardt or Darrell Waltrip or any number of others. A lot of them are tough to beat. And the track itself makes a difference. Some drivers are particularly good on short tracks, and some are world-beaters on superspeedways. I have always felt good on both. And the fact that I've even done well on road courses makes me particularly happy. I mean, it's an ego builder to beat the best in the road-racing world on a course like Riverside in equal equipment, like we use in the International Race of Champions, where everybody drives racing Camaros; but I've done it. A lot of the NASCAR guys have. I think it says a lot for our drivers.

You know, you hear Richard Petty referred to a lot as "King Richard," but I've never felt that he was the king of stock-car racing.

222

I've always felt the name went with *his* name, you know, like King Richard the Lion-hearted. Don't get me wrong, I'm not saying he isn't good, he is. Richard is one of the best, but it's something that you would expect. He started with the best equipment that anybody ever had because his daddy, Lee, was a champion, so he just handed Richard a winning race car and all the knowledge in the world, and Richard has made the most of it. I'm not knocking that; I wish it had happened to me. It would have saved me a lot of years in getting to where I am. But as for "king," I couldn't pick any one driver. It's just like it was in the old days: there are a lot of really good drivers out there, just as many today as there were in the sixties or seventies.

Maybe they're not as tough as, say, Curtis Turner. They don't party all night, go to the track, run 500 miles—up front—and then go back to the party and say, "Now, where were we?" But they're physically tough. You have to be able to herd a 3,700-pound stock car around for 500 miles at speeds of over 200 miles an hour.

The technique that it takes is complicated. Just the drafting alone will get your attention. In case you don't know, drafting is what we are doing when we drive right up on the bumper of a car in front and stay there, a foot away, at 200 miles an hour or whatever he's running. It's one of the things that happens out there that can be explained.

Any moving object, no matter how fast it's going, creates a pocket of air called a slipstream, which is teardrop-shaped. When a car pulls up behind you, it breaks into your slipstream and creates one longer slipstream over both cars. It makes the slipstream more streamlined, it makes both cars go faster and both get better gas mileage. We all do it. And when the car in back breaks out of the draft, it gets a little boost of speed. It's called slingshotting, and you see a lot of it late in a race. It's why I would rather be running second than first on the last lap, because there is nothing the guy in front can do to keep you back there.

When I'm trying to gain speed, I draft anything that's moving. As you're working your way through traffic you can get a draft from even the slower cars; it may be for only a few seconds, but it moves you along quicker. It's why some guys can get through traffic better than others.

Drafting was always around and the drivers were always doing it, but they didn't realize it until the Daytona Speedway opened. With the extra speeds the two-and-a-half-mile track brought, you could feel the effect that much more, so they talk about it being "discovered" at Daytona. They didn't discover it there; they "realized" it there.

But not everybody can do it successfully because, well, because not everybody can handle a loose car, and a car gets looser in a draft anyway, so it makes it a little like driving on wet pavement. Loose, of course, refers to a car that is a little—what can you say?—*squirrelly* on a turn—not too stable. But anybody who came up through dirt tracks like Tiny and Lee Roy and I—and a lot of others—is used to that feeling.

The interesting thing is that people refer to Curtis and me as the best with a loose car, and neither one of us ever professed to be a chassis genius. I can't tell you what it takes under the car to make it handle, but I sure can feel it in the seat of my pants.

Oh, I can tell my crew chief what the car is doing out there, and from that he can determine what should be done. There are screw jacks inside the car, at each corner, and they can jack some weight around, take some off here, and put it on there, or they can change the stagger of the tires, by putting a slightly larger or smaller one on this corner or that corner, whatever. They can alter the tension of the springs. All of those things help in setting up a car.

Once your crew chief is satisfied that the car is set up as good as he can get it, he starts timing other fast cars to see how fast they're going through the corners and down the straightaway. He might find out that you're not in as good a shape as you thought, so it's back to run-and-change.

The track surface can change during a race as it gets hotter and has more rubber on it, so you might have to change your driving style. But when you get the right combination of spring tension, weight distribution, tires, spoiler size, sway bars, and other suspension parts, then it's up to the technique of the driver. The crew chief has done all he can do.

You have to know how to go into the turns and how to come out; in other words, what speed do you go in and how fast can you come off, and where on the track is the best groove? You have to know how to work your way around every foot of the track. And you have to know when to pit. Obviously your pit crew has to keep you informed. Thank goodness for radios today. I really don't know what we did before the two-way radio. Sure, we had pit boards, but a pit board is hard to read when you're going by wide-open and there are a dozen or so out there in about the same place. It's hard to pick yours out.

I don't talk much on the radio, except maybe when we're running slow under the yellow flag. The rest of the time I listen, and my guys keep me informed as to how fast I'm going and where I am in the race and how everybody else is doing. I plan my strategy from that.

At times I've won and been so tired, I couldn't get out of the car. I've played every kind of sport there is, and I don't know of one that takes more out of you, physically and mentally, than racing cars.

But if you're leading, you don't feel tired at all. I don't notice the headache or the ringing in my ears until I get out of the car. Your back can be breaking and you'll never notice it on a good day. But it's terrible when you wind up running fifth or sixth, two or three laps behind. That's when you get in the shower and say, "Damn, man, I need to find a better way to make a living."

One thing's for sure, you never get bored out there, particularly on a short track, because there is always too much happening. Even if I am running badly, I still have to spend every second staying out of the way of other cars. It is one big mess, with no long straightaways when you can scrunch down in the seat and relax your shoulders, and there's *never* a break in traffic. They start forty cars at times on some of those half-mile, high-banked asphalt tracks.

But on a short track we can take out some of our aggressions. There, if you get mad at a guy, you can whale him a good one, and it doesn't hurt a thing. It's much tenser on a superspeedway; you can't take it out on the other guy, because you certainly don't want to make him crash at 200 miles an hour.

The nice thing about a short track is that a guy might do something to you on a superspeedway, and the next week you can take it out on him on a short track and knock the hell out of him.

There are people all the way around those short tracks. It's like being in a big bowl. You can drive down in the first turn, and it looks like you're going to run into the crowd. You could pick out your own mother. And there's never a straight body panel on any car when the race is over. There are black tire marks all over the sides, and the grilles and trunks are all mashed in. That's racing.

Say somebody goes into the corner, gets on his brakes quicker than you do, and you bump into him. Well, if you had a mind to, you could stay mad all day on a short track, but you've got to give a little and take a little. And bump a little yourself. That's just the way short-track racing is. Man, it sure is fun.

If two-ton Dodge cars traveling at 120 miles and hour is "fun," what about the dangers? Well, I'll tell you, crashing is way down on the list of things any of us look forward to. You don't think much about hit-the-wall and limp-into-the-pits types of crashes, but you do think about the crashes like the one I had at Daytona in 1983, when my car flipped end over end half a dozen times. Crashes like that get your attention.

Most of the time you're conscious of everything that's happening, even though it happens superquick. You're always turning the steering wheel and hoping that something else will happen or that you're not going to hit the wall at the angle you think you are. I'm on the brakes and steering or doing something. I've never had time to get down on the floorboards and cover up my head.

There's no one thing I can remember ever flashing through my mind, because I'm consumed with getting out of the trouble I've already gotten into. You can't steer when you're upside down, but I do. I do everything I can to land it.

A short track is a beat-and-bang kind of thing, but you have to take good care of your equipment. I don't mean the body, that's something you don't worry about; I mean the brakes and the suspension. And pitting is more important on a short track than it is on a long one. On a long track you can make up time a lot easier because it's not as tough to get through traffic—it's spread out more. You may be able to draft back in front in a single lap, but on a short track it may take you a hundred laps to get back up front. You have to conserve your brakes, so you don't use them as much as you would like to. You don't run as hard or as deep into the corners; you let the car go in fast, but you let it go in and out more by itself, instead of running wide-open in there and then standing on the brakes.

The tracks have different personalities. Martinsville, for instance, is not a standard short track. It's fairly flat with long straights and tight turns. It's like a drag strip down each side, so you really have to take care of your brakes. It's probably the toughest short track on the circuit—a narrow, slam-bam racetrack with one-groove turns. You have to drive it as much with your head as you do with your foot.

Bristol has a lot of the same characteristics. You have to have your car set up perfectly; otherwise, you'll get lapped in a hurry. On short tracks everybody uses the same groove.

A lot of the superspeedways are one-groove tracks, too—Darlington is. You have to go into one as low as you possibly can, let the car drift up about a car width, and then get back on the throttle. You try to hold that same line through two. On the back stretch you have to stay low and let it drift up close to the wall, staying up near the wall through three and four, then pull it down coming off four. The wall sort of juts out coming off the turn, so you have to have exactly the right line.

At Atlanta you have to search for the right groove because the turns are wide, and what works for you might not work for somebody else. A lot of times I change grooves during the race as the track or the car changes. If I'm running the bottom groove and the track gets slick, I may move up. The man who can find the right groove is way ahead of the game.

A lot of drivers stay with the same groove all day; when it no longer works, they try to make it work, and it usually doesn't. So they lose time and speed. If the car changes—say your tires grow because of the extreme heat—you have to be aware of that and change to whatever tire works at that particular time.

At the speeds we're running today, Daytona is almost a one-groove track. It takes the whole turn to get through, so you have to go in low and let it drift up near the top of the high banks. Talladega is wider than Daytona, and the asphalt is better, so you can pick out different grooves.

But most drivers usually follow the man that's leading, so they can get into the fastest draft. If I'm trying to make up time, I find the groove that's the fastest and combine it with drafting to catch up. In a last-lap situation I may change the groove just to throw the competition off. I may have found a groove during the race that works, but I haven't used it that much, so I save it until the last lap. All of a sudden I'm in a groove that I know but which the other guys can't handle as well.

Strategy means everything.

As for being afraid, I can't even remember the first time I experienced fear, but I have been scared many times. The man who says he hasn't isn't telling the truth. I've already told you that my definition of courage is controlled fear, but there's more to driving than control. A lot of it is instinct. When I first started running the super-speedways and something happened in front of me, I had to think, "Now what do I have to do to get out of this?" By the time I figured it out, I was right in the middle of the problem. But I got to the point where I would get through it and *then* think about it. It paid off. And a time like that, after all, is no time to be afraid.

There have been lots of crashes I saw coming, but I wasn't afraid then. After it happened I might start shaking, but while I was waiting for it, I guess I was too busy to be afraid.

You never stop learning, so I think a driver needs to quit driving when he doesn't want to practice anymore. It means he's scared. If you look at a guy and you can put your hand down between his back and the seat, he's scared. Smokey Yunick says, "That's what was wrong with Fireball, and it killed him."

When you put all of the things together that I've been talking about, you have a winner. And even then it takes a lot of luck. As for losing, well, I guess you would have to say that I'm not a good loser. I don't make a big fuss on the outside like A.J., but I do on the inside. It hurts me to lose.

When you get right down to it, there are only two parts to racing: winning and losing. There's no second or third or fourth. You win or you lose.

I'm a bad loser if you want to know—or maybe I'm what people call a "gracious" loser. Whatever you call it, I just keep it to myself. But it's tough to smile at times when you've been out there all day, working like mad, and you lose. I'm burning inside, but nobody knows it.

When you get right down to it, I'm a dreamer, I guess, and I thank the Lord all the time for making me a dreamer and then giving me the ability to make it happen. But it's not that big a deal, it's just the way I am. Life is just like a parade; some want to play in the band, some want to be drum majors, some want to be clowns, some want to ride on the floats, some want to sit on the curb and watch everybody else, and some want to lead the parade. I always wanted to be the grand marshal. I've always tried to run out front.

THE WALLS OF RACING ARE PAINTED
RED WITH GUYS WHO NEVER LEARNED
TO CONTROL THEIR DESIRE.

15

■

Nobody has ever been able to figure out what it is that makes a great race-car driver. There must be something or maybe even some *things* that make a few guys stand out from the rest; but nobody has ever been able to put a finger on it.

Humpy Wheeler, who used to work for Firestone and now is president of the Charlotte Motor Speedway, has been a friend of mine since my first days of racing, and I guess he has spent more time trying to find out what makes a great race-car driver than anybody. He doesn't know for sure. Nobody does.

It should be a relatively easy thing to find out, but they have been working on it for a couple of decades now, and they still aren't sure. Listen, Humpy has even gotten Ohio University and the University of North Carolina into the act. And none of them has found that single thread they expected to run through all racing greats. None of them seem to have a single trait in common.

Maybe Alan Jones came close. Alan is an Australian and a formula-one driver. It was the day after he had won the Can Am race at Charlotte, and while he was watching the Grand National race as we drafted at 200 miles an hour in our fearsome cars, he said, "It's a bloody black art."

He may be right. Maybe there is no answer and all of them might as well hang it up and go on to something else, like Groundhog Day. But they won't. They will go right on searching.

One of the things that caused Alan to say that, Humpy said, was the way I was driving. My car was loose, and obviously I was fighting it all the way around the track. I told you that in a draft a car gets looser, anyway, but that didn't matter. I was right there, about as close as the chrome on Richard Petty's rear bumper. Maybe it is that seat-of-the-pants sense that is the ultimate part of the black magic. And maybe it *can't* be taught or written down or even told.

We've all talked about it—even the drivers—and there have been as many different answers as there were drivers.

One thing that makes it hard to explain is that nobody even understands what is happening to the machine itself. Oh, they can explain the physics of ground effects, but that's about all. It is impossible to see all of the things that happen to a race car at high speed, particularly a 3,700-pound stock car. You can't see it with the naked eye, so all of the new people who come into the sport spend a bundle to find out. The first thing they do is hook up the cars to computers or whatever, sure that they are going to find out what forces are working out there. "You know, you guys don't know what's happening to the right front tire at Atlanta," they say, "so we're going to show you." Well, Junior Johnson knows what's happening to the right front tire at Atlanta; it gets as hot as hell. And Humpy and the Goodyear people know because they remember tires blistering at Atlanta.

These guys end up with all these mumbo jumbo equations and they don't know what to do with them, so they go to Junior and they tell him he should be running a seven-hundred-pound spring on the right front. "Okay," Junior says. "By the way," they say, "what spring *have* you been running?" "Seven hundred pounds," says Junior. He can't explain how he knows; it's just part of the black magic.

The guys have just spent thousands of dollars finding out what Junior already knew. "Why didn't you tell us?" they ask. "I dunno, it's just what I got out of the back of the truck," he says, which is Southern for, "Why should I tell you, turkey?" It's the way the game is played: All of the guys are helpful until you get to within about thirty one-hundredths of a second of them, and then the information stops. They all understand.

I guess Alan Jones was saying two things: There are things happening out there in the draft that are just as complicated as running around LeMans or Monte Carlo or having to turn right or shift gears; and you literally have to be born in the rural South to understand the language.

I have always kept in top shape, no matter what I have been doing, and I know it's paid off for me. Because of my large bones and my physical condition, I feel that I have been spared from injury a lot of times in crashes. Maybe even death. I mean, I've hit the wall so hard at times that nobody gave me a chance, and I walked away from it. In Texas in the late sixties, when I was running for the Wood Brothers, I was down in the bottom groove of the track and I blew a right front tire. I hit the wall so hard that it stretched my seat belt and my head hit the roll bar. It knocked my helmet down so far that it broke my nose. It even cracked my helmet. I think it would have broken a lot of drivers' necks, but not mine.

There have been a lot of crashes like that.

Another thing that makes physical condition so important in racing is something that Arthur Jones, the guy who invented the Nautilus exercise system, found out: The most exhausting thing anybody can do as far as your muscles are concerned—the one thing that will wear you out quicker than anything—is gripping. Gripping will bring you to exhaustion quicker than pulling or pushing or lifting or anything else. All the muscles required for gripping are close to the heart, and that sends the blood pressure sky-high.

Race-car drivers are not only gripping constantly to control the car, but they are taking out their tension on the steering wheel. After I heard that, I tried not to grip the wheel quite as tight. It works. It's like the boxer who can go fifteen rounds instead of three.

If you went to Stillman's Gym in the fifties and talked with Angelo Dundee, he would tell you that he didn't need to see a guy fight. He *looked* at the guy, at the distance between the back of the head and the front of the jaw and at the symmetry of his neck. A perfect combination produced a fighter that was extremely hard to knock down, like Rocky Marciano or Larry Holmes. Look at most of the great drivers. They fit the mold. They have to. Think of the stress on the neck in racing, particularly the high banks. We're not only undergoing lateral loading but centrifugal loading as well.

And I'll bet that the Glen Woods and Junior Johnsons and Bud Moores can look at a guy and say, "Hey, this cat might have won five hundred races in East St. Louis, but he'll never make it down here."

It's just that you'll never *hear* them say it. You *practice* black magic, you don't *speak* it.

Another important part is that great race-car drivers have an ability to totally wipe out all threat of fear. I have yet to talk with anybody who doesn't admit that he's been scared from time to time, but it's the ones who can go out there the very next day after flipping a race car down the front straight and say, "That happened yesterday. What's happening today?"

Many drivers never do well again at the speedway where they had the bad wreck; they sort of sneak. If you want to know, we have a lot of sneakers. It's like the running back who makes a mistake on an end sweep, when, instead of going back in, he goes outside and gets smashed by two 270-pounders who are running at about 25 miles an hour. He won't make the turn back out to the open field again. But once in a while there's the kamikaze runner who *will* go back out there, and you can bet he's going to score, because the big bruisers weren't expecting him to do it again, so subconsciously they let down a little.

It's the guy who gives 110 percent in a race car, regardless of what's happening around him, who becomes the superstar.

You really *do* have to say to yourself, "I didn't see it. I wasn't there. Man, it happened a million miles away." It's that ability to wipe fear away like you wipe water from a windshield—that it'll-never-happen-to-me attitude—that separates the winners from the losers.

The great race-car driver can handle danger on a daily basis. He looks for it. If I can't find enough of it on the track, I find it in my spare time. I always have. I seem to thrive on fearsome situations. I don't know why, and I don't *care* why. But I do admit it. Here's an example: What do I do for a hobby? Well, for one thing, I have a sawmill. Sure, it's something to fool with, a way to get things off my mind. Besides that, it gives me an endless supply of pecky cypress. But think about it: A sawmill is one of the most dangerous places you can be around. Just look around any big sawmill; there's seldom a guy there with all ten fingers. Or both feet. And you can bet that there's a guy with a great gash across his forehead. Not only is it dangerous, but it also requires a lot of dexterity. Those big logs are always going bananas when you put them up against that sixty-inch blade the wrong way. It's a perfect hobby for a race-car driver. You know, "I want to play, but my playpen has to be a little like the rest of the thing." All of the greats are that way; their hobbies are always exciting, if not downright dangerous. It will be interesting to see what they're doing when they're sixty-five.

Maybe it's something in the genes that causes a person to want to do things that require risks. I understand that psychologists say it's one hundred percent a person's environment, but I think that the good Lord gave out enough different genes to make somebody want to write letters and somebody want to carry them and somebody want to fly the plane to get them there.

I'm no psychologist—far from it—but I would be willing to bet that great race-car drivers are *born* with that ability. And I would also bet that it's the same with other sports; great competitors in racing are no different than great competitors in football or basketball or anything else. Great mathematicians. Whatever.

There are many cases in sports of people overcoming what they lacked in physical stature or ability with a total desire to win, but they always needed someone out there to challenge them. Curtis Turner had a driving school at Charlotte one time, but he never did much fancy driving. Until he hired Paul Goldsmith as a co-instructor. They were both great drivers, so most of the time they ended up out there racing each other while the students stood in the pits and watched. Pops and Goldie just couldn't *help* themselves. The minute one of them passed the other, the race was on and the class be damned.

But they always needed someone to help them challenge that desire. Once it was challenged, they could control it as well as they could the car. They never pushed themselves or their machine past that certain point where there's no return. The walls of racing are painted red with guys who never learned to control their desire.

There are people who have a *need* to be around danger. In the South in the fifties and sixties, stock-car racing gave us the only possible outlet. I would have ended up with some sort of aimless life without racing. I don't know what I would have done, but I probably would have gone nuts around Timmonsville.

Listen, if it had been a thousand years ago, I might have been a Viking. And you can bet that guys like me will be racing in a black hole in the twenty-first century.

So, I think that when all of these things come together in one driver—physical fitness, the ability to react more slowly, the knack of wiping out fear, and the love of dangerous situations—you have a race-car driver they'll probably never stop talking about.

■

In 1984, I got in the hamburger business. Here's how it happened: The Hardee's people decided that they wanted to up their image in racing, so they went to car owner Harry Ranier, who had been around NASCAR for a long time, and they asked him if he would be interested in putting a Hardee's race car on the track.

It's hard to ignore an offer from a big sponsor like that, so Harry asked them what they wanted from him. "Simple," they told him. "We want a race car, and we want Cale Yarborough as the driver."

"It's not that simple," Harry said, thinking that there probably wasn't a chance.

But, as it turned out, M. C. Anderson was getting out of racing, so

I *was* available. Once more, things worked out perfectly for me. I took over the number 28 Hardee's Chevrolet.

In many ways it was like old home week. Waddell Wilson, who was Harry's car builder, and Dan Ford, who worked for Waddell, both had worked for Holman and Moody when I was sweeping floors there in the sixties.

Waddell is one of the top crew chiefs in the business. At Holman and Moody he had been crew chief for Fireball until there was some friction on the crew and he moved over to Freddy Lorenzen's car, where he stayed until Freddy retired. After that, he worked with A. J. Foyt and David Pearson and Bobby Allison, when all of them drove for Holman and Moody.

When Holman and Moody got out of racing, Waddell moved on, leaving behind quite a record. During the many years he worked on Fords he also built engines for Dan Gurney and Parnelli Jones and Curtis Turner and Dick Hutcherson and just about all the top Ford drivers. He built the engines for a long time, and Ford passed them out to whoever they wanted to have them.

Waddell is a real craftsman. He adapted to the Chevy engine quickly, and it's hard to go from one kind of engine to another because there is a real difference. There's not much change between the bottom ends of Ford and Chevy engines—the block and pistons and crankshaft and rods—but there is at the top, where the cylinder heads and intake manifold and all the breathing parts of the engine are. That's where the horsepower is, and you can't carry any knowledge from one to the other, except the basic principle.

During the two years we ran the Hardee's Chevrolet I won the Daytona 500 twice in a row and several other major races. So you can see that Waddell does his homework real well.

But with our heritage you can imagine how happy I was when Ford decided to come back into racing, especially since they asked me to drive one of the new 1985 Ford Thunderbirds. I enjoyed my association with Chevrolet, but going back to Ford was like going home again. They are the ones that really gave me my start in racing.

When we went to Daytona, it was surprising to see some of the same faces that had been there to test with Ford in the sixties. In charge of the Ford crew was Mose Nowland, who came to Ford about the same time I did in the sixties.

Mose told me the Ford racing story. Ford got into Indianapolis racing in a big way in 1935, when Edsel Ford came up with the idea of entering a bunch of cars in the Indy 500, cars that would go like mad and link Ford with speed for all time. It didn't exactly turn out that way. If you really want to know, the entire program was a disaster; so much so that old Henry, himself, stepped in to try to gather up the show.

Edsel had hired the team of Harry Miller and Preston Tucker to put the cars together. Miller was the best of the Indy car builders at the time; Tucker, who everybody remembers as the father of the Tucker Torpedo—the car that never came out—was a slick promoter.

They built the cars well, but Ford didn't have an engine strong enough for the 500. So Henry looked around his shop and called on Don Sullivan, a young engineer who had done much of the design and development work on Ford's first successful V-8, the legendary V-8-60. Sullivan and three other engineers had designed the engine in Thomas Edison's old laboratory, which had been moved to Greenfield Village.

But even Sullivan couldn't save the Ford showing. All four cars were out of the race by the 145th lap. Fortunately for the engine people, they left the race with steering problems.

It was Ford's last full factory effort for many years, until Chevy's success with their new V-8 in the fifties got their attention. The V-8 was Ford Country.

In 1959, Don Frey, who was Ford's executive engineer, began to put together another racing team, with Dave Evans heading it up. And who do you think they put in charge of engines? You guessed it: Don Sullivan. It seems that anytime Ford needed more power in a hurry, they called on Sullivan. This time he laid out much of the original work on his kitchen table. They couldn't get the dyno room, and the Edison Lab was overrun with tourists by then. So they worked on the new engine wherever they could, listening to how it *sounded* as their gauge.

When they thought it was right, they dumped it into a 1959 Ford prototype they had gotten from the press pool, and they sneaked off to run against the kids driving Chevys and Pontiacs at the Detroit Dragway. The first runs were promising, but they faded away before the elimination runs because they didn't want the racing world to know what they were doing. If they hadn't left the manufacturer's license plates on the car, they might have gotten away with it.

The next step was a real test at a real track. So they dummied up a Firestone tire test at Daytona. Curtis Turner was their first choice as driver, but he was laid up from a crash, so they went down the list of NASCAR drivers until they came to Cotton Owens's name. And they got a relatively unknown team to crew the car, the Wood Brothers. They didn't know it at the time, but they had created a dream team. Cotton turned record laps of 145 miles an hour on the new Daytona track.

Don Sullivan went on to help build one of Ford's finest engines, the 289 V-8. Then, after the Ford victory in 1967 at LeMans, he retired. Officially. But, unofficially, the racing people kept in close touch with him by phone.

As we sat in the garage area at the Daytona test, talking about the engine, I asked Mose who designed the engines for my new cars. "Anybody I know?" I asked.

"I think so," said Mose. "The guy who did a lot of the work is Don Sullivan."

"Are you kidding me?" I asked in total disbelief. "Don Sullivan must be eighty years old."

"Exactly," he said. "We needed more power in a hurry, so . . ."

He didn't have to say any more.

It had been fifty-four years since Don Sullivan had built the first V-8-60, but he got things rolling real quick by tracking down the tooling for the old 351 Cleveland engine, Ford's last dream mill. The tooling had gotten down to Australia where a former Ford executive had sent it so that they could build some blocks for his son's race car without a lot of fuss.

Ford ordered 1,000 Cleveland blocks as a "lifetime run," or, in other words, all that would ever be built again. They got 770 blocks before the tooling went belly-up. Sullivan said, "Well, if that's all the

Clevelands we'll ever have, we better get started on designing a new block."

The production 351 block had undergone drastic weight reduction in the seventies because nobody ever expected to turn an engine past 4,800 r.p.m. again. So they beefed up the skirt and pan-rail areas and strengthened the mains—after adding a four-bolt main, of course,—and a new race engine was born.

They called it the 351 SVO, but to a lot of Ford fans it was the answer to their prayers. I hope Don Sullivan is around for another eighty years.

So far we haven't gotten everything together with our Ford racing program. If you want to know the truth, we haven't even finished too many races in the first half of 1985, but it's only a matter of time until Waddell and the boys get it figured out, and then it will be "Katy, bar the door." I promise.

You may know that Bill Elliott, in a privately built Ford, won about everything this year, and nobody has figured out what Elliott has. His Thunderbird is just faster than anybody else's and we don't know why.

There are times when I think that Bill and his brothers have just done their homework well, but there are other times—when he blows right by me—that I know he's got something figured out that the rest of us don't know.

I do know one thing: I don't think there has ever been a time in Grand National racing when any one driver has had as *much* of an advantage as Elliott. There have been times when a whole line of cars or motors have; such as in the sixties when Chrysler's hemi blew everybody's door off; or in the seventies, when General Motors—particularly Chevy—were about impossible to beat, but not just one car.

There *were* times when a driver had a big advantage but didn't show it. He just put on a better show, I guess, and most of the fans didn't even know he could have run away with things. I think some of us are better actors than Elliott.

There were individual races in 1984 when I could have run away from the field, for example, just like he's doing this year, but I didn't.

And I'm not the only one who's concealed the horsepower he had. David Pearson was real good at acting. Why, there were times when he could have lapped us all; I mean, he had some outlandish horsepower, and he would always look like he could hardly make it to the finish line. Man, he is an actor. Richard Petty is another great actor.

Horsepower is something that I don't mind bragging about because, like I told you, I don't have anything to do with that part of the game. There have been times when I knew that I had fifty more horsepower than anybody else, but I held it back and made it look more interesting. For one thing, everybody wasn't trying to find out what I had, like they're doing with the Elliotts. You can't let anybody know you've got that kind of edge if you want to keep it. It works the other way too. There have been lots of times when I had fifty horsepower *less* than the rest of them and I've won by over-driving. It balances out. But right now it seems to be out of balance for everybody but Bill Elliott.

But just wait. We'll catch up. I've had slumps before, and I've never let them get me down. I know a slump has to end, and I honestly feel before every race that this is the day. Who knows, the next race may be it.

I'LL GET OFF WHEN I'M ON TOP.

I'LL JUST STEP OUT AND GO TO THE HOUSE.

Epilogue

■

It's hard for me to believe that things have turned out for me the way they have. Right from the start I knew that I would make it big in racing, but in my wildest dreams I never thought I would make it this big. I mean, all the records and victories and all the honors. I've won more than four and a half million dollars in racing. That's a long way from the first ten-dollar purse or from the five-dollar appearance money I got from time to time.

I have a lot to be thankful for, and there's not a day that I don't thank the good Lord for all of it, particularly for keeping me safe and relatively sound. Oh, I've got a few aches and pains when it rains, and my knee and shoulder give me fits at times, but for the most part I've walked away from some bad incidents,—both on and off the track. I've taken some hard licks.

Sleeping is the hardest part. I go to sleep quickly, but I can only sleep for about ten minutes at a time, and then I wake up and have to turn over. I wear the bed out. I mean, it's like roasting a pig. But every part of my body has been beat and banged and bruised.

One thing I'm real thankful for is that I've never been burned bad in a race car. That's a race-car driver's greatest fear—fire. You know, the worst burn I ever got was when I turned a coffeepot over on myself in a motel room in Charlotte a few years ago.

So, I'm all right for the shape I'm in. I don't remember who said it, but somebody did, and I think it sums up how I feel: "If I had any idea I was going to *live* this long, I would have taken better care of myself."

As far as my business investments are concerned, I'm in good shape there too. I've handled all of the investments myself, without the help of a consultant or anything, and I've been lucky. I did sell off all but three of my dry-cleaning places because they weren't making much money, but that's about the only thing that didn't work as well as I had hoped. I've got a good Honda/Mazda dealership in Florence, South Carolina. I own a Goodyear tire dealership in Timmonsville, and I have a Honda dealership in Savannah, Georgia. And then there are the Hardee's restaurants: I own seven of them. So, you see, when I race for Hardee's, I really race for myself. And I own a company that makes satellite television dishes.

There is a Cale Yarborough Fan Club up in Fredricksburg, Virginia; Carole Bruce is the president of it, and I get a lot of fan mail from that. But I get a lot of fan mail every day, just through the regular mail,—about four or five letters a day. I answer each one of them right away. The only time I don't answer one right then is when it's from a school kid. I always hold it back and wait until the Christmas holidays or the summer, when they're off; otherwise, I'll get letters in the next mail from every kid in his school.

A lot of fans just stop by my farm. The gate is always open, and if they stop, I'll take the time to come out and talk to them for a minute. I figure that if they think enough of me to stop, I should take the time to chat. I even get Richard Petty fans and Bobby Allison fans, because they know I'll talk to them. You see, race-car drivers are heroes in the Southeast, and I'm proud of that. The other day I had my CB radio on and I heard two truckers talking. One of them said, "That Sardis exit there is where Cale Yarborough lives." The other one said, "Yeah, I hear that if you stop there, he'll actually come out of his house and talk to you."

I liked that.

The only time I ever close my gates is during the time of the Southern 500 in Darlington, and then there are so many cars that they're lined up and down both sides of the main road. You can see cars from all over the country.

I've lost a lot of good friends in racing, and there's not a week that goes by that I don't think of every one of them at least once. That's the part about racing cars that I hate the most; it's a pretty tough sport. Even considering the few times I ran at Indy, I've lost many of my friends there; of the six teammates I had up there, Lloyd Ruby is the only one that's still alive.

But I still have a lot of friends in racing. Betty Jo and I are real close with Glen and Bernice Wood and Junior and Flossie Johnson. We're all still family. And I see Banjo a lot at the races, and a lot of my other old friends.

Racing has changed a lot. It's now the kind of place that I wouldn't mind to take my family, except that they don't always want to go. That's understandable, because I protected them from it for so many years. Julie got more of it than Kelly or B.J., because when she came along, we couldn't afford baby-sitters. By the time the other girls arrived on the scene, I had good equipment, so they thought their daddy should win every race. They were bored when I did win and didn't understand when I didn't. Betty Jo goes to some of the races now, but she's pretty busy at home raising the family. It's what she's always done, and I don't think there's a wife in the world who could have done a better job.

That's the part I would like to change in my life—the being away so much when the girls were growing up. I'm sorry that I didn't cut back on my racing schedule sooner than I did. I didn't realize it, but all four of them stayed home and prayed that I wouldn't get hurt, especially when I was running at Daytona or Talladega, where you go so fast. There's nobody who loves to be at home as much as I do.

Over the years I've been to the White House four times, under four different presidents. I've dined with presidents and kings. I spent a few years in politics myself, but that's all behind me. I got enough of politics at the county level to last me a lifetime.

I've driven every kind of racetrack there is, with a fair measure of success at every one. I raced at LeMans in France and in Argentina in an Indy car.

When I'm home, we go to church every Sunday at the same church I've always gone to, the Sardis Baptist Church—Betty Jo and the girls and me. And Mama. Not much has changed with her, either; she still lives in the same house she's lived in since my high-school days, and to keep busy, she manages my dry-cleaning place in Timmonsville.

J.C. lives over on the back of the old farm, near where the original house was. He works for me at my Honda/Mazda dealership. Jerry lives in Columbia and is in the insurance business.

So, you see, not a whole lot has changed in my life.

But NASCAR has changed a lot. For so many years the fans were actually abused; there were bad parking lots and bad traffic and bad food and drink and bad rest rooms, but they still kept on coming. Now, all of the tracks have everything as neat and clean and orderly as they possibly can. And even more fans come.

There are big sponsors everywhere, and at times I think that there's no end to the money. Winston has put so much into racing, and they've improved the sport a lot by what they've done.

Goodyear has the tire battle all to itself now. Firestone gave up a long time ago. That took a lot of the fun out of it, because the "Tire Wars" were exciting. But Goodyear has done even more for the sport; they've brought us the inner tire, which has saved more lives than any single thing, and also the fuel cell, which has almost eliminated the fear of fire in a crash. And I can see the factory days coming back again. It's a bright future.

The sport is definitely better. About the only thing that hasn't changed is the drivers. Oh, most of the names have changed, but their attitude hasn't. NASCAR drivers are still the most unspoiled athletes in the world today. They're just as common as anybody you meet on the street, no matter how much money they've made. And I've never seen any drugs or anything like you hear so much about in other sports.

There are a lot of good drivers out there today, and some of them have been around as long as I have. I personally think that Dale Earnhardt is one of the hardest chargers in NASCAR today, but you still can't pick any one driver when you have guys like Richard Petty and Bobby Allison and Buddy Baker and Darrell Waltrip and a lot of others. It's impossible because they're all good.

Drivers today don't come up through the same ranks we had to. Oh, there are a few like Geoff Bodine, who raced short tracks and modifieds for years before he got to the big league, but many of them today can just buy a ride if they have a sponsor or enough money.

Some of us have gone through a lot: the early days when you stayed out there and made a bad-handling car handle; the rule changes that chased the factories away; a lot of things. Why, it's only been a few years since they introduced the down-size race car and we went from a 115-inch wheelbase to 110 in one year. Those are the cars that did the inside flip, you know, like the one I had at Daytona in 1983. We never had cars that did *that* before. Nobody will ever know how bad those cars handled.

There is going to be a mass exodus one of these days in NASCAR. It has to come; a lot of us are getting older. It's been eighteen or nineteen years since we had an exodus like that, but within a short period, Junior Johnson, Freddie Lorenzen, Pete Hamilton, Marvin Panch, Ned Jarrett, and a lot more retired, as well as Fireball Roberts and all the other guys who were killed. But if you look at the ages today, you'll agree that it has to happen. Race-car drivers are active longer than any other athletes, but our day still has to come. A lot of the older drivers haven't made as much money as athletes in other sports, so they can't retire as early. They have to keep racing.

I guess we're at the point in the book where I have to look at the future, rather than at the past. I can't tell you exactly when I'm going to retire because I don't know, myself. But I can tell you that it won't be too long.

My knee and my shoulder make me think about it a lot, but my reflexes are still good. I think a man's reflexes stay up when he uses them the way we have to. At least, that's my opinion. I've got my own personal test. Several years ago I discovered it. I was in the shower, and I guess I squeezed the soap too hard because it shot up in the air. I grabbed it on the way *up*. "Not bad," I thought. Since then, I do that from time to time. I'm still catching it on the way up; when I start catching it on the way down, I'll think seriously about retiring. If I ever drop it, that will be it.

Even though my reflexes are still good, I have to work a lot harder than I used to, to stay in condition. But I still get butterflies in my stomach before a race, just like I did when I was fifteen and waiting to go on a football field. When those butterflies go away, I'm going too. I mean, when the time comes, I'll be the first to know, and I guarantee you, I won't drag it all the way down the other side like a lot of people do. I'll go into a turn someday and I'll know that I'm not charging as hard as I can, or I'll hang back there in the pack too long, waiting for the right time to pass.

I'll get off when I'm on top. I'll just step out and go to the house.

But for now I still love that sensation of speed as much as I did the first time I drove a race car. And winning—man, I couldn't stand to be out there if I didn't think I was going to win every race.

When those butterflies go away, I'm going to sell cars and hamburgers. Full-time.

Daddy would have been mighty proud of the things I've done. I know that I am. But I don't want people to think of me as anything other than what I am: the kid from Sardis. I want everyone who knows me to be able to say, "You know, that Cale Yarborough hasn't changed one bit since he was a kid slidin' off the roof of the cotton gin."

I've always remembered what Daddy told me when I was real little: "Son, remember, if people don't like you as who you are, they sure won't like you as what you *try* to be."